Existential Time-limited Therapy

WILEY SERIES
in
EXISTENTIAL PSYCHOTHERAPY
AND COUNSELLING

Editor

Emmy van Deurzen

Existential Time-limited Therapy: The Wheel of Existence
Freddie Strasser and Alison Strasser

Case Studies in Existential Psychotherapy and Counselling
Editor: Simon du Plock

Further titles in preparation

Paradox and Passion in Psychotherapy:
An Existential Approach to Therapy and Counselling
Emmy van Deurzen

Existential Time-limited Therapy

The Wheel of Existence

Freddie Strasser and Alison Strasser

With a Foreword by Ernesto Spinelli

JOHN WILEY & SONS
Chichester • New York • Weinheim • Brisbane • Singapore • Toronto

Published by John Wiley & Sons Ltd,
Baffins Lane, Chichester,
West Sussex PO19 1UD, England

National 01243 779777
International (+44) 1243 779777
e-mail (for order and customer service enquiries): cs-books@wiley.co.uk
Visit our Home Page on http://www.wiley.co.uk
or http://www.wiley.com

Reprinted November 1999, August 2001, November 2002

Other Wiley Editorial Offices

John Wiley & Sons, Inc., 605 Third Avenue,
New York, NY 10158-0012, USA

WILEY-VCH Verlag GmbH, Pappelallee 3,
D-69469 Weinheim, Germany

Jacaranda Wiley Ltd, 33 Park Road, Milton,
Queensland 4064, Australia

John Wiley & Sons (Asia) Pte Ltd, 2 Clementi Loop #02-01,
Jin Xing Distripark, Singapore 129809

John Wiley & Sons (Canada) Ltd, 22 Worcester Road,
Rexdale, Ontario M9W 1L1, Canada

British Library Cataloguing in Publication Data
A catalogue record for this book is available from the British Library

ISBN 0-471-96308-9 (cloth)
ISBN 0-471-97571-0 (paperback)

Typeset in Linotype Palatino 10/12pt by Stephen Wright-Bouvier of the
Rainwater Consultancy, Longworth, Oxfordshire
Printed and bound in Great Britain by Biddles Ltd, Guildford and King's Lynn
This book is printed on acid-free paper responsibly manufactured from sustainable
forestation, for which at least two trees are planted for each one used for paper production.

CONTENTS

ABOUT THE AUTHORS

Freddie Strasser, MA, PhD, UKCP Reg. BAC(Acc), AdvDipExPsych.

Freddie Strasser is course leader, tutor and supervisor at Regent's College, London, and elsewhere. He is also a distinguished therapist in private practice. As a founder member of the Society for Existential Analysis, he has specialized in the application of existential concepts, practising existential time-limited therapy and providing clinical supervision.

During World War II, while facing annihilation by both Hungarian fascist and communist regimes, Freddie first became interested in philosophy and psychology. Subsequent wide-ranging experience of clients from many different backgrounds and with diverse need of psychotherapy proved the incentive for him to examine the benefits of existential time-limited therapy. He first became involved in the time-limited approach when supervising therapists in an institution that had changed its former open-ended practice to the time-limited model. During this learning and research process, he became aware that as well as existential philosophy and therapy being conducive to a time-limited psychotherapeutic approach, the structure that evolves from this process can also be applied to longer term therapy.

Alison Strasser, BA Hons, MA, UKCP

Alison Strasser graduated from York University with a BA Hons degree in social sciences in 1978 and then began a career in television. She subsequently studied for an MA in psychotherapy and counselling at Regent's Park College, graduating in 1992. It was during this period that she and her father began developing their ideas on existential time-limited therapy.

A former counsellor for the London-based MIND organization, Alison emigrated to Sydney, Australia, in 1993, where she has a private practice. She has recently introduced workshops on existential time-limited therapy at the Australian College of Applied Psychology, where she is a lecturer.

FOREWORD

The past decade has seen many significant developments in psychotherapy and counselling in the UK. The ever-increasing mandates for both training programmes and professional recognition, not to speak of the significant changes in public awareness of, and demand for, therapy, have served as catalysts for some much-needed reconsiderations as to what models of therapy are most applicable and beneficial in a wide number of settings. Not surprisingly, perhaps, this debate still rages.

Although public awareness of therapy has altered perceptibly over the years, one important distinguishing characteristic remains largely overlooked by its actual and potential clientele: therapy is by no means a united or cohesive system of thought and practice. Instead, a very wide range of competing and contradictory approaches and models exists (somewhat) side by side, each offering a unique perspective on the interventative treatment of human disturbance and disorder.

In 1988, in London, a group of practising therapists first joined together to found the Society for Existential Analysis – an organization dedicated to the promotion and development of existential–phenomenological theory as applied to psychotherapy and counselling. I count myself as being extremely fortunate to have been part of those founding sessions, not least because they proved to be my introduction to Dr Freddie Strasser.

At that time, existential therapy was little known in the UK. Although it has been firmly established as an approach in continental Europe since the first quarter of this century and where models such as Daseinanalysis, Binswanger's Existential Analysis, and Logotherapy continue to evolve and thrive, nothing of the sort had occurred in Britain since the heyday of R. D. Laing and the establishment of the Philadelphia Association in the early 1970s. Nevertheless, the time seemed right. Pioneering texts, such as *Existential Counselling in Practice* by Emmy van Deurzen-Smith had already demonstrated that the desire to know more about the practice of existential therapy was significant and it soon became evident that there already existed a number of disparate individuals who had been applying and extending existential–phenomenological theory in their therapeutic encounters with clients.

The founding of the Society marked a pivotal turning point for existential therapy in the UK. Since its inception, a truly British school of existential therapy has come into existence and, through its regular meetings and annual conferences, its journal, and the academic and professional publications of several of its members, the Society has gained substantial international recognition and respect.

Now, nearly a decade on, has been initiated what might be referred to as the 'second phase' in the development of a British School of Existential Therapy. If the 'first phase' sought to establish the basic principles, or overall 'terrain', of existential therapy in order that it be recognized as a unique approach among rival systems in the UK, the 'second phase', I believe, has moved beyond such and, instead, takes as its focus the clarification and implementation of existential therapy as the principal alternative to the most established schools and systems of therapeutic thought and practice. In line with this, it has become evident that one of the most far-reaching challenges to British therapy as a whole is the development of short-term, or time-limited, models that can be applied in a variety of clinical, educational and social service settings. While current practice in these areas is dominated by psychoanalytic or cognitive–behavioural models, or combinations of the two, the distinctive potential of existential therapy to time-limited practice has been little recognized until now. Thanks to Freddie and Alison Strasser, a valid and important approach to time-limited existential therapy has come into being whose impact and influence will, I am certain, be anything but 'short term'.

Over the several years of regular weekly meetings with Freddie, I have been privileged to witness the genesis and advancement of the model that is being advocated in *Existential Time-limited Therapy*. In spite of the kind words written by Freddie and Alison regarding my contributions to their work, I want to state as plainly as possible that they deserve all of the praise and attention that this highly original and provocative text will undoubtedly receive. It is, I think, an achievement of which they, and British existential therapy as a whole, can be unreservedly proud.

Although the early chapters of *Existential Time-limited Therapy* provide a suitable introductory overview of a number of the principal ideas and concerns of existential therapy, it is the book's exposition of the model from an applied standpoint that ensures its accessibility to a wide number of practitioners and laypersons alike. Further, the actual case material derived from the authors' private practice that is utilized throughout the text truly illuminates and concretizes the more abstract considerations that underlie the model being presented. As will be immediately apparent to readers, the authors' proposals also make plain that, even if time-limited, the approach they have developed makes accessible to therapeutic exploration and clarification many of the so-called 'deep issues' that are usually viewed as emerging only in long-term therapy.

More than this, however, these instructive, and often deeply moving, contributions of the therapists – and, significantly, of a number of the clients themselves – succeed in conveying a good deal of the human 'meeting' that exemplifies the authors' 'way of being' with their clients. This attitude, so expertly represented throughout the text, personifies, far more than any learned technique, the existential approach to therapeutic encounter. That the authors have been able to demonstrate its applicability, and impact, in time-limited therapy is, to me, a primary achievement of their work.

All in all, this text marks an important turning point in the history of British existential therapy. For too long a time burdened with false assumptions and misrepresentations regarding the model's applicability only in long-term therapy and the limited accessibility of its philosophically derived hypotheses, Freddie and Alison Strasser's always clear and straightforward, yet wide-ranging, discussions and explications should dispel these views and reveal time-limited existential therapy to be deserving of far greater attention. All readers who remain open to challenges of their sedimented beliefs regarding both existential and time-limited therapy will find a great deal herein both to stimulate and enrich their work.

Dr Ernesto Spinelli
Chair, Society for Existential Analysis

SERIES PREFACE

It is very telling that this series should be launched at a time when dramatic social and cultural changes accompany the turn of the millennium. As people contend with a sense of crisis and confusion they search for clarity and new ways of living. Increasingly they turn to the professions of psychotherapy and counselling to help them address crucial existential issues.

It is no longer sufficient to talk with clients and patients about their problems as if these were purely functions of intrapsychic mechanisms. In an increasingly complex world, people need to be able to see their own difficulties in relation to the overall contradictions and dilemmas that bedevil human living. They need to be able to make sense of themselves within their own context. Many human troubles are generated by living with technology, bureaucracy and social alienation. Other problems are as old as humanity itself and become more understandable when looked at from a philosophical angle.

The existential perspective on psychotherapy and counselling makes it possible to re-evaluate personal problems in the light of human wisdom. It pays attention to the philosophical, social, cultural and political dimensions as well as to the personal and the interpersonal. It encourages people to examine their lives and rediscover meaning. It makes room for paradox and the acceptance of the inevitable. It allows for questioning and re-evaluation.

Existential psychotherapy has been in existence for almost a century and the theories in which it is rooted go back to the nineteenth-century philosophies of freedom of Kierkegaard and Nietzsche and the twentieth-century philosophies of Heidegger and Sartre, among others. Indirectly it draws on a much longer lineage, in that all of western and eastern philosophy are relevant to such a reappraisal of everyday life.

The approach has not been well documented until quite recently, as many existential practitioners abhor formalization and technology and few have wanted to write about their work, let alone systematize it. This is a pity, for psychotherapists and counsellors need to inform each other of their findings about human life in order to progress in understanding the complex situations in which their clients are caught up.

It is therefore delightful to me that the present series of books with its focus on the application of the existential approach will remedy this situation. Here is a number of practitioners documenting their own particular brand of existential work and showing it to be utterly relevant to their clients.

The present volume focuses on the application of existential ideas to time-limited psychotherapy. Strasser and Strasser show that the existential approach lends itself particularly well to short-term work, which follows logically from the existential focus on human limitations. To be aware of our mortality and our inevitable aloneness leads to a psychotherapeutic approach that aims to be moderate and brief in its nature. Existential therapists do not encourage dependence. They let their clients face stark realities, accepting to be continuously challenged by life. Therapy from an existential perspective is never more than a rehearsal for life. Clients are encouraged to seek out their own sources of coping rather than cultivating a reliance on the assistance of therapy. In a society of scarcity of resources such an approach is extremely topical and relevant.

The book also shows that such a brief and tough approach does not mean that the therapy has to be task oriented or superficial. Existential issues abound in all the material brought to the therapist and this is never more obvious than under pressure of time. The book illustrates how it is possible to allow for the free play of existential concerns and cover much territory in a short period. Clients are able, more than we like to think sometimes, to take enough from a limited number of sessions to continue their development alone.

Emmy van Deurzen
Series Editor

PREFACE

We were very lucky that we were able to establish a father–daughter working partnership in which we could exchange our therapeutic experiences and where we came to harmonize our ideas and theories. The search for our existential world view goes back to Alison's youth, when we were able to rise above our differences and discuss our own issues, and thus sustain an open, honest relationship.

The book began when Alison, who had just emigrated to Australia, needed additional supervision. This was conducted by telephone and later via e-mail. The purpose of the book is a simple one: to convey those experiences that we both came across in existential time-limited therapy with our clients, which were then to be related to the underlying assumptions of the existential approach.

We are deeply grateful to our clients who taught us to be humble, and gave us new insights as well as occasionally confirming our views. Without those clients, this book could not have been written. In this respect we particularly thank James, Sue, June and Edward who were not only courageous enough to give us permission for publication, but who also wrote their own commentaries. As for essential inspiration and guidance, we are grateful to Emmy van Deurzen and express our deep thanks.

This book has taken a long time to write and could not have appeared without the help and support of Dr Ernesto Spinelli. He was not only part of the inception of the project but he also assiduously supervised, guided and ushered the work throughout. For this we are deeply grateful to him.

We particularly thank Julie Reichman for her efficient hard-working editing; Paul Burg for preparation of the manuscript, advice and unfailing support; and Karen Weizel Dixon for her excellent research work.

We would also like to express special thanks to all our students and supervisees. Their contributions were essential to this book.

Finally, we wish to express our thanks to Michael Coombs and the editorial staff at John Wiley. They could not have been more helpful and obliging and it was a great joy to work with them.

The book is written for a wide readership of students, therapists and people who are interested in this field. For clarity we have sometimes stressed the same points more than once. For those who wish to go deeper into the subject of theory and philosophy of existentialism, references to other works are listed in the Bibliography.

AS
FS
1997

1

INTRODUCTION

The purpose of this book is to demonstrate not only the essence of existential time-limited therapy, but also to show that existential therapy is, by its very nature, conducive to a time-limited approach. Although existential therapy has existed since the 1920s and the idea of time-limited therapy has been circulated for almost as long, this is the first time (as far as we are aware) that these two ideas have been combined in a comprehensive practice. A structural view of existentialism can serve as an anchor for both the therapist and the client. The structure of this paradigm does not suggest a mechanistic view of the world, but just the opposite, as it incorporates *Weltschmerz* (world pain) and world joy into the therapeutic encounter. Through this orientation, focusing and goal settings, in their traditional modes, are somewhat superfluous and the existential therapeutic process can produce a shift of perception in clients.

The idea of brief or time-limited therapy has come to the fore since the end of World War II when there was an influx of war-traumatized military personnel who needed therapy of one kind or another. Group therapy such as that introduced by S. H. Foulkes (1975) was one way of coping with the mass numbers, and it was found to be shorter and more focused than the prevailing therapy, which was open-ended psychoanalysis.

In many ways, the arrival of cognitive behavioural therapy, especially the influence of Albert Ellis (1962) and Aaron T. Beck (1976), provided means with which to deal with a client's issues within a few weeks or months.

In 1963 Jay Haley published *Strategies of Psychotherapy* and along with the works of therapists at the Time-limited Therapy Center in Palo Alto – Watzlawick *et al.* (1974) and Weakland *et al.* (1974) – these constituted a significant advance in the range of options available, thus making an important impact in the time-limited therapy field. These therapists implemented a strategic approach that is a more active directive stance with a focus on change, rather than simply growth of the individual.

The last few decades have seen a rise in the number of different schools of thought offering time-limited therapy. There is the psychodynamic approach of David H. Malan (1963), the more solution-focused, but client-centred approach of Steve de Shazer (1985) and Francis Macnab (1991). This book will outline another, more existentially underpinned approach to time-limited therapy, that of 'existential time-limited therapy'.

The time-limited therapy model that we propose consists of a limited number of sessions (anywhere between twelve to fifteen and sometimes even fewer sessions), plus two follow-up sessions, spaced approximately one month apart. We also introduce the modular form of time-limited therapy, which is described in the manner that our development reflects the evolving reformulation of our ideas – such as our realization that there are certain clients who require additional support to the initial sessions offered. In other words, using this modular paradigm we can cater for a longer term type therapy, although still working within a time-limited framework.

The difference between the time-limited and open-ended approaches, discussed in various parts of the book, highlights the point that working within a time limitation brings out a different emphasis and therefore gives different results. However, this book also presents the argument that a well-structured existential therapy is in itself time-limited and hence very conducive to time-limited therapy. Taking the previous argument into account, we will make a distinction between long-term 'time-aware' therapy and what we call existential time-limited therapy.

There are many misconceptions about existential therapy, so part of our aim is to outline how we practise, how we work with clients using the largely philosophical underpinning as a basis for the way we listen, clarify and ask questions. Since Freud introduced psychoanalysis there has been an explosion in the varieties of therapeutic approaches on offer to the general public. There has been an inevitable and indeed positive effect from the cross-breeding and interaction of these different schools of thought. Behavioural therapy now takes into account the possibility of feelings; cognitive behavioural therapy allows for the process of empathy; psychoanalysis has branched off into psychodynamic relational approaches and so on. There are also numerous derivatives of these major schools of thought, so many that they cannot be enumerated here. Suffice to say that Richie Herink (1980) published a book that described 250 different therapies in existence.

In essence, therefore, existential therapy owes much to the continual learning and growth of therapy as a whole. Inevitably any practitioner will be influenced by other schools of thought. The principal point to take into account is that any therapy is a philosophy, in the sense that it contains fundamental assumptions, however implicit, of how therapists view their own world and how they conduct their lives. Whatever the philosophy or therapy adopted these will shape the way a therapist interacts with his or her clients and the type of questions that will be asked, their belief in interpretation or direction. It is, however, important to add that in some respects the therapist's individual personality, such as charismatic or non-charismatic behaviour, will influence the therapeutic process, irrespective of his or her personal philosophical orientation.

Although existential therapy has evolved enormously since the 1920s, it owes its development to the philosophies of the existential and phenomenological movements. Until recently it has been firmly grounded in the open-ended dictum prescribed by the majority of psychotherapeutic traditions emanating from Freud onwards. Although there are plenty of compelling reasons apparently validating the open-ended approach, we argue that the importance of time is so significant to the existential therapeutic process that it requires further examination. The time-limited therapy that this book elaborates is firmly grounded in existential concepts, but its development relied upon numerous hours of experiential practice.

To understand how this therapy works in practice we will outline the origin of existential therapy as it is derived from the philosophy as well as the existential conceptual approach that can be applied to both a time-limited or at a minimum a time-aware type of therapy. We will also examine how we developed a viable method of working. The chapters will provide an overview of the existential orientation to therapy and describe a number of key individual theoretical concepts and their implication and relevance to working as an existential therapist. The conceptual framework and the practice go hand in hand in a systematic relationship that will be presented and discussed using short vignettes and longer case histories to highlight the salient points.

As soon as the idea of time is brought into the process, the nature of the therapy changes, and these are the areas that we want to accentuate. For example, we will examine how time itself has various meanings and implications both for the client and the therapist, how it affects both parties' expectations and how the awareness of the ending is seen as a tool in its own right. Admittedly, many of these features are important in open-ended therapy, as well as in time-limited therapy, but the emphasis of the temporality of the therapy is far more prominent when a time constraint is offered.

One of the important innovations that emerged through our practice was the formation of a structural configuration into our framework that we feel can accelerate and improve the therapeutic process, while still within the bounds of the existential position. While one could argue that structure is not relevant in this uncertain structureless world, we argue as therapists that the delineation of a structure coexists very neatly with how we humans live in the world. The mere fact that we are temporal beings, that is, that we are born and will cease to exist, exemplifies the structure of human existence. This structure is the core of the existential time-limited therapy and it is also shown as a visual presentation in the form of existential wheels.

We begin by outlining some of the historical features of existential philosophy and by introducing the important philosophical concepts that have been consequential in developing an existential therapy. This section also highlights the significance of phenomenology as giving a basis for the therapist 'being' with the client. We also introduce some of the key concepts that have provided the basis for the time-limited approach that the remainder of the book describes.

In our approach the notion of time and temporality has vital importance. We examine the differing perspectives that individuals have regarding time and temporality. Therapies have their own time dynamics and perspectives. For instance, therapies such as Gestalt focus principally on the present time, whereas some, such as the psychodynamic tradition, focus primarily on the past. Others deal with the future, with the emphasis on change, such as the cognitive behavioural tradition. Time has an infinite number of meanings and we examine the time phenomenon from the perspective of several relevant philosophers, physicists and psychologists. From a psychological perspective, time is explored and compared with various biological, cultural, emotional and other existential factors that might emerge in therapy. In contrast, the idea of 'timelessness' and the human disposition to set and achieve goals is examined and related to psychotherapeutic encounters.

We also argue that all existential therapies, whether time limited or not, need to deal with and incorporate this temporal characteristic. Since temporality is part of life it also has to be part of the therapeutic process. It cannot exist without temporality, because every therapy must have a final point, in the same way that a person's life must end. Following this argument we present the idea that any type of existential therapy, whether time limited or long term, is by its nature a 'time-aware' therapy. If time is ignored, as implied by the concept of 'open-ended therapy', then the therapy has lost its existential nature.

Time and temporality is one of the core features of existential philosophy in the sense that we all need to come to terms with limitations and uncertainty, and the unpredictability and inconsistency of the nature of existence. These kinds of reflections are of concern in existential time-limited therapy.

Following this reasoning the theory is put to the test. The therapy we describe is not a solution or goal-focused therapy in the traditional sense, although goals are implicit in the process, both by the client and therapist. It is impossible to partake in any therapy without some kind of expectation, even if this is only the desire to understand oneself better. Goal-setting per se influences both the therapist's and the client's perception of psychological time, which is discussed in terms of the positive and negative aspects of having a limit to the number of sessions. We discuss our reasons for existential time-limited therapy and the introduction of the modular approach.

The structure of existence in the world is then introduced and represented in the graphical figurative form of existential wheels. The wheels consist of ten segments. Wheel I delineates in each segment a notion of universal limitations and possibilities that the world imposes on human beings. These are termed by existentialists as 'givens' (Heidegger, 1962; van Deurzen-Smith, 1988; Spinelli, 1994). Conversely, Wheel II relates in each corresponding section to the application of this concept into therapeutic practice.

In Chapter 5 all the notions of each segment are analysed and then systematically expanded, segment by segment until the circles are closed. The relevant segments are printed in bold. Throughout this chapter case vignettes are discussed to underpin or to further explain the concepts and the methods in practice.

The book continues, with case vignettes, to 'bring to life' the theoretical constructs and then separately analyses them. The structure of the wheels also demonstrates how each of our attitudes towards these existential 'givens' is very much based on our reactions to them. That is, our attitude will dictate whether we see the 'givens' and life in general in terms of possibilities and ways of moving forward, or as limitations and restrictions on the way we live our lives. Juxtaposed within these ideas are the concepts of taking responsibility and freedom of choice.

We have sought to reduce complex philosophical notions to commonsense level and we decided that repetitions were sometimes necessary to make the context of the book clearer.

Case studies are written in this book with the consent of clients, three of them with their own verbatim comments on the therapy. Names are disguised to ensure anonymity and some of the vignettes are composites. At this point in the book we reached a stage when we could connect all the philosophies, theories and therapies to case studies. There is a long case study about bulimia which demonstrates how a rigid and entrenched belief system affects the client's life. The last case study demonstrates the way a rigid belief system, however moral and noble it may appear, can have devastating effect on human life. We have avoided mentioning the name of the therapist (Freddie or Alison) to protect some of the clients' identities. We have used the pronoun 'we', at times, to mean the authors of this book; but usually to mean human beings.

The conclusion summarizes the similarities as well as the divergence of case studies, how universally we human beings respond to the ontological 'givens' and at the same time how differently each individual is affected by them. It is also concluded that each case history is characterized by the fact that all clients' individual issues are interconnected with one another and with all the segments represented graphically on all wheels. We also conclude that as much as all our clients universally responded to the 'givens' of the world, so much more did they differ in their responses. At the same time clients had the opportunity to exercise their free will and choose at least their meanings and attitudes.

2

OVERVIEW OF A COMMON-SENSE EXISTENTIAL APPROACH

Existential philosophy and phenomenology are complex words that require simple, commonsense explanations, not least because the outstanding feature of existential philosophy lies in the emphasis on what it means to be a human being.

Many people associate existential philosophy with complicated ideas and negative truths. They hear words such as death, anxiety, isolation and meaninglessness, without realizing that they form only one part of the whole. While all these concepts denote negative connotations, existentialism also incorporates positive affirmations. For example, as we come to terms with the idea that a certain degree of anxiety is a normal and even essential part of living, we have not just increased our awareness, but also opened up the choices that are available to us.

The word existence has its roots in the Latin word *ex-istere* that can be translated as 'to stand out', to emerge, proceeding forward in a continuous process. It stems not from a traditional, objective, rational, scientific focus or impetus, but from an examination of how humans intersubjectively understand themselves in the midst of their lived experiences. It does not preclude the past, because the way we exist in the present is a conglomeration of our current interpretation of experience and expectation of the direction our life will take in the future. Rollo May, the distinguished American protagonist of existential philosophy, defined this approach in his book *Discovery of Being*:

> For the very essence of this approach is that it seeks to analyse and portray the human being – whether in art or literature or philosophy or psychology – on a level which undercuts the old dilemma of materialism versus idealism. Existentialism, in short, is the endeavour to understand man by cutting below the cleavage between subject and

> object that has bedevilled Western thought and science since shortly after the Renaissance.
>
> (May, 1983:49)

Existential philosophy is thus concerned with the science of being – that is with ontology (*ontos*, Greek for 'being'). What kind of attitude does one adopt towards it, and what can one do about it? This can only be comprehended if one understands that every individual has made his or her own unique pathway in the world and experiences an individual existence in that singular way. Within this unique pathway, however, each individual exists in a relational or co-constituted mode to others and to the world. In other words, as soon as we exist we are inexorably connected to others.

Among the protagonists of this philosophical movement are Kierkegaard, and Nietzsche from the last century, and Husserl, Jaspers, Heidegger, Sartre, Merleau-Ponty and Buber from this century. There are many differences in the way the philosophy has been interpreted into psychotherapy. However, broadly speaking there are two divisions, consisting of the European school and the American school. Among the European existential analysts and therapists are Ludwig Binswanger, Medard Boss, Viktor Frankl, Emmy van Deurzen-Smith and Ernesto Spinelli, while Rollo May, Irvin Yalom and James Bugental represent the American school of thought.

From the mid-1950s, the existential movement has had an immense impact on a number of psychological movements. Indeed, the humanistic schools sprang from the essential tenets of existential phenomenological philosophy, taking on board such concerns as the importance of freedom of choice and the notion of the interrelationship between observer and observed. The notion of the subjective interpersonal relationship has even influenced the Post-Freudian schools.

For instance, Harry Stack Sullivan, the psychoanalyst, developed an interpersonal theory of psychiatry that postulates 'that recurrent interpersonal situations characterize a human life' (1953:111). Neo-Freudians such as Alfred Adler (1969) and Karen Horney (1951), moved away from the Freudian notion that humankind is totally dependent on instinctual drives, and recognized the importance of the interpersonal relationship between therapist and patient.

Some authors, however, contend that existential philosophy is not a stand-alone philosophy, but rather a mood that embraces a number of disparate philosophies (Friedman, 1964). In many ways this is a response to the fact that there are numerous differences between the individual existential thinkers. Despite this, existential thinkers and proponents are still united in their reaction to the static and purely rational theories of human existence. Indeed, this idea is corroborated by Irvin Yalom (1980), who postulates that psychotherapists are not philosophers but practitioners.

THE THEORETICAL AND PHILOSOPHICAL BACKGROUND

Existential philosophy and phenomenology are two connected philosophies, and in terms of a practising existential therapy they are firmly linked. Phenomenology concerns itself with how human 'beings' subjectively interpret things to themselves (Husserl, 1977), as opposed to the natural science framework that emphasizes finding the true objective nature of reality. The importance of phenomenological exploration is that it excludes the notion of true objective reality, instead seeking a subjective explanation of the individual's relationships with objects, others, and his or her sense of own being. Existentialism extends this exploration and focuses on human existence, yet uses the phenomenological methods of investigation as an important tool for inquiring into the client's world. Existential therapy, therefore, cannot exist without the phenomenological system of investigation.

PHENOMENOLOGY

The founder of the phenomenological approach was Edmund Husserl (1859–1938), who attempted to establish an alternative method for scientific investigations at the height of an era of reductive scientific reasoning, where objectivity was the only accepted method for scientific research. Husserl questioned this Cartesian dichotomy between mind and body, the split between 'subject' and 'object' (Husserl, 1977). He developed a theory that incorporated the importance of understanding the world as it is experienced in our consciousness, as distinct from viewing it as being constituted of remote entities that are in some way separate to our perception of them. Through the lens of subjective interpretation, phenomenologists can observe how people interact with themselves and with others, as well as the meaning they gain from their existence. Husserl's focus was not only with objects but with people as well – he called it *Lebenswelt* ,'the living world'.

When we describe phenomena this cannot be achieved without the 'inseparable relationship' between human consciousness and the world. Husserl described this inevitable human characteristic in terms of 'intentionalism'. He depicted human consciousness as always being directed toward the world to give meaning to it. In the process of gaining meaning, the person must at the same time interpret it in his or her meaningful (subjective) manner. That is to say, if I am conscious, I am always aware of something: when I become aware of my anger I might also notice that my anger is directed towards something or someone (Husserl, 1977).

One of the important factors that came from this new awareness was the experiential 'proof' that the world in which we live is constantly reshaping itself with regard to the meaning we give it. From a therapeutic viewpoint, any kind of change evokes anxiety: not the neurotic self-perpetuating and self-defeating behaviour pattern with which we are all too familiar, but the anxiety that promotes a wealth of emotional behaviour such as fear, joy, desperation, confusion and indifference. Change became the cornerstone of phenomenology. Husserl devised a method to explore and investigate observable human behaviour that incorporated the importance of change. This is where the phenomenological exploration becomes the primary method in an existentially oriented therapeutic approach. Spinelli (1989), following Ihde (1986), describes three phenomenological 'rules' that relate and define phenomenological investigation and these are also the rules that we apply in time-limited existential therapy. They are bracketing (or epoché), phenomenological description, and that of applying the rule of equalization.

Bracketing

As part of the therapeutic process, existential therapists have to learn and understand what it means to experience the 'thing in itself'. To do this, we need to attempt to suspend all theories and other preconceived judgements to experience the real situation. If, for example, a therapist has strong views about fat people, he or she needs to suspend this bias in order to focus on the primary data and to experience the client without the initial bias. Husserl called this suspension 'bracketing', or epochē, which means to place all those biases, expectations and prejudices temporarily into a bracket or holding position. After further clarification with the client, which includes all aspects of the phenomena, we can then compare this additional information with our original bias. This process allows our attitudes to become more open to our immediate experience.

This has several implications. First, it avoids the need for impulsive or ill-considered questions. Second, it obviates concerns about the constant need to formulate questions. The important factor here is to listen and understand what the client has to say.

Admittedly, total suspension of all our biases and assumptions is impossible, yet just the awareness of this process can make an impact on interpretation and intervention in a therapeutic situation. Through these means we facilitate the client to explore the relational world of the client, as the client experiences it. It is, however, our own relational world view which is focused at this stage.

Phenomenological description

Phenomenological description is a rule that relates phenomena so that they 'remain at a descriptive level of interpretation to focus upon the immediate, or primary data of experience' (Spinelli, 1994). That is, it represents the way to recount an experience, rather than the need to explain it; it investigates meaning in contrast to searching for objective facts. This is a qualitative, rather than quantitative, method that focuses on the way something appears and what it expresses.

This analysis brings us to another fundamental phenomenological assumption, which is that our view of the world is always biased by our present world view, our present opinion. It is always, in Spinelli's words, an 'interpreted world' (1994). Thus, we can never speak of an objective true reality, only of inter-subjective experiences as they are at a particular time.

Equalization and horizontalization

The third rule of 'equalization' (Spinelli, 1989) explains that any initial description of phenomena must be made without priority or hierarchical importance. By applying these rules clients can assemble and narrate their experiences in an atmosphere that is not biased or judgemental. On a practical level, this means that clients are seen and heard for what they are, for what they are saying. We do not attach labels and we recognize that what may be important for a client one week may have shifted in significance the next. More pertinently, the therapist does not immediately presume to know what is important in a client's initial statements.

The practice of methods

By implementing these three steps, the phenomenological method provides an atmosphere in which clients can explore their relationship with the world. It is an approach that enhances the existential phenomenological philosophy so that people have to be understood in their own unique environment. The emphasis lies in how human beings experience and perceive their world and in their awareness of their relationship between themselves and others, and between themselves and with others. This is not just for the client. The therapist, too, is part of the relationship and has a need to view himself 'self-in-relation' to the client, their relationship with others and with their own self. This is rather different from the 'self' as a separate, fixed and complete 'entity' (Spinelli, 1994:342). In the therapeutic encounter the relationship between self and clients is the most significant. In this mode of being, the therapist maintains his or her non-judgemental position as much as possible and through empathy is able to enter the clients' internal world and to reflect it back accurately.

THE PRINCIPAL CONCEPTS OF EXISTENTIAL TIME-LIMITED THERAPY

This section will examine the principal concepts of the time-limited existential model and will also discuss the main differences between this and the notion of the open-ended approach. As we have already stated in Chapter 1, the main differences between time-limited and longer term existential models lie in the emphasis of various concepts. For instance, in the time-limited model the focus centres on temporality, the limit of time, the use of the structural model and the therapists' and clients' expectation of the outcome. This section will highlight these concepts and show how the structure can form the basis of existential time-limited therapy .

Certain existential approaches to counselling and psychotherapy are diversified by the schools and authors of individual approaches. For example, there is a significant diversion between the approaches of Boss, Yalom, van Deurzen-Smith, Laing and Spinelli. While there is considerable divergence in style and sometimes in methods, there is a common cohesion between them, underpinned by the basic tenets of the phenomenological and existential approaches. Van Deurzen-Smith summarizes the main goals of this type of therapy:

> The goals of existential therapies are: first, to encourage the client to become authentic and relinquish self-deception;

> secondly, to assist the client in clarifying and grasping the inner value-system and mode of existence in the world; thirdly, to enable the client to come to terms with life, by building up confidence in and reliance on inner self and reality; and fourthly, to explore with the client what are the client's priorities and to eventually determine a new direction for living.
>
> (van Deurzen-Smith, 1988:162)

While there are very different interpretations for setting goals, in our approach one of the important goals is to facilitate clients in realizing limitations that are imposed on them by the world, and to distinguish them from the limitations that they impose on themselves. Gary, for example, realized during therapy that he had lived his life firmly believing that not only should he eliminate all his anxieties but also that it was imperative that this happen. As therapy progressed he realized that he had set himself an impossible task. Indeed, Gary's belief that life had to be without anxiety had grown into a rigid way of thinking. In the process this thinking had become counterproductive. He had imposed his own limitation that was to fight against and avoid each and every anxiety at all cost. His sedimented belief surrounding anxiety was also paradoxical, because the more he tried to avoid it, the more he generated fear and anxiety.

The one important distinguishing feature of time-limited therapy is the limitation of time itself. So, although the goal is to achieve the same kind of awareness as outlined in an open-ended approach, the aspect of time becomes a tool in itself when employing a time-limited therapy model.

Once there is knowledge of an end, of a limit to the process of therapy, a different atmosphere is created instantly. The constant reminder of the ending elicits its own pressures for both the client and the therapist. It heightens the anxieties and intensifies the tension for the client, who expects to be 'cured', and for the therapist, who wishes to help the client.

This tension has both positive and negative ramifications, in that the overwhelming desire to cure the client will usually have a counterproductive effect in therapy. As described previously, this obliges therapists to 'bracket', or to suspend, as far as possible, their intensive desire to help clients. Instead, they need to return to the basics and allow themselves to concentrate on the relationship with the client. An anxious therapist who desires a positive outcome will impede the process of enabling the client to reflect and challenge their own discrepancies.

However, the implicit certainty of ending will often intensify a client's commitment to the therapeutic process. Anxieties that may not emerge over a longer period of time are more likely to surface in time-limited therapy, as well as the anxieties surrounding the prospect of ending. These and other aspects of time will be discussed further in Chapters 3 and 5 (and below, see Structure).

Expectations

Clients' expectations of any therapy are usually very high. They count on an instant cure and complete elimination of their presenting problem so that they can return to 'normal'. In existential time-limited therapy, these kinds of expectations need to be addressed from the outset, the aim being to reduce any expectation on behalf of the client to a feasible and workable position.

Our own expectation as therapists is to help clients to clarify issues and to promote awareness both on a cognitive and emotional front. In any time-limited approach it is not feasible to cover each and every issue. We hope that clients can not only alleviate their initial problem but also learn and absorb the method and procedure of this process. In this way a client will be able to deal with new issues in a different manner.

Interventions

Our experience shows that the frequencies of clarifying questions and challenging interventions are more common in time-limited therapy than in the open-ended therapy approach. We attribute this to the intensive nature of time-limited therapy, which catapults the client into self-disclosure and working more assiduously on issues. The therapist, too, is made aware of the pressure of time, and will therefore act differently. This is further supported by the outline of the structure of their existential therapy that provides a basis on which the therapist can work when searching and challenging a client's world view. Naturally, not all interventions will be challenging and the use of associative interventions is also employed to prompt self-expression and disclosure. It is important to note that in existential time-limited therapy we as therapists do not interpret but facilitate and prompt clients to make their own interpretations. These types of questions and reflections are elaborated in Chapters 4 and 5.

Ending as a therapeutic tool

As acknowledged before, the simple fact of knowing that there is an ending tends to evoke stronger emotions. These largely centre on the issue of separation, so for instance emotions such as fear, anger, sadness and the recollection of previous losses and rejections help clients to identify their value and coping strategies.

Length of course of therapy

We usually agree to between ten and twelve sessions with two follow-up sessions, which occur at six-week intervals after termination, when working in a time-limited therapy mode. Another module, or series of sessions, can be contemplated after the second review. In Chapters 4 and 5 these points are discussed in more detail.

Focusing and goal setting

It is not the aim of the existential time-limited approach to focus on one particular issue or to set specific targets or goals. The reason behind this thinking is our assumption that all clients' issues are inextricably linked.

STRUCTURE

We believe that the emphasis on the existential structure is the linchpin of time-limited therapy. We will show how it functions at a conceptual and practical level both in the following section and in succeeding chapters. We have found that the use of the structure can facilitate therapists in understanding the client's world, challenging their discrepancies and aiding the therapist to link or interconnect their issues into a more holistic framework.

If we accept that from the moment we are born we are faced with inescapable uncertainties and inherent limitations, then it also becomes apparent that we all strive in our own way to form and create a framework or structure upon which we hope to depend. This is the starting point of the structure that we use in existential time-limited therapy. The structure that we propose mirrors the possibilities and limitations that face human beings. Possibilities are inherent in all of us. Acknowledging our possibilities gives us our freedom, our freedom to choose the way in which we view the world and the decisions that we make.

Freedom to choose the way in which we view the world and its limitations, on the other hand, is also inherent in everything we do and every choice that we make. The best examples of human limitations are those of birth and death, as they are both inescapable universal predicaments. There are, however, many others, such as the colour we are born, whether we are short or tall. All human beings and the world are marked by certain ontological characteristics embraced by these limitations and possibilities. In existential terminology they are called 'givens', or facts that we are either born with or encounter during our life which cannot inherently change. Although the 'givens' might be immutable, the way we perceive them or the attitudes we take towards them are always open to reinterpretation.

For example, short clients might initially see their height as a limitation, but on reflection, they may realize that this could give them an advantage or possibilities that a tall person may not have. In just the same way a tall person might feel uncomfortable with his or her height and may need reassurance. It is a question of perception and upon reflection, they may realize that rather than being handicapped, their height might give them an advantage that a short person may not have. The 'givens' that we describe in the wheel are, for example, anxieties about our safety in this uncertain and unpredictable world; our need for interpersonal relationships; the value system that we create; the self-concept that we build up in this period between the beginning and the ending.

Yalom identified these in his book *Existential Psychotherapy* (1980) as the four 'ultimate concerns of life: Death, freedom, existential isolation and meaninglessness'. All of these are incorporated in the existential wheel. The 'givens' are represented on the structural wheel of concepts as shown in Figure 2.1.

Each section of the wheel represents one of the concepts of the universal 'givens' that strikes every individual. This conceptual wheel is subdivided into sections that are printed in roman script and those which are printed in italics. Sections 1, 2, 3, 7 and 9 in roman script represent those ontological 'givens' that are outside human influence. These are inexorably imposed on us by the world and can be considered as inherent limitations. Sections 4, 5, 6, 8 and 10, printed in italics, represent the reaction and responses to those inevitable five 'givens' that are printed in roman letters. These are:

1. The uncertainties and inconsistencies to which we humans are exposed and which the world imposes on us.
2. The interpersonal relationship that every human being experiences

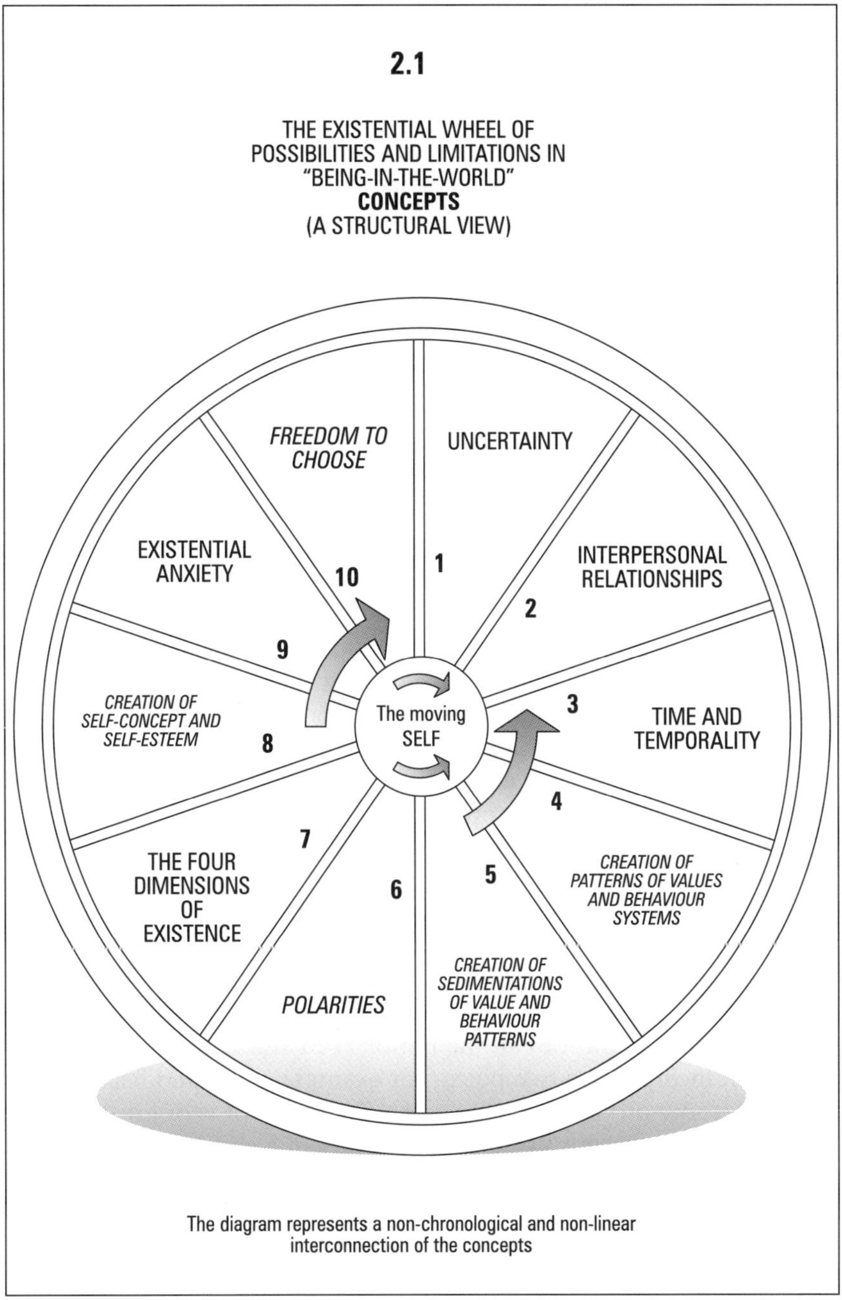
2.1
THE EXISTENTIAL WHEEL OF
POSSIBILITIES AND LIMITATIONS IN
"BEING-IN-THE-WORLD"
CONCEPTS
(A STRUCTURAL VIEW)
1
UNCERTAINTY
2
INTERPERSONAL RELATIONSHIPS
3
TIME AND TEMPORALITY
4
CREATION OF PATTERNS OF VALUES AND BEHAVIOUR SYSTEMS
5
CREATION OF SEDIMENTATIONS OF VALUE AND BEHAVIOUR PATTERNS
6
POLARITIES
7
THE FOUR DIMENSIONS OF EXISTENCE
8
CREATION OF SELF-CONCEPT AND SELF-ESTEEM
9
EXISTENTIAL ANXIETY
10
FREEDOM TO CHOOSE
The moving SELF
The diagram represents a non-chronological and non-linear interconnection of the concepts

Figure 2.1

from the moment of coming into this world. 'Being-in-the-world' also means 'being-with-others'.

3. Time and temporality: nobody can escape from the fact that our life and our mode of living are influenced vastly by our finitude and our transitory mode of being and relating to the world.
4. The four dimensions of existence. In Chapter 5 we describe the dimensions of our existence: physical, public, private and spiritual worlds. No human being can avoid being regulated by the physical environment and being motivated by the same principle. We are also social animals and are inevitably interacting with the world and other human beings. Through the private or personal dimension we are connected with our internal world and preoccupied with our self-concept and self-worth. On the spiritual dimension we connect to the world of ideas, to the metaphysical world and to the meaning of being.
5. Existential anxiety is the emotion that is in the background and rooted in all human existence. In Yalom's words (1980:485), 'We must all face inevitable death, groundlessness, isolation and meaninglessness.'
6. Humans create patterns of values and behaviour systems to make life liveable in the face of these inextricable limitations. For example, to combat the uncertainty of the world, different cultures created divergent safety measures. These include values and patterns. To be a good citizen, for example, comprises an idea of a value and encompasses a behaviour pattern.
7. Sedimentation is described in detail in Chapter 5 and means that there is a human propensity to harden, ossify and make some of these values and behaviour patterns rigid. For example, if somebody believes that the only way to exist is to be modest, or to be superman or perfect, then he or she cannot contemplate existing without conforming to these sedimentations.
8. Polarities are built in all the notions of values. Each value judgement incorporates two poles. For example, good and bad, modest and 'show-off' are opposite poles. This concept is of great importance in the therapy. Exploring the poles of a client's sedimentation is a basic skill in existential time-limited therapy.
9. We create our self-concept and we can choose to increase or diminish our self-esteem. This is a question of attitude.
10. In Chapter 5 we quote Sartre who states that we are forever choosing ourselves and we are condemned to be free. If we accept this premise then this section should be printed in roman letters, as

> according to this we would have no choice in the matter, of choosing or not choosing. Yet, we believe that while certain circumstances limit our freedom to choose, most of the time we have the potential to choose even if sometimes only attitudinally.

The centre of the wheel, however, represents the self in process and is constantly in a relational mode with each of the sections. This relational mode is characterized by a non-linear and non-chronological fluid interaction. All these concepts are individually analysed in Chapter 5 and connected with Wheel II (with corresponding section numbers) that illustrates the practical applications of these concepts in therapy. Furthermore, each section is exemplified with a case vignette.

Of course the paradox is that existentialism by its very nature cannot provide anybody with a framework that guarantees safeguards or stability. Using a loose but clearly defined structure, however, can also highlight the uncertainties of being thrown into this world and the certainty of leaving it. Van Deurzen-Smith confirms this notion when she writes that: 'Although an existential approach is essentially non-technological, I also believe that one needs some methods, some parameters, some framework, in order to retain one's independence and clarity of thinking' (1988:6).

Sartre, too, acknowledges the importance of structure as the basis of ontology, which for him is the 'study of the structures of being of the existent taken as a totality' (1958:633).

The structure and its graphical representation in the form of the 'existential wheel' also serves therapists to delineate their own world views and their own issues. This, in turn, will facilitate them to tolerate and understand their clients' issues and world views. We start from the premise that any of the clients' issues will in some way resonate with some of our own issues. This is of vital importance in our paradigm, as we do not believe that our own issues will impede therapy. On the contrary, if we become aware of it and we can process our issues, it could be an important tool to identify with the client's problems and pains. At the same time this will facilitate the therapist to move out and look at a situation from a perspective and identify clients' discrepancies and contradictions.

A typical illustration that exemplifies this and demonstrates how clients' own problems can strike at the heart of the therapist's issues, is a story of one of our supervisees. Matthew was counselling a lifer in a prison. In one of the supervision sessions he brought in his own enigma. His client 'vividly' described how he had stabbed his girlfriend, yet managed to deny this act vehemently with full conviction. He maintained that it was not he who had put the knife into his girlfriend's back, because in the client's words, it appeared 'as though I wasn't there'. The client, at the same time, revealed his anger, anxiety and violent emotions while he related the physical act of the knife penetrating and exiting from his girlfriend's back. It was quite clear in this session that the client's anger was directed against himself. He then proclaimed: 'It was not me, it was one of my other selves that I did it.'

Through this incident Matthew became aware of his own strong issues and anxieties and how sometimes just a hair's breadth divides us from each other. Matthew realized in his supervision sessions that he too, carried within himself a seed of aggression, as all human beings carry an element of everybody's issue. Through his own issue Matthew could deeply identify with the client and also identify the discrepancies and challenge them.

Before we continue we need, however, to bring an element of caution to this idea. While we have found that the structure provides both an anchor and an invaluable tool in therapy, we must emphasize that the structure of the wheel needs to be considered only metaphorically and not as a literal representation of the world. Its only purpose is to facilitate the therapist to listen and intervene at the right time. If it gets too technical or is taken too literally, the structure can easily become counterproductive. Technique and theory can impede the natural flow of the relationship between client and therapist. In phenomenological terms, therefore, we must attempt to 'bracket' both the structure and the wheels when working with a client and attempt above all to remain 'human'.

In this way the structure provides a background for the therapist to facilitate clients to explore and become aware of their own world views and issues. Therapists will thus be able to give impetus to clients to challenge their own perceptions, to learn the process and continue to do so even after the therapy has ended. This way of relating to clients is very different to an open-ended, free flowing, dependence inducing therapy, although such therapy might be appropriate at times.

In the final part of this section, before we go into detailed descriptions of other 'givens', we describe the interpersonal relationship, anxiety and freedom of choice. All are those ontological 'givens' with which human beings are universally concerned and which are considered fundamental in existentialism. They are not only interconnected with each other, but also interconnected with other sections of the wheels. They are depicted on the existential wheel and represent both the limitations and possibilities of existence. Each individual will have his or her own special idiosyncratic way of dealing with these concerns, described here and further elaborated in Chapters 4 and 5.

INTERPERSONAL RELATIONSHIP

The interpersonal relationship in existential terms is seen as one of those 'givens' because it is not only the basis of all human interactions but is also a sine qua non of living. In other words, we cannot live without interacting with others from the moment we are born, that is to say it is a sine qua non of living to interact with other people. The significance of interpersonal relations is at the heart of most philosophy but Kierkegaard was the first to emphasize the importance of subjectivity to the individual.

Kierkegaard

A good deal of the background to the existential phenomenological approach stems from Sren Kierkegaard (1813–1855), a Danish Christian philosopher. He was influenced not only by his father's sombre, gloomy and guilt-ridden religion, but also by the Cartesian mind–body dichotomy that was the basis for the scientific and technological revolution then. Kierkegaard felt that the restrictions imposed by the scientific, objective rationale meant handcuffing human beings to an extremely narrow point of view. He claimed that in the process of objectifying reality into an abstraction or, that is, analysing reality from a distance, without experiencing it, was contrary to the human movement of existence. In Mary Warnock's words: 'The myth which Kierkegaard aims to destroy is the scientific myth that everything is causally determined, and that therefore in principle a complete and objectively true account of the behaviour could be provided, if only we took trouble and observed enough' (1970:8). 'For an abstract thinker to try to prove his existence by the fact that he thinks, is a curious contradiction' (ibid:281). He wanted to free humanity of this shackle and to open their eyes to a new viewpoint, which involved that of experience.

Kierkegaard has thus moved away from the accepted rational notions of investigation and suggested that in essence truth can be understood only in terms of subjective experience (1941). Through understanding the relational notion between 'being-in-the-world' and 'being-with-others' human beings become and always are in relational mode. The two can never be separated from each other. This was such a radical departure from the then current thinking and had such an impact on science and in particular psychotherapy, that it is worth exploring and contemplating further.

Kierkegaard's discovery took place in the period that was dominated by the Cartesian mind–body dichotomy and by Hegelian thought, which was characterized by the rational, systematic way of thinking that had prevailed in Europe for the previous two centuries. A typical Hegelian explanation of human thoughts was 'what is rational is actual and what is actual is rational' (1952:6). This kind of reasoning dominated European scientific and philosophical thinking as it marched through its technological successes of the industrial revolution.

Even though Kierkegaard wrote about this during the first half of the nineteenth century it was not recognized until the first quarter of the twentieth century. Freud, for instance, ignored these concepts and his theory still rests on the premise of strict scientific rationale. The conscious and unconscious psyche was studied in a neutral fashion and the mind and body was split, with the individual driven by unconscious conflicts that existed between the id, the ego and the super-ego. The therapist's function was to unravel and interpret the repressed material, making the patient discover the unconscious processes. It was all based on the scientific model of the mind.

In spite of this scientific edifice, as the psychoanalytic endeavour progressed, various authors began to use the notion of interpersonal empathy as a tool. Ralph Greenson, an American psychoanalyst and ex-chairman of the Scientific Advisory Committee, Foundation for Research on Psychoanalysis, writes:

> The ability to empathise is essential for psychological-mindedness and is dependent on the capacity for temporary and partial identification with others. It is necessary for effective communication between patient and analyst and must be present in both.
>
> (Greenson, 1967:54–55)

Although Martin Heidegger was a philosopher (a student of Husserl), he exerted great influence on modern existential psychotherapists, in particular on the Swiss existential psychotherapist Medard Boss (1979). He resurrected the Kirkegaardian relational theory in 1926, and expounded it in his voluminous book *Being and Time* (1962). Here he began to use the term 'being' as it related to the world: 'Everything we talk about, everything we have in view, everything toward which we comport ourselves in any way, is being; what we are is being and so is what we are. Being lies in the fact that something is, and in its Being as it is' (1962:26).

From this book's stance, however, the principal emphasis is to explore how human beings relate to the world and to others. Heidegger used the word *Dasein* to designate his perception of what it is to be a 'human being', which is translated as 'being-there' or 'being-in-the-world'. The hyphens in 'being-in-the-world' are present to suggest that these concepts are inseparable. The two notions are interconnected, in that 'being' cannot be investigated without exploring the notion of *Dasein* (human being) and only humans are capable of this kind of exploration. This position holds that the very fact that humans are aware of their existence implies an inseparable relationship between being human (or *Dasein*) and the world. Indeed, this relationship starts from birth, in that as soon as we are 'thrown' into the world we are immediately confronted with others. As such Heidegger demonstrates that humans have an inescapable relationship with one another, hyphenating the words so that the notion becomes 'being-with-others' (1962).

Our natural state is the state of communion with people who participate in one other's private world. This is an interdependent world and fundamentally a world of togetherness. The relationship that is established between two people contains aspects of caring and the expression of concern.

Heidegger's interpretation of 'being' and *Dasein* has become the underlining tenet for the existential philosophers such as Sartre (1958) and Merleau-Ponty (1962), and for therapists such as Boss (1979), May (1983), Yalom (1980), van Deurzen-Smith (1988) and Spinelli (1989).

It is also true to say that the psychotherapies of Carl Rogers (1961), Abraham Maslow (1968) and Fritz Perls (1959) took these notions and developed them into what is known as the Third Force of psychotherapy. All these theories are based around the idea of 'being with the client' and as such rely on the interpersonal relationship between client and therapist; they do not depend on the 'scientific' investigation of the mind.

The existential model is sometimes confused with the humanistic schools. It is true that they sprang from the original ideas but most of the humanists have strayed away from some of the basic philosophy. However, they have retained elements such as the importance of 'being with' the client and the notion of being always in relation with others' togetherness.

Contemporary existentialists

In general, existential therapists place particular emphasis on the importance of this type of model for relationships. Van Deurzen-Smith, for example, talks about the ideal relationship, which she calls the 'I–Me' relationship. This is the perfect relationship that, unfortunately, to a large extent, is only a Utopian one, but whose formulation allows us to understand the elements for which we strive. She writes that, 'In this type of relationship the individual surrenders her aspirations to selfhood and strives for something greater than herself instead' (1988:208). She compares this type of relationship with a couple's total commitment to one another:

> Neither tries to enslave or be enslaved by the other. Neither tries to be open to the other's subjectivity, both are just together in the harmony of unity. Almost invariably such experience coincides with a joint project which is highly desirable to both and for which each would be willing to cease to exist as an individual if this were necessary.
>
> (van Deurzen-Smith, 1988:208)

Existentially, this type of 'unifying I–Me' relationship is what we aim at in the therapeutic relationship, the client and therapist may experience a feeling of 'togetherness'. These are the moments when there is an intense understanding of how the client gains his or her meaning, when there is a combining of two understanding minds working towards the greater whole.

A slightly different interpretation emerges from Spinelli, who believes that the relationship between client and psychotherapist can be broken down into several elements consisting of self-to-self, self-to-other, and self-with-other.

Spinelli argues that what is different about existential phenomenological therapy is the focus on this third mode of relating, the 'self-being-in-relationship-with-the-other':

> While most therapeutic models emphasise and work with either the first or second (or both the first and the second) relational realms, they rarely attempt to the third, or indeed to the conjunction between the therapist's and client experience of 'self-being-in-relation-with-the other'. Yet it is precisely this third realm which existential phenomenological theory, as applied to therapy, illuminates and provides with its unique 'take' on therapy. In this way, it argues that it is through the exploration and clarification of this real 'being realm of between-ness' that the remaining two realms are more adequately disclosed to clarificatory challenge.
>
> (Spinelli, 1994:332)

Before we return to the question of 'specialness' and its importance in therapy, Carl Rogers must be considered, as he was one of the first psychologists to put these ideas on the world map. Rogers summarized his central hypotheses of his client-centred approach:

> Individuals have within themselves vast recourses for self-understanding and for altering their self-concepts, basic attitudes, and self-directed behaviour; these recourses can be tapped if a definable climate of facilitative psychological attitudes can be provided.
>
> (Rogers, 1980:115)

The facilitative attitude he refers to consisted of three elements: Genuineness, Congruence and Empathy. In short, a caring, empathic and congruent relationship creates a particular specialness in the therapeutic encounter. From these, clients can grow in a constructive manner when 'there is a close matching, or congruence, between what is being experienced at the gut level, and what is present in awareness, and what is expressed to the client' (Rogers, 1980:115).

Nevertheless, although Rogers emphasizes and in many ways based his early work around the importance of the interpersonal stance, he did diverge from other existentialist therapists, namely in the stress on his belief that all human beings are inherently good and all strive for self-actualization. From an existential point of view, human beings become and create themselves according to their own perceptions. The very idea of self-actualization implies that this is something good that must be strived for, which contradicts the notion of self as relational and self as constantly changing. This is discussed in more detail in Chapter 4.

From a historical perspective, it is interesting to note that until the middle of the twentieth century there were essentially only two dominant psychological orientations: the psychodynamic and the behavioural approaches. While both were employing different theoretically based models, they were united in their employment of the scientifically based exploration of the mind. As previously mentioned, the neo-Freudians and object relation theoreticians did give credence to the interpersonal element in therapeutic encounters. None of them, however, has promulgated this idea to the extent of the existentially underpinned therapies.

What is so different is that they remain largely preoccupied with the intra-psychic relationship. This in contrast with the existentialist stand that relates inter-subjectively with each other.

It must be clear by now, that from an existential stand the natural primordial state of human beings is the state of 'being-in-the-world' and through this inseparably 'being-with-others'. It is one of the intrinsic human 'givens' that being with others points to a communion among people and a natural interdependence of human beings. Moustakas (1994) quotes Tillich:

> A person becomes a person in the encounter with other persons, and in no other way . . . . Every human being is an absolute limit, an unpiercable wall of resistance against any attempt to make him an object. He who breaks this resistance by external force destroys his own humanity.
>
> (Tillich, 1961:15–21)

Interpersonal relationships are a universal 'given' that is characteristic to all human beings. In our work in existential time-limited therapy this 'given' has provided us with a launching pad from which to connect all the other universal human givens or concerns, which are graphically presented on the existential wheels.

Thus, using this special client and therapist relationship, we engage with the client in an existential exploration. The therapeutic encounter always reflects the client's behaviour in his or her 'outside' world as the microcosm of the therapy room reflects the macrocosm. In both of these worlds we find authentic and inauthentic ways of being.

While different authors have different views about the purpose of this special relational mode of working in a therapeutic situation, all of them would converge in accepting the premise that through this interpersonal mode, whether we call it togetherness (Sartre), 'I Thou' (Buber) or self-with-others (Spinelli), one promotes a change in clients' perceptions, or co-present as R. D. Laing used to do.

In existential time-limited therapy, we contend that a shift of perception occurs as a result of an interaction between experience, comprehension and apprehension. Apprehension in this context means mentally grasping the phenomenon, in other words, having an 'insight' experience. This is based on various experiential learning theories (Kolb, 1984) and is described and applied to a case study in Chapter 6.

We also experience and believe that a crucial conducive condition to precipitate these experiential processes is that of a special inter-subjective 'self-with-other' relationship. Through these relationships we engage with clients in an existential exploration of their world view. All relationships can develop into either authentic or inauthentic mode, although different authors have differing views on this.

Authenticity

Heidegger describes in *Being and Time* that authenticity is the ability to stand on one's own:

> Because *Dasein* in each case essentially its own possibility, it can, in its very Being, 'choose' itself and win itself; it can also lose itself and never win itself, – or only 'seems' to do so. But only insofar as it is essentially something which can be *authentic* – can it have lost itself and not yet won itself. As modes of Being, *authenticity* and *inauthenticity* . . . are both grounded in the fact that any *Dasein* whatsoever characterised by mineness. But the inauthenticity of *Dasein* does not signify any 'less' Being or any 'lower' degree of being.
>
> (Heidegger, 1962:68)

While Heidegger did not apply any value judgement on authenticity or inauthenticity, it is also true that as authentic humans we need to be open and able to accept all kinds of experiences, including all those ontological 'givens' that characterize our being between birth and death. As such, we are left alone to choose our attitudes and our decisions even facing and being aware of the ultimate finitude. Heidegger writes:

> Anticipation reveals to Dasein its lostness in they-self, and brings it face to face with the possibility of being itself, rather after itself, in an impassioned freedom towards death – a freedom which is a release from the Illusion.
>
> (Heidegger, 1962:311)

Thus, the true authenticity of human beings is to face and be aware of the temporality of our existence. To borrow Solomon's phrase from *Continental Philosophy since 1750*, 'This prospect of death gives him the most important choice to be authentic or not' (1950:227). For Sartre, on the other hand, inauthenticity means 'bad faith' and for him 'through bad faith, a person seeks to escape the responsible freedom for being for itself (1958:629). This means that inauthentic living (or in Sartrian terms 'bad faith') denies freedom and responsibility and denies anxiety, and instead various 'musts' and 'shoulds' imposed by class, religion and parental upbringing become the basis for inauthentic actions.

Authenticity, as described above, is a theoretical notion and can never be completely achieved. In practice, it is, however, more of an ideal to strive for authenticity than to live constantly in an authentic mode. It must also be realized that these authors believe that human beings oscillate between inauthenticity and authenticity. Without inauthenticity there can be no authenticity, and vice versa. From a practical point of view, however, authentic living is, as van Deurzen-Smith writes: 'becoming the author of one's own destiny. Quite simply, being authentic means being true to oneself' (1988:48). To make authentic decisions means discarding (or 'bracketing') preconceived judgements and opinions imposed by society or significant figures and gaining insight into one's own intentions, purposes and inclinations. Indeed, an authentic approach will precipitate anxiety, as the crutches that have kept clients safe and secure are being discarded. Anxiety may be temporarily suspended by finding new inauthentic support until such time as this fake security is proven false. The therapist must guide the client to realize that it is a sine qua non to accept that existential anxiety or 'angst' is not only part of life but the basic unease or malaise which humans experience as soon as they become aware of themselves. Existential anxiety is also, as previously stated, an ontological human characteristic.

Many different philosophical discourses have been written about the importance of authenticity. However, for this book, we will describe authenticity as simply a behaviour pattern, where decisions stem from being 'true to oneself', and are made through conscious awareness. Conversely, we would define inauthentic behaviour as stemming from compulsive, out of awareness kind of action. For example, when a bulimic individual binges, but at this moment is unaware of her motivation, she is acting inauthentically. As she becomes aware that she might be compensating or escaping from feelings of rejection and low self-esteem, she has at least become aware (or authentic) about her decision to binge.

ANXIETY

Another core of existential concepts that underlies the construction of the wheel is that of anxiety. This is inherent in every human interaction. Anxiety is another 'towards' relation of the 'being'. It is not a faculty which humans acquire but is, rather, and more important the centre of one's existence. It is not a peripheral threat or fear that may be classified with other reactions, but something that is rooted within man's existence. 'Existential anxiety' must be distinguished from 'fear'. Maybe the best way to describe existential anxiety (anguish or dread) is as not only a threat to being, but in May's words: 'Anxiety is the experience of the threat of imminent non-being' (1983:109). Anxiety is thus again an emotion towards others, namely the fear of loss of others.

Death anxiety, loneliness and isolation go hand in hand. This also applies to the recognition of our temporality. When we recognize that we are finite, that we must die, we also learn that we are inexorably alone. That our choices are limited is most clearly exemplified in death – we all have to die.

Existentialists believe that awareness of death gives significance to living. The characteristic of human being is the ability to think about the future and the inevitability of death. This need not be a negative prospect. The realization of death can provide us with zest for life and creativity. The denying of death is not only inauthentic but as Rollo May has said, it is 'self-alienation' (1961). Existentialists, therefore, do not view death negatively, but hold that awareness of finitude gives significance to living. Yalom postulates that the recognition of death may help us transform a stale mode of living into a more authentic one (1980).

Even on the simplest level, such as being asked by a female friend to decide which film to see, our immediate reaction may be tainted with anxiety. Before any conclusion, we might contemplate questions like: 'I don't know – what does she want me to say'; or 'I don't know – I'll think about it'; or 'If I choose this one, will she want to see it too?' Whatever the response, a choice includes an element of anxiety. Without anxiety, we would remain static, unable to move forward and unable to take responsibility for ourselves. Existentialist philosophy acknowledges that living is unknown and unpredictable, and from this premise of uncertainty it tries to explore how people go about living within this kind of world.

Clients sometimes come to therapy to be liberated from all their anxieties. Gary was one of those clients who had this belief. He met what he called his 'first setback in life' when his relationship with his 'great' girlfriend broke down, and he found that unexpectedly 'the repercussions were huge'. Until then Gary had seen his life as one of undiminished progress and success.

At the onset of therapy Gary believed that the process was concerned with the elimination of all anxieties. He felt that until this point in his life his academic, athletic and work successes had been achieved without difficulty. As Gary began to clarify and further illuminate on these successes, he became aware that in reality it was only his fantasy that his life had been free of anxiety. Indeed, his conviction was part of an illusion that juxtaposed neatly into his belief system, which incorporated the idea that one could and should go through life without meeting with anxiety.

Gary wrote after the completion of therapy that, 'When I could no longer deceive others and myself and – in other words when I could not maintain a fiction any longer – I had what I can only summarize as a breakdown.' It was only when Gary started to challenge himself and become aware that some of his anxieties were a normal part of living that he was able to contemplate an alternative range of choices and possibilities. Human beings need a degree of anxiety to realize that they are in a particular situation and that decisions need to be made.

FREEDOM OF CHOICE AND MEANING

From an existential point of view if human beings exercise their freedom of choice in experiencing others in the world, they also experience the uncertainty of their interpretations. Furthermore, human beings realize that all their interpretations are fluid and cannot depend on any certitude. Ultimately, this and the realization of temporality and knowledge that the relation to the world will always remain incomplete leads the individual to the conception of an existence that is meaningless. This does not mean that purpose or meaning of life are denied. On the contrary, faith and meaning are important factors in existential therapy. Van Deurzen-Smith writes:

> Existential counselling can be seen as a process of exploration of what can make life meaningful. The despair and the sense of futility that clients start out with is construed as a necessary first step in a quest for meaning.
>
> (van Deurzen-Smith, 1988:3)

Nevertheless in an authentic existence, man's relation to the world and to its meaning will always be tinged with doubt and uncertainty. Hence, in a final analysis man's existence is without intrinsic meaning and meaning has to be created. In spite of this, human beings always have the possibility to choose. While the limitations, as the existential wheel depicts, are substantial, so are the possibilities from which humans can choose. If apparent choices are not available, there are usually alternative ways of viewing the situation. For example, imagine two individuals incarcerated in two separate singular cells, who develop very different attitudes to their predicament. While the one can become completely desperate and search for possibilities to commit suicide, the other could find meaning in spirituality or in writing a book telling the story.

SUMMARY

In this chapter we have introduced some of the philosophical and theoretical background behind time-limited existential therapy. Although the basic concepts for both time-limited and long-term existential therapies do stem from the same background, we have pointed out the major distinctions in terms of emphasis, between the two models. Phenomenology is the primary tool for existential investigation, and its rules for explorations that are needed in existential time-limited therapy have been looked into. The differences between the emphases of time-limited and longer term existential therapies have been discussed. Under the heading of structure some of the fundamental concepts of existential time-limited therapy have emerged, graphically presented and described. Interpersonal relationship, starting from Kierkegaard onward has been discussed and anxiety, freedom to choose and authenticity have all been looked at, connected and presented in a graphic form. These core existential concepts are illustrated to introduce the reader into more specific elements of the time-limited therapy approach. Other concepts such as safety, temporality, values, behaviour sedimentations, the four worlds and paradoxes will be further elaborated upon in the following chapters and are outlined as part of the structure of the wheel.

3

THE MYSTERY OF TIME

Although very few of us could imagine life without the reality of living in the present, dreaming of a future or remembering the past, it is nevertheless extremely hard to define our perceptions of time. It is certainly a shared human experience that our perception of time will vary from time to time and from place to place. An hour in a therapeutic session can sometimes feel as short as a few minutes, while at other times the same hour can seem as long as three. From this we can deduce that our perception of time does not correspond with actual chronological time. The way we perceive time is very much dependent on our particular emotional state, which has its own implications for time-limited therapy.

Philosophers, scientists and psychologists have argued for centuries about the correct explanation and meaning of time, but there has never been a clear consensus of opinion both in regard to physical reality and time or psychological perception. Extensive literature exists and numerous arguments abound, but they all conclude in paradoxes. Examples of these circular debates date back over the centuries to St Augustine and John Locke.

St Augustine, the major Christian theologian, argued in the fourth century about the necessary relationship between mind and time. He asserted that 'if there is no mind there can be no time' (Boscolo and Bertrando, 1993:30). In contrast, Sir Isaac Newton, physicist and mathematician, author of *Principia* (1687), formulated his Theory of Mechanics, which argued that if time exists in the universe it must also be measurable by the motion of matters in relation to their space. Time is thus distinct from temporal things, and exists in its own right. Thus the notion of time is not an invention of the human mind, but it subsists in reality, irrespective of human existence.

In the same century, however, John Locke, the English philosopher, argued that nothing exists in the mind except that which resides in the senses. In other words everything is relational to that of our mind:

> When anyone says that Queen Elisabeth lived sixty-nine, and reigned forty-five years, these words import only that

> duration to some other, and mean no more but this. That the duration of her existence was equal to sixty-nine, and the duration of her government to forty-five annual revolution of the sun; and so are all words, answering, How Long?
>
> (Locke, 1952:217–218)

Thus, according to some authors and contrary to Newton's scientific theory, time cannot exist as an external reality except in the minds of observers. These two views demonstrate how we can perceive more than one kind of concept of time. According to the scientific rationale, time exists in its own right in that it is external and not reliant on the presence of humans. It must also be measurable and is the basis of chronological time or clock time. Psychological time or subjective time, on the other hand, is defined as our capacity to perceive the passage of time in our own particular subjective manner. Precisely because of this subjectivity, time is therefore linked closely to our temporal existence and does not necessarily correspond to clock time. Psychological time depends on our emotional state, that is, whether time passes quickly or slowly is dependent on our particular mood, on our state of being.

It is interesting that *Webster's International Dictionary* defines temporality as 'concern with time and as (human) relation to time and the world rather than to eternity'. Indeed, temporality means that every human experience, including our own existence, is by its nature transitional.

Translating these concepts in terms of our experience, we find that the language of existential philosophy aids us in our understanding of time. Existential philosophy is about the investigation of human existence and 'temporality'. It is the most essential part of human existence, because it also relates to a person's mode of being and relationship to the temporal dimensions of the past, present and future. How we relate to these three dimensions of time reveals important aspects about our relationships to ourselves.

Some people convince themselves that they live in their past: they might blame the past for all their ills, or they might view their past as something that was so wonderful that they seek to return to that time of bliss. By living in this way, these people have a tendency to ignore their present and their future. Other people stay in the present, they live their lives as if they had no past and certainly no future. Present time becomes a safe haven because the future is too uncertain and the past is too frightening to contemplate.

Finally, there are people who wait for the future to happen, but invariably it never does, or rather not in the way they had anticipated. Doreen was one such example: she was brought up with the cultural expectation that she would stay at home until she got married. From an early age she fought with her mother, became exasperated with her father, but knew in the back of her mind that everything would turn out for the better 'when she got married'. In her early thirties Doreen did get married, but she soon found, after the novelty of being a married woman had worn off, that her life was not progressing in the direction that she had expected. She still had a difficult relationship with her parents, she still felt a great unease about life and she was having problems relating to her husband. She buried herself in various self-help books relating to strategies at work, hoping that she might gain satisfaction by being promoted at work. In therapy Doreen gradually came to understand how she always lived in the future and what this implied in terms of her dissatisfaction with her life. As she started to live more in the present, the future began to take care of itself. Understanding each person's sense of their past, present and future can help guide a client towards a more balanced position between these three states of time.

Death, too, is an important part of our sense of temporality and how we incorporate death into our sense of living. In *Being and Time* (1962:372), Heidegger proposes that human beings disclose themselves either authentically or inauthentically. Indeed, our attitude towards death is our foremost concern and can also be either authentic or inauthentic. For Heidegger authenticity and our awareness of our finitude are closely related. Death is closely related to nothingness. He says that by accepting the encounter with nothingness, we can muster and organize our possibilities in life. That is, we can project ourselves into the future:

> Anticipation reveals to Dasein its lostness in the they-self, and brings it face to face with the possibility of being itself, primarily unsupported by concern of solicitude, but of being itself, rather in an impassioned freedom towards death – a freedom which has been released from the illusions of the 'they', and which is 'factical', certain of itself, and anxious.
>
> (Heidegger, 1962:311)

The only way we can avoid experiencing temporality is by inauthentically denying and escaping from it. In fact, in contemplating time and temporality, we are always moving in a self-reflecting loop, since we have no possibility or power to extricate ourselves from temporality or from the notion of time. For existentialists, all our experiences are temporal or subjective in nature. Time is so much part of our existence that we argue that no therapy which takes into account the existential themes can be called open ended, for this would imply that the temporal aspect of life which includes endings would be excluded from the therapeutic process. Therefore, whether we work with clients on a time-limited or longer term basis, the concept of time is paramount. In the following sections of this chapter we will examine the factors that influence our psychological time, i.e. those psychological and biological aspects which change our perception of time in relation to chronological time.

PHYSICAL CHRONOLOGICAL TIME

Our inner feeling of temporality, our perception of the duration of time, is always related to what we believe is a fixed certainty, and that is the certainty of chronological time. All mankind's activity and thought is calibrated to clock time. So what and where does this idea of clock time come from? Official public time was not invented by scientists but originates from the observation that the passage from day to night changes in the position of the sun, moon and that other star and seasonal changes followed a pattern. Scientists only entered the picture when more accuracy was demanded. Technology required the subdivision of days into equal intervals in order to determine an accurate reference point and stemming from this, clocks were invented to monitor the passage of time. Chronological time arises from the need for public time and has been adopted globally to suit our purposes.

BIOLOGICAL TIME

Although to a certain extent our biological sense of time is capable of adjusting to both our external and internal subjective circumstances, the body is governed by biological rhythm. The 24-hour biological pattern is called the circadian cycle. During this period we usually sleep for approximately eight hours and are awake for sixteen. While we are asleep, voluntary muscle activities almost disappear and there is a decrease in metabolic rate, respiration, heart rate and blood pressure. During our wakeful hours our mental and physical functions are most active. The natural time signal for the circadian pattern is the change from darkness to light. Changes such as our metabolic rates, respiration, heartbeat, hormone secretion and many other alterations take place according to the cycle.

It might appear that our circadian rhythm is one of the fixed points as regards the universal time measurement, but this is not so. Drastic shifts in the circadian cycle cause our bodies to readjust and there are individual reactions to these changes. The jet-lag syndrome is one good example. Travelling from San Francisco to London there is a time difference of eight hours in which all the biological cycles need to be reset. Some people can readjust in a few hours, while for others the adjustment can take days. It has been shown that pilots who are continuously shifting their circadian rhythms suffer not only from physical fatigue, but may also experience mental health problems. The same applies to shift workers, such as nurses, who are continually changing their circadian rhythms from day to night. Another additional factor to how well a person will cope with a change in their circadian rhythm is their particular emotional, physical and psychological state at the time of the shift.

One can conclude that changes in the circadian rhythm will in turn disturb or modify our psychological sense of time, which will therefore be at variance with clock time. As any disturbance of the circadian pattern (such as lack of sleep) will have an effect on our emotional state, the awareness of this phenomenon in therapy is necessary.

Another interesting phenomenon is related to seasons in the year and the differences associated with the northern and southern hemisphere. For instance, summer in the northern hemisphere is considered to be June to September, while in the southern hemisphere the warm weather months are December through to March. Moving from one hemisphere to another can have an enormous effect on one's sense of being. It is interesting that 'markers' such as Christmas, Easter, Hallowe'en, the blooming of spring flowers or the falling of autumn leaves, which have their particular associations with months, seasons and sense of continuing time in the year, become irrelevant when changing hemispheres. Time in relation to the movement within the year becomes meaningless.

Time can also become meaningless in certain psychological situations. For example, some clients in a catatonic or total depressive state can completely lose their sense of time.

PSYCHOLOGICAL TIME

Psychological time and temporality are multi-faceted. People's sense of time, inside or outside a therapeutic session, depends greatly on their emotional, biological and physiological state. In a therapeutic situation the therapist is concerned with the client's subjective perception of 'reality'. Indeed, reality from an existential phenomenological perspective is nothing but a human perception, as Spinelli notes:

> True reality is, and will forever remain, both unknown and unknowable to us. Instead, that which we term reality, that is, that which is experienced by us as being reality, is inextricably linked to our mental processes in general, and in particular, to our in-built, innate capacity to construct meaning.
>
> (Spinelli, 1989:2)

Individuals in a depressed emotional state, for example, often feel that time does not seem to pass. The same person, in another emotional state, may perceive clock time as their only reality. Sometimes there is too much time and sometimes there is never enough. Jane recounted how she often lost track of time completely when she spent what she considered to be happy times with her partner. Yet, when she felt jealous and he had left her waiting for hours, she would count every minute and every second and time would go by very slowly.

The emotive feature of temporality plays a great role in our perception of time, which in turn is subjective and can deviate from chronological time. The way we sense time depends on how we are experiencing the immediate present, which in turn is linked to our emotional state. Fear, terror, horror, panic, dismay, as well as joy, happiness and love, can alter one's perception of duration. There are many factors which can determine our internal perception, including our attitude to stress, particular motivations, and the degree of urgency for accomplishing a goal. Drugs too will radically change both the emotive state and often the subjective sense of time.

In therapy, the manner in which a client experiences these different manifestations of time can be a useful tool for exploration. Changes in emotive features can be picked up through modifications in body language and often by a switching in rhythm of a client's tone of voice and language.

One of the themes commonly heard is how people experience near-death encounters. They usually describe how time slowed down to the extent that a few seconds seemed endless, where all senses became heightened. Some say that sequences of their life flashed before them. Another example is how people describe their holidays when they are away from their daily routine. Maria went away for three weeks and used her stay for a combination of relaxation and reading, as well as enjoying a full itinerary of tourist attractions. While she was there time seemed to fly, but on her return she realized that the time frame seemed much longer than when in her usual routine of work.

A corollary of these incidents related to time is that therapists can use the opportunity to tune into clients' perceptual framework and gain a deeper understanding of the way in which they run their lives according to time.

TIMELESSNESS

Marie Bonaparte, one of Freud's early collaborators, elaborated in some detail how she interpreted the notion of timelessness in her book *Time and Timelessness* (1938). She described a period of infancy, which is devoid of any notion of temporality, as a state of paradise. Through the phenomenon of time, human beings are burdened with fear of death, uncertainty and unpredictability. They constantly try to escape from this harness and invent the notion of eternity and permanency, in order to return to this eternal bliss of timelessness. According to Bonaparte one of the ways humans escape automatically from the yoke of death anxiety is through dreams:

> This flight from the tyranny of time which we are able to review each night seems . . . to represent one of the greatest wish fulfilment accomplished by the dream for the benefit of human beings who remain harnessed to time's chariot while days lasts [sic].
>
> (Bonaparte, 1938:461–462)

The wish for eternity, the desire to escape from anxiety or isolation and occasionally to escape from the dread of difficult decision-making drives humans, without even being aware of why are they doing so, to return and to re-experience these childhood moments of timelessness, which Bonaparte calls the paradise.

The therapeutic contract between client and therapist is drawn up in order to create a safe environment. The framework for this contract is designed to be conducive to hold clients in a trusting and safe setting. This notion of a safe boundary is described in detail in Chapter 5. Within this wholesome therapeutic boundary, the safe holding environment is re-enacted. On some occasions clients are able to re-experience this euphoria of oblivion, or rather a sense of timelessness. Rebecca was reliving her anguish over her mother's death, describing the dreams she still had and generally talking about her thoughts and feelings. The only interventions during the session were to allow Rebecca to delve deeper into her thoughts. At the end of the session, Rebecca stood up in a daze. She could not believe that 50 minutes had passed and described the experience as one of 'timelessness'.

Van Deurzen-Smith describes in *Existential Counselling in Practice* (1988) how a therapist–client counselling relationship which is conducive to this safe and holding environment is akin to Buber's notion of the I–Thou human relationship. She recounts this process as a desirable concept of the therapeutic session:

> In the unity of the shared project individual differences become unimportant for the moment. All that stands out is the awareness of an underlying motive which binds people together. The energy and enthusiasm generated in such a moment of merging with an absolute notion of one's own destiny can be considerable. Many religions, especially more primitive ones, build their ceremonies around this type of experience. Healing rituals do the same thing.
>
> (van Deurzen-Smith, 1988:209)

In this nurturing, caring therapeutic environment the temporal perception of time may sometimes become irrelevant and the everyday life sense of time gives away to a different reality: a perception of timelessness.

GOAL-SETTING IN RELATION TO THE SENSE OF TIME

One of the most important factors influencing the time horizon is the individual's attitude towards personal goals. Goal-setting and expectations are inherently intertwined with the perception of the duration of time. People commonly take the attitude that goals, once set, should be realized in the shortest possible time. Our emotions will move from a state of calm to that of extreme stress according to the importance and urgency of the particular goal. These emotive changes, needless to say, influence our perception of time and in turn constitute material to work upon in therapy.

For example, clients who come to their first session with a specific problem often expect that problem to be 'cured' within a limited time period. Stephen had a fear of flying. He had put his own time limit on therapy as he fully expected to jet around the world without fear within fifteen weeks. He also came armed with his own theories, having read many books on the subject of phobias, and was insistent that he needed a label. Once he had one, he felt that he could find a specific 'cure'. He took to the process of therapy 'like a duck to water'. He appeared to be enjoying the process of exploring, clarifying and challenging many of his beliefs and behaviours. He also did a great deal of writing in between sessions, where he would clarify his thoughts. But time was ticking away and Stephen, feeling the pressure of this, became angry in the sixth session because he believed he was no closer to getting on his aeroplane. He felt cheated and manipulated by the therapist. Instead of taking the more obvious route around Stephen's anger, the rest of the session was devoted to his sense of time, and how he felt when it was out of his control. He began to piece together several instances when time was an important factor. For example, for work he often had to fly to different locations, which would mean getting up early in the morning, working until late and then taking the last plane back. It emerged that again he felt cheated because his employers were too penny-pinching to put him up in a hotel overnight. Essentially, he resented having to work under these conditions. Again, when he flew to exotic places for holidays, he felt cheated. Holidays were supposed to be fun, but instead he would feel restless and lonely, wondering what he was doing. The pressure of time, including his expectations of his goals and the sense of feeling swindled, were intricately interrelated.

In time-limited therapy the client tends to emphasize goals more than in an open-ended approach. Indeed, the limitation of time can be considered almost an inhibition to the attainment of the desired therapeutic atmosphere, since both the therapist and the client may feel that they must achieve something. This pressure is compounded if one takes into consideration the existential phenomenological approach of this book, which holds that the desire of the therapist to help the client and the resulting pressure which the therapist may place on the client is counterproductive (Spinelli, 1994).

If we take into consideration that both therapists and clients are affected by time then this aspect alone may constitute a very powerful argument against using time-limited therapy. And yet, it can also be argued that it is just because of these changes and the changes of the dynamic in the therapeutic relationship that the existential approach enables the therapist to challenge this pressure and to turn these negative aspects into an advantage. In the following chapters it is precisely this kind of pressure, in terms of the impending ending, that will be described. The ending itself is the catalyst for both therapists and clients to challenge clients' discrepancies and contradictions.

It is sufficient for now to argue that in an inter-subjective and personal relationship it is important to become aware that the pressure of time needs to be addressed. If the therapist is able to suspend all prejudices, the desire to pursue goals, the need to cure the client, and to 'be there' with the client in an interpersonal relationship, then paradoxically, this may enable the therapist to create the desired therapeutic atmosphere described earlier.

There is also a cultural perspective on time. The Hopi Indians, for example, have no tenses in their language and therefore do not distinguish between past, present and future (Boscolo and Bertrando, 1993). This draws attention to the fact that the therapist must become cognisant with each individual's relationship with time in order to understand the client's unique perceptual framework. It is also true that becoming aware of a client's sense of time can lead to themes around behaviour and general attitude about life. At the same time this kind of exploration allows the therapist to enter into the client's perceptual framework, and by sharing his or her concept of time aids in creating the 'relationship' that is paramount to the existential approach; this is described in further chapters.

THE ECONOMY OF TIME-LIMITED THERAPY

Another increasingly important aspect of time is the financial element or the economy that a time-limited approach offers, compared to open-ended therapy. Psychotherapy in the UK is available through the National Health Service, voluntary organizations such as MIND (for mental health), the Terrence Higgins Trust (specializing in HIV and AIDS), or through the private sector. As the National Health Service waiting list for clients is so extensive (on average six months for the first assessment), offering counselling or therapy for a limited time would drastically reduce delays. In some cases this is already being done.

Not only does taking a time-limited approach help to relieve financial burdens, it is also argued that for many cases it is more conducive for processing problems and issues than the more traditional open-ended therapies. Furthermore, it will be argued that at times the longer term therapies can be counterproductive, and may initiate their own dependency issues, both for the client and for the therapist.

SUMMARY

Various authors and theories have divergent views concerning the nature of time. Time can be seen as a physical, natural phenomenon which is measurable by instruments, and can also be conceived as a subjective construct of the human mind. Psychological time is multi-faceted and depends on human beings' emotional, physical and physiological state. From an existential perspective, human beings are inextricably welded to their own and others' sense of the world as well as their submersion in their particular temporal existence in time.

Since changes in clients' sense of temporality are intricately related to their emotional and physiological state, these notions have important implications in the practice of therapy. The list of emotional factors influencing and altering a person's view of temporality is almost endless and therefore using a client's 'in-the-moment' perception of time is extremely useful. In addition to the verbal content, changes in body language can also be worked with. Often clients can verbalize how their body 'feels' before they can verbalize anything else. An important function of the therapist is to tune into a client's perceptual framework and using time can aid this process.

We exist in the present, but upon reflection our current experiences are always extrapolated from, and validated by, our reconstruction of the past (even the immediate past) and an aspiration or direction toward the future. This has therapeutic implications. The process can be advanced by the pressure of the time limitation imposed from the outset of the time-limited approach. The restriction of time alters the dynamics of interaction taking place between the client and the therapist. Many say that this could have an adverse effect on therapy, but it is argued here that the existential approach can turn this negative aspect into an advantage.

4

EXISTENTIAL TIME-LIMITED THERAPY LIMITATIONS AND POSSIBILITIES

The purpose of this section of the book is to illustrate the practical aspects behind the existential 'time-limited' approach under discussion and to consider how these relate to some key existential concepts. In order to present what are often complex and abstract ideas in a straightforward and clear manner, graphical representations and case studies will be used.

WHAT IS EXISTENTIAL TIME-LIMITED THERAPY?

Some confusion exists regarding the definition of time-limited therapy. While some authors employ the term 'brief therapy', others prefer to speak of 'time-limited therapy'. Semantics aside, what is being expressed in a variety of terms is that important differences exist in the many underlying assumptions and techniques employed by the practitioner.

Of the various existing models, Mann (1973:16), for example, has developed a time-limited model consisting of twelve non-negotiable sessions. In contrast to this, Budman *et al.* (1992) and Dryden and Feltham (1992) argue against a rigid framework and suggest that sessions can range in number from one to approximately twenty. Dryden and Feltham stress the importance of the client's need to find a focus. Here 'time-limited therapy' is more an attitude adopted by the therapist and client at the start of therapy, highlighting that there is a definite end to the course of therapy. This is a very different stance from open-ended therapy, where part of the process for the client is not to know when he or she will conclude the course until this is mutually – or at times individually by the therapist – agreed upon at some stage in the process.

However, there are some similar theoretical concepts inherent in all these brief therapies. First, it is argued, there is less likelihood of clients becoming dependent on the therapy or the therapist. Second, the aim is to use the structure of time in a more economical fashion, knowing the self-imposed time pressure. Third, as in all therapies, the underlying belief is that clients are able to carry the acquired experiences beyond the confines of therapy, so that change will occur as a natural progression.

While the existential time-limited approach accepts these three underlying principles, it also believes that all of the client's presenting issues are interconnected to his or her life experience and therefore it is largely irrelevant which issues become the focus. Thus, this approach does not find it necessary to have a focal point other than the exploration of the client's being-relations. He or she does not set any kind of goal that might impede the natural flow of the client's self-disclosure. Our aim is to initiate a self-disclosure that can precipitate an inter-subjective relationship which can induce exploration of a client's own discrepancies. This in turn may precipitate experience of insights and a shift of rigid sedimented perception.

It must also be re-emphasized that in existential terms the notion of time is paramount, whether it be limited to the twelve-week modular approach or incorporated into longer term therapy. Time, and the clients' awareness of its importance in their lives, become part of the learning process. Since our existence in this world is to all intents and purposes ultimately temporary, this 'given' is accompanied by core anxieties. The fear of ending, whether it is separation from a friend, a job or the ultimate – death, is raised in therapy and possibly made explicit when a limit of time is part of the intrinsic process.

Therefore it is one of the fundamental features of our position to highlight the concept of the temporal nature of existence in therapy. To be aware of the great variety of aspects of time and temporality in therapy is a vital characteristic of both the existential 'open-ended' approach (as it is called) and the time-limited therapy approach advocated in this work. Excluding or not incorporating time awareness in open-ended therapy subverts the concept of open-ended existential therapy. 'Open-ended existential therapy' thus becomes a misnomer, since 'open-ended' might mean that the 'time' element of the therapy has not been considered at any point. Without a perception of chronological and psychological time, true existential therapy does not exist. Therefore any practitioner of existential therapy must integrate the time component into the process, whether it be the time-limited therapy approach described in this book or in a longer term therapy. We thus arbitrarily term existential therapy that consists of no more than 20 to 40 sessions as time-limited existential therapy, and those with no specific number of sessions as long-term or open-ended existential therapy.

THE REASON FOR TIME-LIMITED THERAPY

The expectation for both therapist and client has traditionally been that therapy is long term, open ended and may last for years. However, current life styles and changing social conditions mean that people cannot afford to spend either time or money on long-term therapy. Indeed, this trend towards briefer courses of therapy had already appeared to have taken an accelerated momentum after World War II. This is exemplified by James Mann who already in 1964 instituted a programme at Boston University School of Medicine and Medical Center for time-limited psychotherapy (Mann, 1973:IX–X) In addition, recognition of the value of therapy by the National Health Service and business corporations has led to significant pressure to shorten the process to accommodate financial constraints.

Various other therapists such as Malan (1963), Macnab (1991), Budman *et al.* (1992), Gustafson (1986) and de Shazer (1985) are all involved in this paradigm. Dryden and Feltham describe in *Brief Counselling* how therapists both in the USA and UK have reduced the duration of therapy considerably. For example, Dryden and Feltham note that in the USA, 70 per cent of clients attend an average of six or fewer visits (1992:209). Student population research in England points to similar figures. According to Dryden and Feltham:

> For the year 1990/1991, for example, Leicester Polytechnic Counselling and Welfare Service saw 490 clients from a total student population of 11,922, who attended an average of four sessions (74 per cent of clients attended for only one session): University College London Counselling Service in that same period saw 250 clients from a total student population of 9138, for an average four to five sessions.
>
> (Dryden and Feltham, 1992:51)

There are certain situations where a time-limited approach is the only option available to the therapist, although we have found that there are also distinct advantages, even when the constraints of time or money do not exist. Yet, rather than simply follow a curtailed version of open-ended therapy, it is vital for the therapist to have an understanding of the implications of working within time-limited frames.

We began to formulate this particular approach to time-limited therapy work for different reasons and in different places, yet there was an outstanding similarity in the methods we had begun to investigate. Initially, we were both working in private practice as existential therapists within an 'open-ended' paradigm. Freddie had begun supervising at an institution that had changed its working approach from open-ended therapy to one that offered a maximum of twelve sessions. At this time, Alison decided to emigrate to Australia; if she wished to continue to see new clients before she left, she would be forced to work within the short time available.

As we have said before, we do not believe that a time-limited approach is suitable for all clients. The initial sessions are therefore very important to assess whether the option is feasible. If we feel that the client would benefit from time-limited therapy, and the client agrees, the terms of the contract are subsequently elaborated and agreed upon.

ASSESSMENT

Clients are seen at our practice on an average of between ten and twelve times and the therapy always ends with two subsequent review sessions at not less than four to eight weeks later. These terms are agreed upon in the first session and are not offered if the client wants open-ended therapy or we believe that this type of time-limited therapy work would not be favourable. During initial negotiation of the contract we incorporate, by mutual agreement, a contingency for additional sessions. Situations occasionally arise where the therapist and the client need to renegotiate the time frame which may result in an additional block of sessions. For this reason, we developed the modular system (see below, Modular time-limited therapy approach). In such cases, we recommend waiting for a specific period of time to elapse, usually between four and six weeks, before entering into another series of sessions. The reason for this long interval is to give clients breathing space and the opportunity to apply their learning from the counselling experience to their daily relations outside the therapeutic setting and the security of having recourse to a therapist. Clients should become acclimatized to working through and resolving their issues themselves, without recourse to a therapist.

We have found that it is not desirable to be rigid about which clients are more suitable for existential time-limited therapy and which are not. In many ways, the therapist has to assess the type of client that can best adapt to this type of therapy. There are some situations where the time constraint is imposed from the outset, due to the client's own circumstances. In general, our experience suggests that clients who present themselves with a very specific problem, but are not too inflexible in the way they perceive themselves and who are prepared for self-examination, are most suited to this approach. Clients who are too dogmatic in outlook, or have a long history of alcohol abuse or drug addiction, for example, would be less suitable. Clients who have not experienced a loving role model and find it hard to express or even acknowledge emotions will generally gain more from long-term therapy. However, these guidelines can be misleading, for we have seen clients suffering from eating disorders and those with extreme anxiety problems who on the surface would appear unsuited, but have achieved a reasonable therapeutic outcome.

MODULAR TIME-LIMITED THERAPY APPROACH

When we first began using the time-limited approach, we conformed to the strict ending procedures that some of the existing models suggested, such as Mann (1973), Strupp (1992), Budman *et al.* (1992) and Ellis (1992). However, we began to see that there were occasions when the twelve weeks, plus the two follow-up sessions, proved to be too time limited. For example, one of our clients, Denise, completed her twelve-week course and her two follow-up sessions. Her initial presenting problem of depression appeared to have dissipated and she had explored various issues in the process, among them a sedimented behaviour pattern of optimum control. Among the sedimented issues, the behaviour pattern of optimum control appeared paramount. Without this optimum control she felt lost, and without self-importance or self-concept.

A few months later she returned to therapy, not due to depression, but because she had begun to be overwhelmed by her negative emotions and by anxiety. She said, 'It felt as if the first few months only lifted the lid off the Pandora's Box. Now I need to know where to go with all these feelings and thoughts.' In such a situation, we recommend a different approach. After a series of clients who, like Denise, demonstrated that a rigid non-negotiable framework could sometimes appear incomplete, we modified our procedure to allow for a more flexible setting of boundaries.

The more adaptable approach means that further sessions are available for those clients who are in an agitated or confused state and need additional time to explore some of their unresolved issues. To retain the framework and maintain the context of a time-limited therapy approach, we draw clients' attention to the possibility of further modules of therapy and follow-up sessions in the initial outlining of the contract. It is interesting that Dryden and Feltham (1992) realize that:

> There is no one right way to terminate counselling, as we have said. It will be apparent . . . that there are different approaches to time-limited counselling and its management. . . . There is also the question of fixed or staggered or tapered endings; of serial counselling (repeated courses of counselling over a span, perhaps, of years); and follow-ups.
>
> (Dryden and Feltham, 1992:71)

The drawback to open-ended therapy is that clients lose some of the impetus and incentive associated with the absolute finality that strict time limitation provides. We acknowledge that sometimes humanitarian reasons take preference over perfectionism. However, we believe that it is necessary to accept that clients have differing and changing needs. Some will find that the first module only begins to touch the surface of the issues they want to explore. In our opinion, incorporating this flexibility into the framework considerably outweighs the disadvantages involved. What remains crucial in any case is the adherence to a fixed series of sessions that delineate the boundaries of any module and which imbue it with its independence and completion.

There are occasionally situations where clients are terrified of clear-cut endings. Separations can become very awkward and due to the strict boundaries of time-limited therapy the therapist needs to remain rigid about time limitations. The modular approach introduced at the beginning of the therapy could eliminate this problem. Shirley's case exemplifies this perfectly. Shirley, a client of a supervisee, came to therapy outlining a problem of deep depression, insomnia and panic attacks. The institution where the supervisee worked had only allocated eight sessions. It transpired that Shirley was a transsexual who had been born a man and had undergone a sex-change operation. She told a story of an extremely unhappy childhood, throughout which she felt that she had been born the wrong gender. She had been absolutely convinced that being a woman would bring her total happiness. Although the operation had been a technical success and some of Shirley's peers accepted her new persona, she could not find the complete fulfilment she had hoped for.

Despite her lifelong dream being realized, she descended into a state of suicidal depression. The therapist involved felt overwhelmed and frustrated. It seemed impossible to overcome such an intensive problem in a set number of sessions. We explored various possibilities that might prove suitable and effective for both the client and the institution. We arrived at a framework of a module of a further eight sessions followed by two review sessions that we hypothesized would be accepted by the institution. There was also an option that, if necessary, either of them could have recourse to another series of eight sessions. This brought a sense of relief not only to the supervisee and the client, but also to the institution that had agreed to this structure.

The method of working in blocks proved rewarding for everyone involved. We adopted the term 'modular time-limited existential approach' to encompass the idea of seeing clients in either a single module (for example, twelve plus two sessions) or a series of such modules. At the end of a course of therapy some clients may not feel ready to embark upon independent exploration, believing that they have been abandoned by an uncaring therapist. One of the advantages of the block method is that clients do not feel rejected should they need to negotiate another series of sessions.

Should either the client or the therapist, however, find that additional sessions are required, and the client had been under the impression of a fixed ending, it could then appear that the therapist had made an error in the initial assessment of a client's needs. Thus a question of the therapist's credibility may arise. In allowing for the provision of further modules in the initial contract, the therapist maintains his or her credibility and the trust of the client. Admittedly, a strict frame usually results in a more intense type of therapy, since time-limited existential therapy uses the impetus of time as a tool itself. However, we have found great benefits in demonstrating flexibility rather than conforming rigidly to one module of twelve weeks.

We also discovered that keeping the aspects of time limitation always in the foreground intensified the clients' working on their issues not only during sessions but in between, and that the gap between one module and another usually results in many insights that in turn, as explained earlier, may initiate change of perception.

CASE EXAMPLE

Pia exemplified the way in which we were able to incorporate this more malleable approach into the structure. She completed one module of sessions, during which we worked on her compulsive behaviour that manifested itself in the way she interacted with people. For example, she would take enormous risks, such as bringing her lover home, even when her husband was there. She took pleasure in entering into relationships with men without thinking of the consequences of her actions. Pia also developed an involuntary trembling of her hands when she had to face what she termed as 'important' people in a work context. By forcing herself to smile and make light-hearted conversation, Pia was able both to divert her own attention away from her trembling hands, and to distract others from noticing.

While exploring these strategies and her method of coping with her increasing loss of self-esteem, we began to look at those value systems that had begun the cycle. Pia realized that her nervous condition was associated with her view of her father, who on one occasion had been so violent with her that he had broken her lower arm. She became aware that this incident had made her feel totally rejected and alone. She had been unable to understand who she was and how she should relate to people. In the following sessions the incident served as a metaphor to explore her various coping techniques, which she used to avoid the devastating feelings of low self-worth.

One year after we had finished the module, Pia telephoned from abroad in a tearful state to ask if we could meet. She told me that she had met Martin while she was abroad on business. She had fallen in love with him, divorced her husband and married Martin within the space of three months. She had great doubts about her decision and had become deeply depressed. We agreed on a modular contract of five sessions and began examining Pia's compulsion for excitement in her life. She became aware that rushing into her new relationship with Martin was also part of her pattern of needing a new exciting experience that ultimately did not fulfil her needs. It was obvious to Pia that these sedimented behaviour patterns now served the purpose of avoiding her feelings of low self-esteem that had begun in her childhood.

At the fifth and final session Pia was in a state of utter distress. She truly believed that she would not find the happiness and stimulation that she needed within this marriage. We then explored the process of our present therapeutic encounter. I challenged her assumption that the only way to 'live fully' was either to chase men or to pursue what she considered exciting experiences:

F. Pia, we've discussed before how you enjoy taking chances, whether it be through the men that you see, or by travelling to new places, and generally how you seek new excitement.

P. (*after a longish silence*) Yes, for me living means living life to the full, otherwise it is not worth living.

F. It appears to me that you are feeling quite anxious now – am I correct?

P. Yes, very much so. For me to live an ordinary life is a treadmill existence and I have been very successful in avoiding that all my life. I also want to continue avoiding it.

P. (*long silence*) . . . but I pay a price for it. (*She cries.*)

F. Pia, how do you feel now in your body? What about your breathing?

P. I feel a knot here (*she points to her chest*) and I'm only breathing up to here (*she points to her lower chest. Then as her breathing becomes deeper and her thoughts become quieter, she starts to sob.*)

P. (*after another long silence*) This is the first time in my life I have felt that maybe even in this quietness and silence I could find a quality that could replace the constant race to live a 'full' life.

Pia then contemplated the possibility of finding some other kind of meaning and value in her life, of perhaps finding positive aspects to remaining restful. We then explored the potential of finding purpose and interest even in the drudgery of everyday life.

On parting, Pia questioned me about whether she could contact me in the future. I referred to our previous discussions, noting that it was preferable to allow a few months to pass before starting another module, to learn and benefit from the sessions. However, should she need further help, it would be possible to engage in another series of sessions. Pia had known from the outset that although it was important for her to gain independence, support was there for her when and if she needed it. This knowledge, encompassed in the therapeutic contract, helped Pia to trust the process and gave her the means to negotiate a new module.

The ability to trust is intrinsic to the entire therapeutic process. It is important that the sense of trust is not marred by an ambivalence that can so easily be created if clients feel they have been left with unresolved issues when a module ends. Therapists who adhere to a strict number of sessions may find themselves in an awkward position, questioning whether to prolong the therapy or allow the client to finish at that point (see the case of Edna, Chapter 6). The modular time-limited approach eliminates this ambiguity and allays fears of interminable therapy. We find that clients are often relieved when the option of a specific number of sessions is offered. The thought of visiting a therapist regularly for an unspecified length of time, possibly years, although comforting to some, may be a daunting, undesirable or unrealistic prospect to others.

ELEMENTS OF THE EXISTENTIAL TIME-LIMITED APPROACH

Time as a major tool in the time-limited therapeutic process

While we were both familiar with other focus- and goal-oriented time-limited therapy approaches, it soon became apparent that their views differed from our existential phenomenological approach. In addition, there was no literature available that could absorb both the time-limited and existential factors. We realized that the time factor and the knowledge of the end date had both positive and negative repercussions (as elaborated in Chapter 3). The positive side manifested itself in the necessity to enforce a particular kind of commitment for the therapist and the client. There had to be greater emphasis on the ending. The disadvantage, however, in setting a fixed ending was that on occasions the pressure of the time limit brought its own inherent problems both to the therapist and the client. However, the skill of the therapist to suspend his or her preconceived ideas of what should or should not happen in the therapy could alleviate the pressure to achieve something in the available time.

While the idea of time and its relationship to both the therapist and client has been discussed, it nevertheless needs to be re-emphasized that one of the most important advantages in the existential time-limited therapy is the time element itself. By its very nature time-limited therapy is about time and the impact of terminating contact between therapist and client. Therefore time is always in the minds of both the therapist and the client and is a constant reminder of the temporary nature of their relationship.

Van Deurzen-Smith explains this in terms of a person's inevitable progression throughout life:

> Progress, from an existential perspective, is seen as the ability to live in time. Living in time is that mode of existence where a person is aware of their own inevitable progression from birth to death. This progress is not avoidable and therefore change and transformation are not avoidable. Progress is therefore defined as an active management of one's ageing and developing process.
>
> (van Deurzen-Smith, 1988:222)

Existential time-limited therapy exactly mirrors this format both in individual sessions and in the course of therapy in its entirety, for each session represents a microcosm of the necessity to be aware of temporality. This awareness is a constant progression from the awareness of living in time as a progression from the beginning to the end of the session and as such represents a continuum from the beginning to the end of therapy.

Clients often express their feeling about the temporality of the therapy either explicitly or implicitly. In many cases clients express great relief that therapy need not be an endless commitment, but contained within this frame. Another element in which the emphasis on existential time-limited therapy manifests itself to a greater extent than in 'open-ended therapy' is the constant awareness of ending.

Ending

The knowledge of ending and separation frequently has the effect of evoking strong emotions, such as the fear of rejection. This can take many forms, including anger, sadness and relief, all of which can be worked through as clients learn to identify their value and coping mechanisms.

Edna manifested these feelings about separation in therapy. On the surface she had worked rapidly, becoming aware of how she needed to please others to avoid her fear of rejection and realizing that this fear was connected to the notion that other people would recognize that she was a 'naughty' promiscuous girl. During each session, the impending ending was discussed, but Edna did not manifest any special concern. It was only during the tenth session that she brought up the issue, without any prompting. Approximately twenty minutes into the session, Edna became angry, verbally attacking me on the fact that she was being abandoned and treated in the same way as she had been by her father, mother and her boyfriends. After a few minutes of crying uncontrollably, Edna suddenly shrieked that she remembered what it was all about.

Her anger at the fear of being abandoned had somehow prompted her to remember the discovery of her mother in bed with her boyfriend. This recollection evoked the revival of all her feelings of rejection, which were worked through in the remaining two sessions. She recognized that she had created a strict routine and value system around her life to ward off any form of rejection. In doing this, she may have thwarted her potential as a writer.

It can certainly be said that by the very nature of limiting the therapy to twelve weeks, the imminent ending and separation from the therapy brought up Edna's feelings of abandonment and rejection. She could then piece together what she had discovered about herself in the previous weeks and the additional emotional input that had occurred in the tenth session.

The therapist's and client's expectation of the therapeutic outcome

One of the factors that we found important regarding time limitation was the client's initial expectation of what therapy can do both during the process and after. Most clients who have never had close contact or experienced therapy themselves often expect either an instant cure and complete elimination of their presenting problem or some particular method or tool that can specifically help in overcoming their dilemma. It is therefore essential that both the client and therapist address these kinds of expectations from the outset.

Indeed, one of the aims of the time-limited approach is for clients to alter their expectations from those that are unrealistic to those that can be achieved. This view very much conforms with van Deurzen-Smith's notion that:

> Existential counselling aims at enabling clients to abandon false hopes of a smooth and perfect life, where the past would be all achievement and the future all promise. The existential counsellor does not promise a nirvana of accomplishment in the savouring of an always fully experienced now.
>
> (van Deurzen-Smith, 1988:222)

During Lottie's initial session, it emerged that she enjoyed consulting various step-by-step, self-improvement books ranging from how to improve one's finances to how to create a positive self-image that would alter relationships both at home and at work. She expected that therapy would be a speedier way of achieving these goals and that the therapist would have the necessary answers that would be imparted, without pain, during the sessions. Much of the first session was spent exploring these expectations and explaining that Lottie would find her own answers through her self-exploration.

Closely linked with the concept of clients' expectations is their perception of their own limitations, together with their assessment of these limits and whether they are realistic. It took Lottie well into the second modular block of twelve-week sessions to realize that life was not as black and white as she had imagined. Each week she would sit down and give a progress report on what she felt she had achieved. She would write copious notes of what she had to do to be her ideal person, but as she began to accept the idea that living also involved a struggle, both her progress reports and her notes ceased. Lottie had begun to recognize her own limitations and to realize that she needed to accept herself as she was in the present.

In fact, the whole process of Lottie's therapy was one of a gradual reduction of her original expectations. From her unrealistic demand of needing an instant cure, it took Lottie two modules to accept that a transformation of attitude was a necessary component of change.

It is sometimes difficult for clients to accept that there are limitations. They often believe that their path to happiness lies in the elimination of all anxieties. Yet, adopting this attitude can lead clients like Lottie along a false path where they expect that by developing strategies such as positive doing and thinking, or becoming more assertive, they will achieve happiness. If and when they realize that in spite of all these efforts, they can still fail, the primary existential fear and anxiety takes on a different nature, creating a self-perpetuating loop of anxiety. The fear thus becomes fear of the fear, and the anxiety, anxiety of the anxiety.

Only when Lottie accepted her predicament and realized that even within the limitations she did have choices, did she begin to trust herself enough simply to accept her own natural course. She became aware that she need not become totally frustrated by not being the 'ideal' person who would live without obstacles and anxiety, but she had the choice of accepting these and herself as a reality. Part of this was also acknowledging that she was to become a mother and that her life would change radically in any case.

Dependency

Within a limited time structure, unhealthy dependency is less likely to occur. Dependency is no longer intrinsic to the therapeutic relationship as it is in open-ended therapy, where it is often difficult to eliminate. It can occur for various reasons that are related to the client's own sedimented value system, such as the need for approval or disapproval, fear of rejection or the need to maintain the status quo, as in the case of Hannah.

Prior to coming to see me, Hannah, 31, had been in therapy for five years and during that time had become totally dependent on her therapist. Her presenting problems were a combination of panic attacks, an inability to have satisfying relationships with men, insomnia and frequent suicidal tendencies that she alleviated by frequent telephone conversations with the Samaritans. She realized after a few months of therapy that when it came to her sexual behaviour, she had developed a strong moral code which had emerged from her parents' sexual value system. Hannah constantly felt guilty and over the years had acquired a coping strategy of withdrawal and shyness. While she became cognitively aware of this, she was unable to discard her compulsive behaviour patterns. Indeed, it was impossible for Hannah to shed the notion that her parents might find out about her sexual behaviour and her fear that, as a consequence, they would reject her. For a long time, every session revealed the same underlying theme.

As time progressed, however, Hannah began to realize that she might have some vested interest in maintaining the status quo, that in some way she benefited from remaining in familiar circumstances. Part of this was reflected in her reliance and dependence on her therapist, and on the permanency of the therapeutic sessions. By perpetuating her behaviour and not moving forward, she could stay with her therapist. As Hannah realized this and we concentrated on the impending ending and as I emphasized the time limitation, she began to work through her dependency syndrome and her fears of separation, so that termination of therapy could be seriously contemplated.

A dependent person can often remain dependent on therapy unless the issue is addressed early on. Within the twelve-week model, due to the concentrated time span, dependence is less likely to be a problem. Instead, dependency is taken as part of the capacity to trust, where trust is creating the environment in which the client feels comfortable in divulging without being judged.

Dissociation

In the process of existential time-limited therapy, the client at some point will become aware of certain repeated patterns of feelings and emotions that may come as a complete surprise. For instance, Janice, who had an alcoholic father, was sexually assaulted by an uncle when she was 17. She entered the Church as a novice nun at 22, was cast out ten years later and continued to live an isolated existence until her parents died. She then realized that she needed help to overcome her depression. Initially, in therapy, Janice felt that she had dealt with her sexual assault and no longer blamed herself for the incident. As we began, however, to explore the various events of her life, Janice realized that she had shut out a great deal of her emotions in order to move forward. Some of these repeated feelings were her inherent dislike of getting close to anyone physically, while she also experienced a desperate need to be with people who were 'straight and honest'.

In therapy she traced her stance back to the time when, as a young girl, she had hated being in close proximity to her father, especially after he had been drinking. Following the sexual assault, this became a fear of being touched by anyone, even close friends. Entering the Church was in many ways an escape from having to come to terms with this fear. She expected it to be a safe and honest place, but unfortunately, this hope was not fulfilled when, after a disagreement with her Mother Superior, Janice was told she was not suitable to be a nun and had to leave with only the clothes she had worn upon arrival.

Although Janice's purpose was to find a 'real' interpersonal relationship with someone she could trust, she was unable to accept any emotional closeness because at some point it would involve physically touching. This created a dissociation between Janice's feelings and her behaviour pattern, which she maintained thereafter. In spite of knowing that it was important to surround herself with trustworthy people, she had not understood the significance of how her behaviour decreased her chances of finding the right friends. Again, until a friend put her arms around her and she shrank away in horror, she had not realized how much she abhorred any physical contact. These insights gave Janice an awareness, and put into context some of the decisions she had made.

This kind of dissociation is very common among clients. In therapy an awareness of dissociation of feelings from the actual behaviour causes overwhelming emotions. After the death of her parents, Janice's siblings decided to sell the family home, without her consent. Janice could now acknowledge that she felt betrayed, that she did not trust her brothers and sisters. She felt very isolated, depressed and for the first time cried about the loss of her parents. She then became aware of and challenged her own behaviour patterns: that deep down she had an overwhelming longing for closeness and physical contact and yet she was unable to achieve this intimacy because of her lack of trust of others and her low self-esteem. This example of dissociation conforms precisely with Spinelli's statement: 'The question of dissociation revolves around an individual's self-concept in that it supposes a dissonance between beliefs about one's self and the experience of one's self' (1994:222).

Personal meaning – recognition of inner strengths and trust

Most clients whose presenting problem is one of deep depression suffer from the impression that they lack a meaningful human existence. That is, they have lost their purpose in life and they flounder aimlessly in a 'senseless' world of nothingness. Until modern times, the majority of societies were equipped with beliefs, whether in a God, several gods or the supernatural, that acted as a guide through their lives. This firm belief system provided people with a day-to-day meaning and also carried them through the greatest of tragedies. It furnished them not only with religious purpose but also with faith and trust in God, others and in themselves. The advent of scientific exploration of religion and that of existence has deprived some human beings of a vital stability and moved them to search for other meanings.

As discussed in Chapter 2, some of the existential authors (Sartre and Camus) do not believe that the world or indeed life has any significance; it is totally meaningless. Camus, for example, describes how the irrationality that 'surrounds man until his ultimate end', is in direct contrast to the way humans long for clarity and meaning (1960). It is one of the paradoxes of existence that humans cannot accept life without meaning, and yet there is no clearly defined meaning to life. Existentialism became known as the atheist philosophy, but writers such as Kierkegaard, Tillich and Frankl do view existence from a spiritual viewpoint, emphasizing the notion of spirituality and meaning. Frankl bases his 'Logotherapy' entirely on man's search for meaning. Only when clients in the depth of their depression begin to develop a trust in something, either in some sort of spirituality, transcendence or trust in themselves, do they begin to re-establish a kind of meaning to life.

The strength of time-limited therapy is that because of the time limitations and the therapist's structural approach a connectedness between the client and the therapist can be established early in the therapy. In other words, therapists through their own structure can connect with the clients' pains and problems. As a result of this clients can be facilitated to challenge their own discrepancies and through this method can experience insights and discover new meanings.

Marianne typified this connectedness between therapist and herself and soon found a link between depression and meaninglessness. She complained of suffering from insomnia and depression, and at times was so greatly incapacitated that she was unable to work. This was in spite of her high-powered job and her good reputation within her profession. She attributed her depression to her permanent squabbles with her superiors in the office. It took many weeks of therapy for Marianne to shift her focus from her business to her private life and to become aware that the nature of her relationship with her partner made her life appear without purpose. Her partner was a married man with children.

In therapy, Marianne soon became aware of her lack of meaning in life, and that her longing for something that at first she could not express was nothing else but her search for meaning in life. However, even when she realized that what she wanted was a meaningful relationship and to have children, her behaviour pattern continued. She understood her behaviour, but had difficulty in altering her depressed state. Once in therapy, she started to became aware of her mental and bodily inner strengths that helped her to develop faith in herself and others. Only then did she begin to challenge her own behaviour patterns and to comprehend her previous relationships with her partners and others. Before the conclusion of therapy she managed to assert herself with her partner and to clarify their relationship and just before her last session she announced that she was pregnant.

One year later Marianne rang for an appointment, wishing to introduce her son. Her life had changed completely as soon as she realized that her purpose in life derived from her interpersonal relationships with her family and in bringing up her children. Simultaneously, her working life also improved, in the sense that as it became less important, the disputes that she had with her superiors became far less significant. Thus, it can be seen from the above example how discovering or acknowledging a meaning can alter the world view of clients and indeed their direction in life. Meaning, in our experience, need not to be attached to some 'positive' moral value. It can take many forms: for instance, meaning can be attached to material economic progress, to writing, or to painting, to name but a few; it can take the form of creativity or to work at an achievement.

In our experience clients very often come out of their depression when they develop faith in something and realize that the highly limiting attachment to their old meaning is no longer working for them. They can then move forward with a new meaning. In Marianne's case, her old meaning was the value she had attached to her position and status at work. Her depression masked the fact that as she grew older her needs were changing and until she could recognize that her old meaning was no longer valid, she could not move forward.

Focusing

One of the theoretical concepts behind some of the time-limited therapies (Malan, 1963; de Shazer, 1985) is that of focusing or goal-setting, whereby the client and therapist agree on a focal concern in the first couple of sessions that can be worked through in the ensuing weeks. It is believed that by focusing on one area it is possible to keep the process within the limited time frame, and that a great deal of the client's material is thereby excluded. It is also felt that if clients could resolve one area of their lives, other areas would automatically change.

At first, we too believed that finding a focus was important to keep the therapy time limited, but we soon found that no matter which focal concern was chosen, it became inapplicable, as will be described in subsequent chapters.

This predicament is manifested in the case of Philippa. Philippa's presenting problem was one of an inability to separate from her mother, who was now old and largely confined to an old people's home. Philippa knew that she wanted her own life but each time she attempted to assert her independence, her mother would stubbornly become moody, causing Philippa to feel guilty about her intentions. In the first session the obvious choice was to use the twelve weeks to focus on Philippa and her mother. Indeed, several entire sessions were devoted to their relationship, but many other facets of Philippa's life were covered, including her relationship with her father, her religious beliefs, her fear of rejection, as well as a strong recurring theme of her fear of loneliness and death. She gradually began to recognize other sides to herself that she had never acknowledged. She started to reconstruct and realize the significance of other people in her life, and saw that her existence did not revolve entirely around her mother. It is important to note that the focus on Philippa's relationship with her mother was only one of the many ways of centring on an issue. I could have focused with equal efficiency on her relationship to her father. Each issue and all the existential 'givens' are enumerated on the wheel (as is shown in the following section).

It is also our belief that it is possible but problematic to divide one's life into segments, since it is clearly shown that our beliefs and values overlap to such an extent that all issues interconnect.

Structure and the interconnections of all concepts

We claim to be theoreticians of existential therapy only insofar as we can use and apply theory to the practice of psychotherapy and for the purposes of everyday life. Theory as applied in this way is more akin to a philosophy of life.

Our basic assumptions derive from the existential phenomenological model as described in Chapter 2, where we also explain what are known as the universal concerns (or 'givens'), which affect all human beings. The basic premise is that everyone, without exception, is subject to his or her genetic, environmental and cultural 'givens'. Within these constraints, and between birth and death, human beings create a unique mode of existence. The essence of existential time-limited therapy lies in the clarification of clients' attitudes towards the concerns that life imposes on them. The 'givens' that this point of view encompasses include the need for safety; the importance of having interpersonal relationships; our attitude towards time and temporality; the way we form, develop and cope with our belief and value systems and how we fix (or sediment) them; the way we exist in our natural, private, public and spiritual worlds; the contradictions and paradoxes that living creates; the anxieties that we all endure; the realization that we all suffer from guilt and loneliness and how these relate to our self-esteem; and that in the final analysis, we have free will and choice.

The two existential wheels in Figures 4.1 and 4.2 demonstrate these 'givens'. Figure 4.1 represents those existential concepts that encompass all human concerns throughout a person's life. These can be subdivided into those elements that the world universally imposes on human beings (printed in italics on Figure 4.1) and those which human beings create as a response to these universal limitations (printed in roman script on Figure 4.1). We believe that the ten segments of the wheel (Figure 4.1), from 'uncertainty' to 'freedom of choice', cover both the 'givens' that encompass the limitations of the world and the possibility for human responses. Within this universality each human being creates his or her individual answer with all the potential that humans create; the aspirations, concerns, anxieties, fears, ambitions and joys that collectively comprise one's existence in this world. The assumptions that lie behind these ideas stem wholly from existential and phenomenological ideas.

Figure 4.2 represents the method or the practical way to apply the underlying concepts. Each segment of this figure dovetails with the corresponding segment of Figure 4.1. For example, the notion of the human concern with 'uncertainty' is shown in the first segment of the Figure 4.1, which links with the first segment of the second existential figure. Thus, the idea of 'uncertainty' is manifested in the practical concern of setting the boundaries and framework, as well as the methods employed to provide that safety.

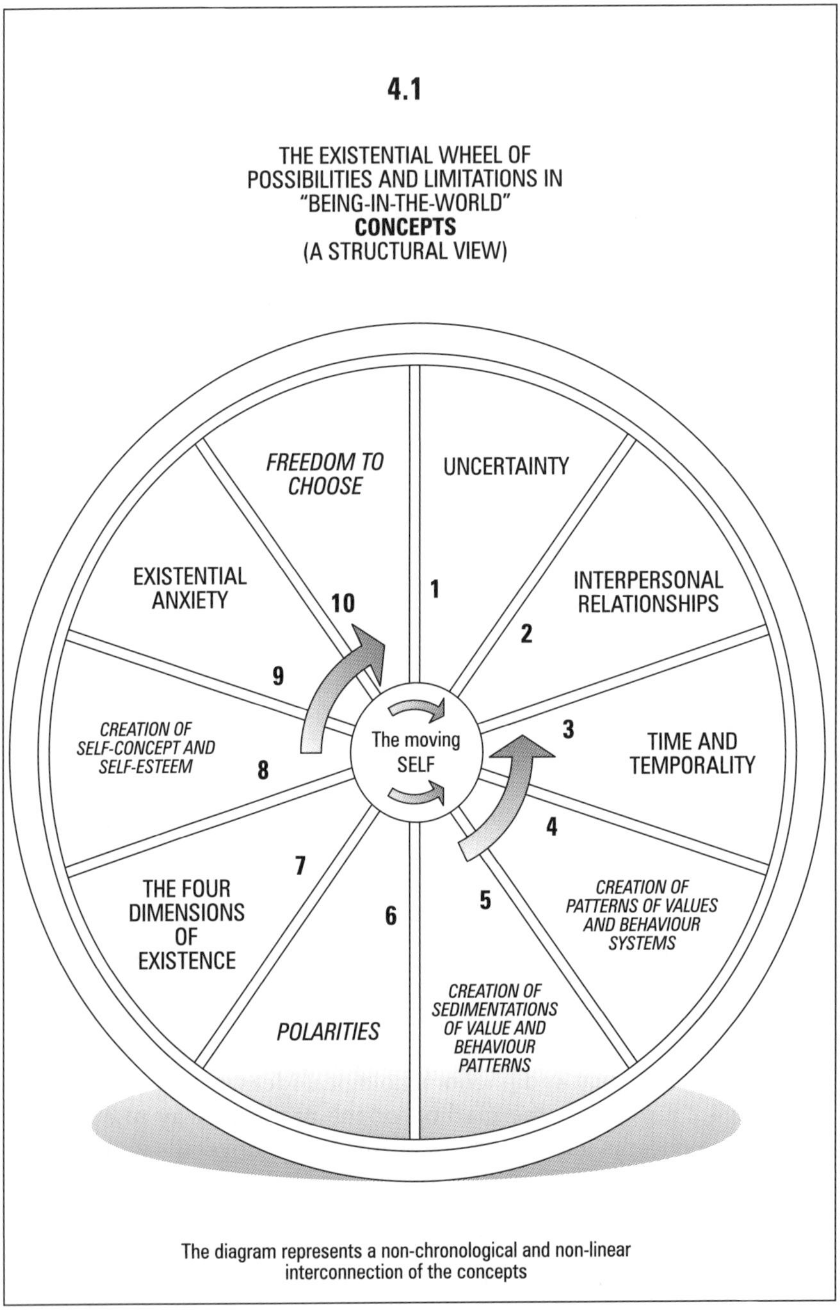
4.1
THE EXISTENTIAL WHEEL OF
POSSIBILITIES AND LIMITATIONS IN
"BEING-IN-THE-WORLD"
CONCEPTS
(A STRUCTURAL VIEW)
FREEDOM TO CHOOSE
UNCERTAINTY
EXISTENTIAL ANXIETY
INTERPERSONAL RELATIONSHIPS
10
1
2
9
3
CREATION OF SELF-CONCEPT AND SELF-ESTEEM
The moving SELF
TIME AND TEMPORALITY
8
4
7
5
6
THE FOUR DIMENSIONS OF EXISTENCE
CREATION OF PATTERNS OF VALUES AND BEHAVIOUR SYSTEMS
POLARITIES
CREATION OF SEDIMENTATIONS OF VALUE AND BEHAVIOUR PATTERNS
The diagram represents a non-chronological and non-linear interconnection of the concepts

Figure 4.1

4.2

THE EXISTENTIAL WHEEL OF
POSSIBILITIES AND LIMITATIONS IN
"BEING-IN-THE-WORLD"
METHODS AND SKILLS
(A STRUCTURAL VIEW)

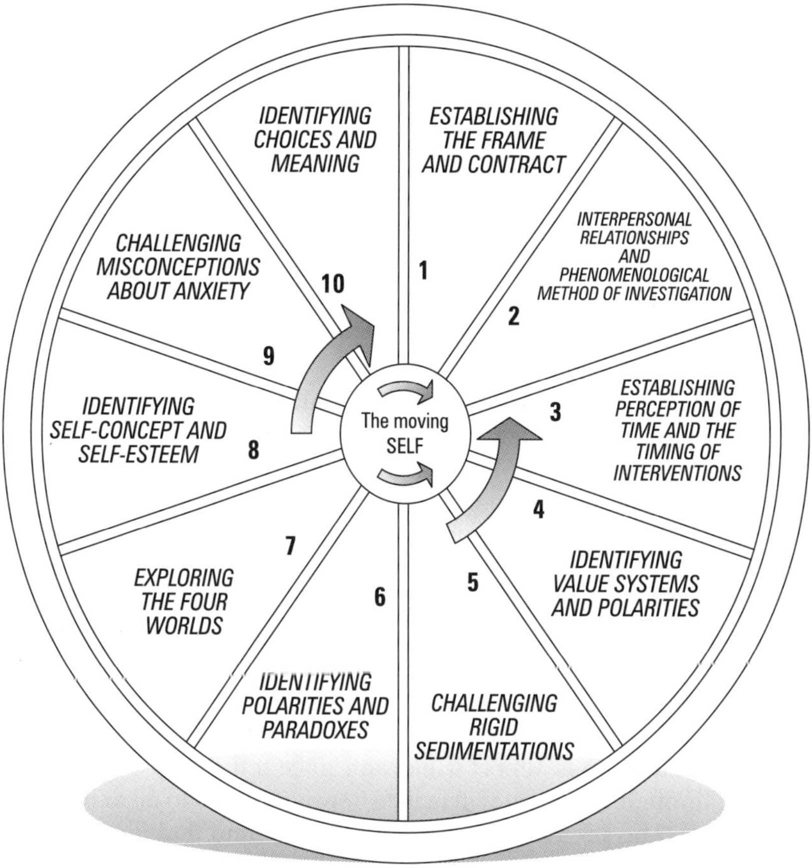

The diagram represents a non-chronological and non-linear interconnection of the methods

Figure 4.2

From the start of our practice it was apparent to us that working within a 'structure' was important in the time-limited approach. Traditionally, existentialists would deny structure and method in therapy, even though in our therapy some methods and framework are claimed to be necessary as discussed and quoted in Chapter 2. The usual way of existential therapy is open ended and depends on flexible relations between the therapy and the client but not on the structure. Yet we found the structure already paramountly evident by the fact that we have been thrown into the world as temporal beings and we are going to die. This in itself is an existential facticity, which gives an existential 'structure' to the therapeutic endeavour.

'Structure' in itself, therefore, gives a different perspective to existential therapy. We found that the analysis of this and the awareness of it provides therapists with both an 'anchor' and an 'oar'. That is, it gives therapists a point of reference as well as a valid tool for recognizing and understanding the issues raised by many clients. We find that by way of this diagrammatic avenue we are able to comprehend at a much earlier stage some of the key aspects, such as how clients view themselves in the world and how their belief and value systems have been formed. This helps us to identify and challenge our clients' discrepancies and contradictions from the outset of therapy.

Another unexpected advantage of the figurative wheel is that having a structure helped us to 'bracket' (the need to suspend and 'horizontalize' our preconceived self) our own prejudices and to distance ourselves from the situation in order to give us a wider perspective of the client's viewpoint. This notion of suspension is described by Spinelli in *Interpreted World* (1989:17–19). This is probably because knowledge of the framework gives us a sense of security and thereby reduces the necessity or the desire to make those all too frequent incorrect assumptions about clients.

Furthermore, the structure highlights the existential–phenomenological hypothesis that all issues always interconnect and express themselves throughout all facets of the client's world relations. It follows that what the client focuses on is almost irrelevant, since if the subject is properly followed through, the client will realize how it is linked to all of his or her other issues. This idea is highlighted in the diagram that illustrates the interconnection of all the concepts in relation to the shifting self.

This can be clearly seen in the case of Lynn. During one session Lynn began to focus on a particular situation where she had felt rejected. She told me that as a young child she had enjoyed being an extrovert and had taken pleasure in getting attention. Her mother disapproved, however, and had reprimanded her for 'showing off'. This reaction, it transpired, related to many other issues. We deduced from this account that Lynn's value system, at least in part, consisted of the positive and negative ideals that 'showing off' is bad while remaining modest is good. This links directly to her sedimentation, in that the only way for her to be accepted by others is to be reserved.

Examining these ideas further, Lynn's self-concept and self-esteem are also connected. When she was scolded as a child, Lynn's sense of self as an extrovert became the 'wrong' way to behave and she felt rejected for who she was and who she wanted to be. Therefore, behaving 'modestly' was met with approval by others but was not acceptable to herself. The cycle of rejection–self-doubt and confusion–lack of self-esteem repeats itself, for when she feels rejected, her self-esteem evaporates. This creates a deep concern about who she is and what is expected of her. Apart from the benefit of recognizing these sedimentations, if Lynn were able to choose a different attitude towards her original values and behaviour patterns, and thus change this pattern, it would provoke another set of anxieties. Hence we can see that all these issues are connected to both the limitations and possibilities that Lynn has to confront.

The shifting relational self

In the centre of the existential wheel is the 'relational self', which is 'the self' as non-chronological and non-linear, and which interacts with all the sections of the wheel. In existential terms the self is not fixed or entity-like but instead is seen as a process that continually reinterprets and reshapes its identity from the multiplicity of derived experiences.

The relational self as a process is represented on all the wheels as a moving self that interacts with all sections of the wheel. Thus, the self is the product of all our experiences. At the same time the self that creates and recreates itself does not possess any hierarchical value, for each time we change or present another self, that changed self has no higher or lower value than the previous self. One cannot say that the 'new' self is any better than the 'old' self. Spinelli refers to this concept of self as the 'relational self':

> On initial consideration, the existential–phenomenological model's view of the 'self' may strike many readers as being either odd or absurd. For this model argues that the question of whether or not a 'self' exists, in the sense that each of us 'has' a self that is real (as opposed to 'unreal selves') fixed or (relatively) stable, and which seeks to express, or actu-

> alise, itself, is, at best, open to doubt. Instead, this model prefers to view the self as a focal point in relation and, as such, speaks only of the 'self-in-relation' rather then the 'self' as a separate, fixed and complete 'entity'.
>
> (Spinelli, 1994:342)

Some therapists of different orientations, however, such as Rogers (1961), believe that human beings have a core self. When clients project an image of themselves of how they should be, or would like to be perceived, then they believe that the 'self' is incongruent; that indeed they are concealing their 'core' or 'real' self. To 'actualize' oneself, in this paradigm, the true self must be discovered. By implication this notion has a hierarchical value, for one self is seen as better than another self. In existential time-limited therapy we consider every 'self' presented by the client as a congruent self that has a valid meaning. There are times, however, when clients appear to be incongruent because they are ashamed to disclose something. From an existential point of view this is just the self in a process of becoming another self, that is to say a person is ashamed of him or herself. Spinelli describes this phenomenon as 'splitness' and argues that this can only be removed:

> Once we consider the 'self' to be an impermanent, plastic construct that exists only as an outcome of relational factors. As such, the self-construct is 'grounded' in relation and can only be said to be 'real' insofar as it is *that which reflects and is reflected on in any given experience*. In other words, the self-construct reveals *the self that is being experienced when it is being experienced*.
>
> (Spinelli, 1994:347)

In therapy, each state of the self as a phenomenon needs to be explored and clarified. When clients feel uncomfortable about a particular state of self, it is the self that feels uncomfortable. Clients who become aware of this will then examine what it is that this self hesitates to reveal.

Rebecca was a client undergoing a short module of therapy. On one occasion she arrived at our session with some drawings she had made. She showed them to me and said, 'This is not the real me, it is just an illustration that I can sell. My real self is represented by much deeper work.' When I reminded Rebecca that both types of work had been created by her and were as such a part of her, she was taken aback. She had never considered this phenomenon, and it was a revelation for her to see that different aspects of her self, all equally valid, could be manifested. Rebecca re-examined her interpretation of the so-called 'shallow' drawing and to her amazement found aspects that had equal profundity to those she had believed to be present only in her more in-depth work.

It is remarkable how this attitude towards the 'real' self is embraced in the minds of the public. (It is actually diametrically opposed to the phenomenological position and is a very important feature to challenge in therapy.) Rebecca considered the self that created the 'popular' drawings superficial and therefore undesirable. She wanted to be perceived as a person with deeper values. Yet when we explored her other more 'in-depth' paintings, she still found conflicts with those values. In this sense she was still unable to achieve what she had desired. In not accepting her present self, Rebecca found that she was always in search of the other 'self' that constantly eluded her.

When we take into account the notion of the 'plastic' self, the self that is not stagnant, that is ever-changing, the process of therapy must also be deemed as continually shifting. Therefore both the client and therapist must reflect on these changes as they naturally occur. It also highlights the significance of the therapist retaining an open mind and not becoming fixed in his or her own comprehension of what the client's perception of self might be. This allows the client to find his or her own path.

In this chapter we have described the existential time-limited approach and how we arrived at it. We have also delineated some vital elements of the time-limited existential approach that mark not only its vital characteristics, but also emphasize the differences between the open-ended existential and time-limited approaches. The structure described in Chapter 2 was further discussed here on a more practical level and the two existential wheels were clarified. The existential concept of self as a process was expounded and shown as the centre part of both wheels.

Chapter 5 will lead up to a description of a concrete therapeutic method applied in practice with some concrete vignettes.

5

CONCEPTS AND METHODS

This chapter deals, in a concrete form, with the structure of the existential notion of being in the world. The concept of limitations and possibilities which enhance or limit human existence will be described and their relevance in therapeutic practice established. With reference to the figures in this chapter, the segments of the wheels shown in bold letters represent the relevant topics.

UNCERTAINTY

In this section we will demonstrate the implication of the 'uncertainty' in existential time-limited therapy. Namely, the everyday uncertainties and ambiguities of life are substituted in the therapeutic environment with an artificial boundary that provides a modicum of safety for the client. This will be evident from Figures 5.1 and 5.2. 'Uncertainty' is a universal 'given' that affects all human beings. We have, therefore, marked this in bold on Figures 5.1 and 5.2 in order to distinguish it from the other sections.

From the moment of birth, one clear basic need is to feel safe and secure. It is an incontrovertible fact that upon first opening our eyes we are 'thrown' into a world that is inherently full of insecurity and uncertainty. As babies we seek the warmth and nurturing environment of our parents or carers. These feelings of comfort and safety remain as a memory, which even as adults we constantly desire to return to.

Maslow also argued that after we have satisfied our basic needs, such as the need for food and shelter, we strive for protection and safety to exist in the world: 'after the bodily needs are taken care of [our needs] are for [one] protection safety, security' (1968:199–200).

From a phenomenological existential point of view one of the main features of the structure of human existence is a person's own despair and existential anxiety. In Rollo May's words: 'the anxiety of a man facing the limit of his existence with its fullest implications: death, nothingness' (1977:118). Between birth, death and nothingness we struggle for safety, yet we cannot eliminate entirely this existential anxiety of not being able to fulfil our potential during a life span. Following this reasoning, a perennial search for safety and security in a world that is replete with uncertainties and unpredictability is one of the paradoxes of our existence. We struggle continuously and fight against this paradox, trying to eke out some kind of meaning, some kind of security, against which we can measure ourselves as constant and safe. As adults this can take many forms, such as our desire for relationships, an urge for religion or a passion for work.

One of the presenting problems of some clients is that they cannot accept this 'given' as a fact of life and will constantly strive to acquire permanent stability. A fundamental contradiction is that we both seek and strive for this elusive notion of safety in a world that cannot provide it. Searching for security in itself generates 'existential anxiety' as discussed in Chapter 2. In the process of trying to alleviate this anxiety we learn an infinite amount of coping strategies to protect the little security that we do find.

Gary, for example, believed from a very early age that he could go through life without encountering obstacles or anxieties. He needed only to stay within the parameters of conforming to his parental values that were to be an obedient boy, a conscientious student and a good athlete. By achieving these goals he could become a happy person. When his first major crisis occurred, Gary collapsed completely. He did not want to experience, nor could he cope with, any negative feelings or even a hint of anxiety. To a certain extent he succeeded in this by not taking risks, withdrawing from relationships and generally removing himself from all social contact. These were all strategies to avoid connecting with his inner torment. At the same time he retreated to the frame of safety to which he was accustomed.

Gary kept a diary so as to analyse the therapy. He said, 'My problems seemed mountainous. I needed to offload and I needed to hear a different point of view, one that challenged my own – over and over again. In my belief that life needs to be smooth and anxiety-free and in my judgement the norm was based on conformity. I could only exist in a positive way if I lived without obstacles and anxiety. When [my] relationship did not work out, and finally met with failure, the repercussions were huge!'

There is an infinite number of coping strategies which people adopt. Under the section 'Polarities and paradoxes' we list a number of typical methods that clients may use. In time-limited existential therapy we attach great importance to this notion of safety. A good therapeutic situation is provided by the setting of firm boundaries within which the clients can rely on a consistent and predictable environment. To some extent, this can be perceived as an almost artificial situation, especially

5.1

THE EXISTENTIAL WHEEL OF POSSIBILITIES AND LIMITATIONS IN "BEING-IN-THE-WORLD"
CONCEPTS
(A STRUCTURAL VIEW)

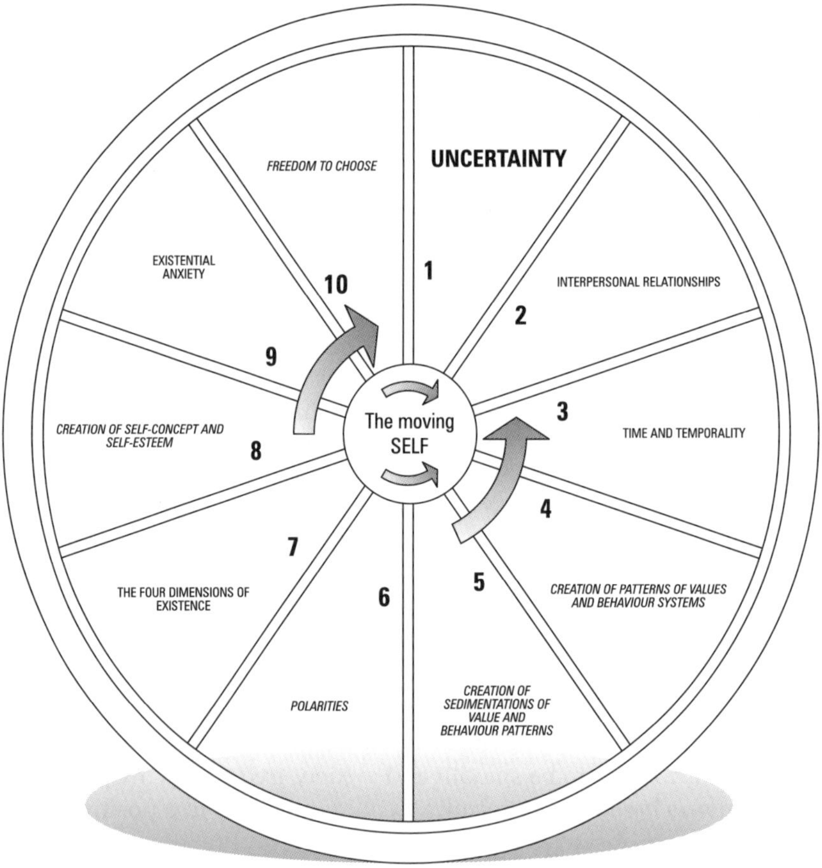

The diagram represents a non-chronological and non-linear interconnection of the concepts

Figure 5.1

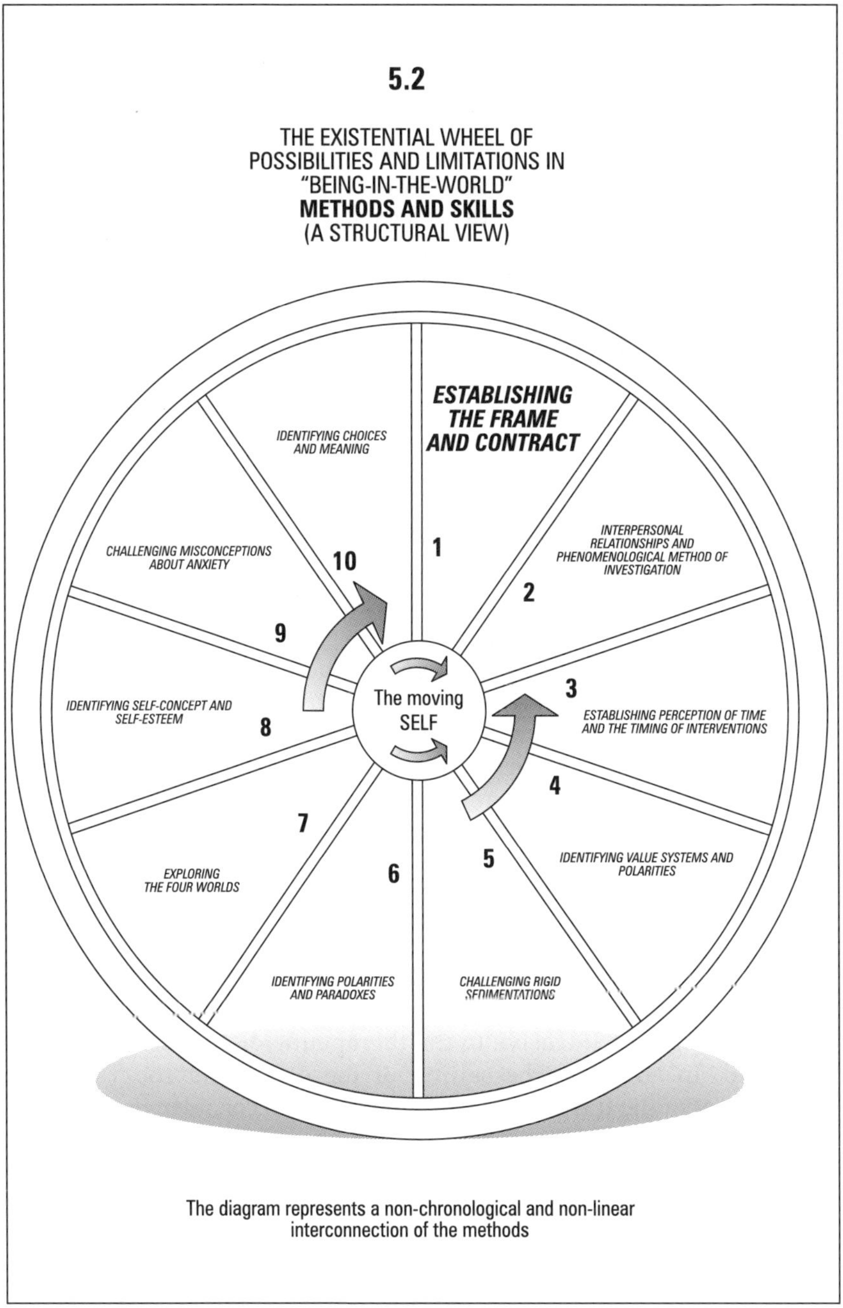
5.2
THE EXISTENTIAL WHEEL OF
POSSIBILITIES AND LIMITATIONS IN
"BEING-IN-THE-WORLD"
METHODS AND SKILLS
(A STRUCTURAL VIEW)
ESTABLISHING THE FRAME AND CONTRACT
1
INTERPERSONAL RELATIONSHIPS AND PHENOMENOLOGICAL METHOD OF INVESTIGATION
2
3
ESTABLISHING PERCEPTION OF TIME AND THE TIMING OF INTERVENTIONS
4
IDENTIFYING VALUE SYSTEMS AND POLARITIES
5
CHALLENGING RIGID SEDIMENTATIONS
6
IDENTIFYING POLARITIES AND PARADOXES
7
EXPLORING THE FOUR WORLDS
8
IDENTIFYING SELF-CONCEPT AND SELF-ESTEEM
9
CHALLENGING MISCONCEPTIONS ABOUT ANXIETY
10
IDENTIFYING CHOICES AND MEANING
The moving SELF
The diagram represents a non-chronological and non-linear interconnection of the methods

Figure 5.2

when contrasted with clients' everyday struggles with the exact opposite. However, by creating this kind of environment and a base clients can become aware of the illusory nature of their notions of safety.

From the onset of therapy, the salient points of the framework are agreed upon. This typically consists of the duration of each session, the frequency of sessions, the intended time span, that is whether open ended or time-limited, and an agreement on fees. By adhering to this framework clients are provided with a sense of safety. One client poignantly expressed it as the feeling that, 'If everything else goes wrong with my life at least my therapy remains consistent. The four walls are there, the therapist is exactly on time and the atmosphere of the therapy is always consistent.'

Stability in therapy is provided through establishing the therapeutic framework and the verbal contract that is drawn between client and therapist. David Smith quotes Laing and offers ten components required for a secure frame. Although Smith is a communicative psychotherapist, where the entire therapeutic process is based on securing the frame, some of his points are equally relevant to existential time-limited therapy. He writes that 'a sense of basic trust' and 'a powerful sense of being held well and of appropriate containment' (1991:173) are important components in securing that frame.

Admittedly, because of the different stances of communicative psychotherapists, clients' experience in a communicative frame would differ from an existential time-limited approach. Nevertheless, in our attempt to allow that trust and security to emerge in a therapeutic environment we put forward as the structure of a frame the main ingredients: the setting; fees; confidentiality; modular approach and ending.

THE SETTING

The consulting room should provide maximum privacy. Disturbances such as telephone calls, a receptionist, clients in the waiting room, or anything that might be intrusive to the therapeutic dialogue are not to be permitted. In addition, the setting of the consulting room and the arrangement of the furniture are also important to consider. Sessions and the duration of each session need to be agreed with the client. The important point here is that sessions take place on the same day of the week, at the agreed hour and are always of the same duration. This can create a holding situation that can be associated with consistency and thus safety.

FEES

The fee should be set and if possible not altered. Absences such as holidays or illness and the period of cancellation notice required for either the client or the therapist should also be agreed upon.

CONFIDENTIALITY

A vital ingredient is for a client to trust the therapeutic relationship. Only through trust can a client feel safe in the therapy. To reach such a trusting relationship the issue of confidentiality must be resolved. Clients should feel free to divulge their innermost secrets, knowing that this information will remain in confidence. It should be noted that clients whose cases are related in this work were asked permission for inclusion. Confidentiality should therefore be agreed and ethical issues discussed. If the therapist has a supervisor then this fact needs to be discussed with the client. If there are other factors such as a client who has a legal or social welfare case pending, which may lead to a break in confidentiality, then this too needs to be clarified.

MODULAR APPROACH AND ENDING

In existential time-limited therapy the client and the therapist discuss and decide the duration of the programme and the follow-up sessions. Usually in the first or second session, after the assessment and other aspects of the frame have been established, the subject of the length of therapy is discussed. The duration of the programme will be mutually agreed according to the client's need and the therapist's allowable time frame. This is usually a contract of between twelve and sixteen sessions. Two follow-up sessions take place at a minimum of four to six weeks after the conclusion of the original course of therapy.

The modular approach, as described in Chapter 4, is agreed upon and the client is reassured that, should the need arise, a further module can be renegotiated after the review sessions. In some cases 'outside' fixed limits may have to be arranged. To recapitulate, it is vital that the possibility of a further module is mentioned at this stage so that the client has a clear picture of the parameters. It is important that the client does not feel 'on trial', which could happen if the whole modular scenario is not explained well. Clarifying the ending and putting across the notion that clients need to work towards gaining their independence is crucial in the practice of time-limited existential therapy. As discussed in Chapter 4, the emotional impact of ending may precipitate clients getting in touch with their feelings of abandonment. It can, however, be employed as a tool in therapy.

Discussion of clients' expectations also belongs to the framework. The importance of establishing and clarifying what clients anticipate from the process is of great significance. It is not uncommon for clients to hold unrealistically high expectations. We therefore prompt the client to explore from all angles what they believe they could expect as a whole; what they in fact expect from the therapy and from our therapeutic relationship. At the same time we encourage the client to explore whether his or her expectations are possible within the limitations of the world. Sometimes this process takes the full duration of the course of the therapy.

We articulated the importance of establishing and maintaining the framework. It is also worth noting that the main objective of these strict boundaries is to provide a safe and secure environment for clients to disclose and express themselves freely. Sometimes therapists employ the strict frame and forget the reasons for it. To take an extreme example: if a client suffers a heart attack, no therapist would restrict him or herself from helping the client even if the boundary has to be violated by calling an ambulance and thus ensuring safety. It is, however, often the accidental deviations from these boundaries that can facilitate a dramatic change, if used as a way of talking about the issues involved.

The following example may make this somewhat complex issue a little clearer. During the eighth session with Paul, believing it to be the tenth session, I asked him how he felt about having only two sessions left. Paul was visibly distraught and expressed profound bafflement, saying, 'This is only our eighth session and I'm sure we have another four left before we finish.' I responded by showing my own disappointment about this important mistake. After further discussion, Paul revealed that at that moment he had lost complete confidence in me. He felt that there was no concern or care about his own well-being: had I known the correct ending date, he would have felt confident that I would continue to care for him even after the therapy ended. During the following sessions Paul continued with this line of thinking and eventually came to the conclusion that the therapist, too, was only human and capable of making mistakes. He realized that the therapeutic environment was also subject to the same kind of uncertainties which he experienced in everyday life. From this realization the way he responded to unpredictable situations in general could be further explored.

In many ways, providing a safe environment for clients is a paradoxical exercise. While therapy strives to provide safety, it also aims to allow clients to become aware that the world inside and outside the therapeutic walls is not one of safety and security. It is necessary for clients to find their own potential within the realms of uncertainty.

INTERPERSONAL RELATIONSHIP

The necessity of interpersonal relationship is the basis of the time-limited therapy and for this end it utilizes a phenomenological method of investigation. This is exemplified on the two wheels shown in Figures 5.3 and 5.4. Figure 5.3 shows that interpersonal relationship is a universal 'given' which is imposed upon all of us by the world. From the moment that we are born we are with others and we cannot escape from this until our end.

The interpersonal relationship is also the fundamental underpinning of the existential approach. We have discussed various aspects of this notion in Chapter 2. In this section we will explore how these ideas work in therapy.

Any type of interpersonal relationship involves the acknowledgement of others as separate beings. It is impossible to avoid being with others from our very first moments of existence. As such we are always 'with' other people, which can be expressed in such ways as relating, disclosing and manifesting ourselves. This is one of the universal human concerns that is a prerequisite of living. Yet it is also a limitation imposed upon us, namely because we cannot exist without others and without expressing ourselves to others. Sidney Jourard writes: 'Everything and everybody in the world discloses themselves by one means or another as long as they exist' (1971:19). It is part of the human condition to relate to others, to be with others. Indeed, it is yet another of the 'givens' of existence.

We all have many different types of relationships, each with their own patterns of communication and levels of disclosure. There are also numerous ways of disclosing ourselves. We can decide to be open and honest and to reveal ourselves freely or we can decide to conceal ourselves behind a mask. The position we choose will depend on the nature of the relationship and how much we need to protect ourselves. Jourard argues that 'throughout the history of humanity we have camouflaged our true being in front of others in order to protect ourselves against criticism or rejection' (1971:VII).

From an existential point of view we can disclose ourselves either by deceiving ourselves when we disclose something other than our true experience, or we can disclose in line with our lived experience. Both are disclosures, the former we could call inauthentic while the latter would be an authentic disclosure.

In the therapeutic relationship we create a condition for clients to disclose themselves unguardedly. In doing this we (the therapists) also enter this relationship, as explained in Chapter 2, on three relational realms (Spinelli, 1994:331). First, as therapists, as we listen to or are with our clients we consider our own issues, experiences, listening capacities and precon-

5.3

THE EXISTENTIAL WHEEL OF
POSSIBILITIES AND LIMITATIONS IN
"BEING-IN-THE-WORLD"
CONCEPTS
(A STRUCTURAL VIEW)

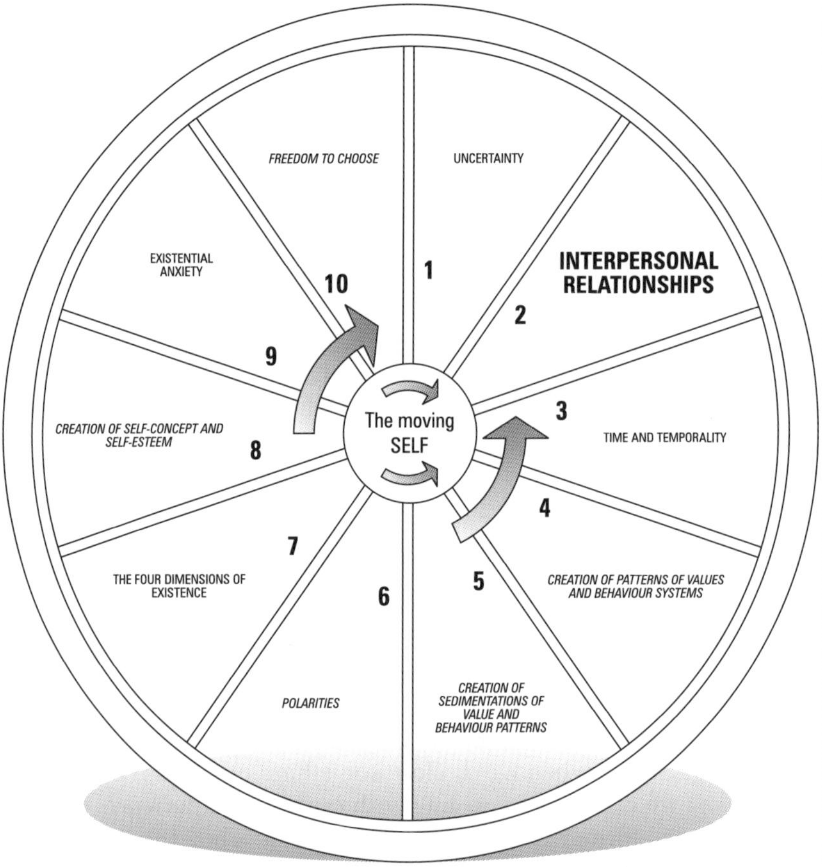

The diagram represents a non-chronological and non-linear interconnection of the concepts

Figure 5.3

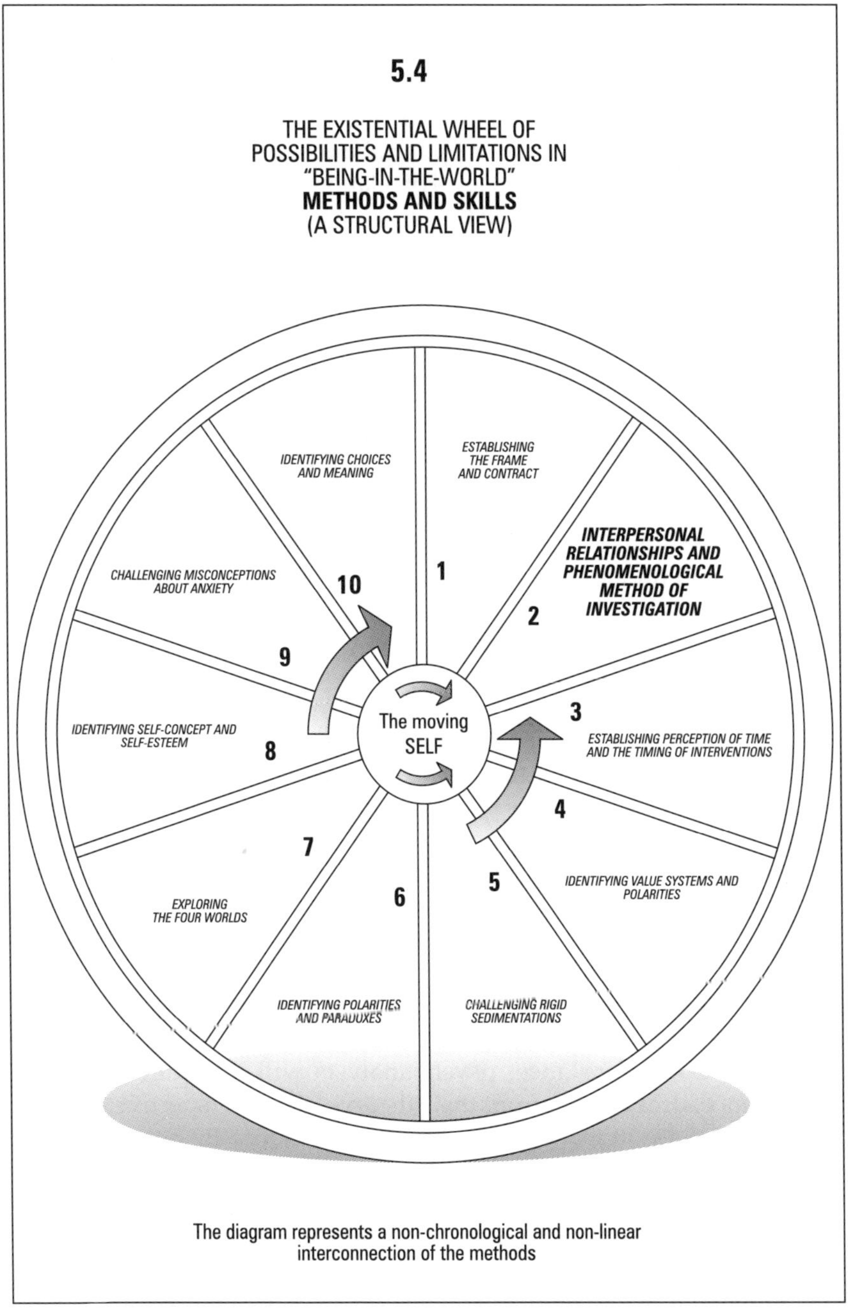
5.4
THE EXISTENTIAL WHEEL OF
POSSIBILITIES AND LIMITATIONS IN
"BEING-IN-THE-WORLD"
METHODS AND SKILLS
(A STRUCTURAL VIEW)
ESTABLISHING THE FRAME AND CONTRACT
1
INTERPERSONAL RELATIONSHIPS AND PHENOMENOLOGICAL METHOD OF INVESTIGATION
2
ESTABLISHING PERCEPTION OF TIME AND THE TIMING OF INTERVENTIONS
3
4
IDENTIFYING VALUE SYSTEMS AND POLARITIES
5
CHALLENGING RIGID SEDIMENTATIONS
6
IDENTIFYING POLARITIES AND PARADOXES
7
EXPLORING THE FOUR WORLDS
8
IDENTIFYING SELF-CONCEPT AND SELF-ESTEEM
9
CHALLENGING MISCONCEPTIONS ABOUT ANXIETY
10
IDENTIFYING CHOICES AND MEANING
The moving SELF
The diagram represents a non-chronological and non-linear interconnection of the methods

Figure 5.4

ceived ideas and emotions. In this process we also attempt to bracket our biases and monitor our own sense of being. In the second realm of being, in relation to the client, we experience and consider the client's value system and, within it, the possible inherent discrepancies. We also consider our understanding of the client's perception about his or her relationships with ourselves and others. The third level of relationship is, according to Spinelli (1994), however, the crucial and the most meaningful involvement in therapy. In this realm of relationship we focus on our immediate interrelationships (or being 'with' relationships) with the client.

In this process we explore and clarify what emerges from the interaction between the first two relationships, and how we experience ourselves being in relationship with the client, and the client with the therapist. Through this unique mode of 'betweenness', not only can clients honestly and genuinely disclose themselves, but therapists will reveal themselves as being in relationship. In this therapeutic relationship therapists will reveal themselves to the client as simply 'being-there' and not necessarily through verbal disclosures. In this climate clients' mundane behaviour patterns could unfold themselves; that is, clients' macrocosmic behaviour patterns repeat themselves in the therapeutic encounters. Usually, after the endings of the therapy certain changes take place in both parties.

In the example of Paul, where I made a mistake in the timing of the sessions, he realized that I am also human and I realized I had made an error. Even mistakes can be useful tools in therapy.

The purpose of intervention in any therapy is to interpret and clarify client's issues. Following this reasoning the question must be asked: who should interpret in a therapeutic encounter, the client or the therapist?

Interpretation

The next question is whether existential therapists interpret at all. Historically speaking it is only possible to interpret if there is a theory to interpret from. So, for instance, psychoanalysts will interpret resistance, transference, dreams, etc. from their theory-driven perspective, in order to aid the process of making unconscious, conscious. 'By interpreting we go beyond what is readily observable and we assign meaning and causality to a psychological phenomenon' (Greenson, 1967:39). The response of the client and the client's history and personality are also taken into account, but essentially interpretation involves understanding the theory and applying it to the client.

Chambers Twentieth Century Dictionary defines the word interpret as 'to explain the meaning of . . . to translate into intelligible or familiar terms'.

In existential therapy, the therapist is the facilitator of interpretation as opposed to the interpreter. After a combination of challenging and associative type questions, the therapist might conceive a notion about the client and may link certain themes together and ask more specific questions until the client can make his or her own connection and interpretation. Often it is between sessions that clients make their own interpretation. For example, Rebecca kept saying that she went blank when certain types of questions were asked which related to her feelings. She also had the habit of laughing and making jokes at these junctures. Her reaction when the questions became too probing was pointed out to her. In the following session Rebecca said that she felt as if she had been hit in the stomach, and that she now realized that she had so many feelings associated with inconceivable pain, which was why she blanked. Thus no interpretation in the traditional psychoanalytic term was necessary. Rebecca was allowed to make her own interpretation.

In our work we distinguish between contemplative (associative) versus active and challenging intervention.

Associative intervention

The first type of intervention stems from 'associative' thinking. This facilitates clients to narrate their story in an almost free associative mode so that a contemplative, almost hypnotic state emerges. This is that 'timeless' or 'mindless' condition which was talked about, where the perception of 'clock time' disappears. Indeed, clients frequently comment how time becomes suspended during sessions.

During this sequence of therapy an inter-subjective understanding between therapist and client may develop and therefore it is important that any intervention from the therapist is carefully timed and premeditated, so that the flow is enhanced rather than interrupted. The most common interventions will consist of careful listening and 'being' with the client; reflecting back moods, feelings and content; summarizing; noting any body language signs; monosyllabic prompting and most important of all, the ability to remain silent.

Again, the communicative method has an important message, since this psychoanalytic approach relies entirely on the content and derivatives of the stories told by clients. Inter-subjective understanding between clients and therapists is important in this paradigm as, according to the communicative approach, only through this relationship can clients express their derivatives and reveal their unconscious messages. David Smith writes that it is only through our unconscious system that we are specifically able to understand inter-subjective reality: 'According to communicative theory, each of us carries within us a brilliant psychoanalytic intelligence, and each of us is, unconsciously, a natural psychoanalyst' (1991:134).

Although existential therapists will not necessarily subscribe to the communicative concept of the unconscious process, they would accept and have experienced the 'timeless' merging of the thoughts and emotions between therapist and client. Some authors would describe these moments as insights. Carl Rogers, in a dialogue between Martin Buber and Maurice Friedman, said: 'The moments in which people do change are the moments in which perhaps the relationship is experienced the same on both sides' (Friedman, 1964:489). For Buber these are the Thou and I empathic moments that are the result of 'human effective dialogue' (ibid., 1964:489). Furthermore, Buber says, 'Meaning by dialogue (is) not just talking. Dialogue can be silence' (ibid., 1964:489).

Challenging and active intervention

The very nature of 'challenging' and the notion of active intervention will by definition interrupt the clients' associative and narrative mood. It will provoke them to transcend into a different plane, that of active thinking. Active interventions challenge the client's perceptions and pick up on any discrepancies that might have emerged. In so doing, they evoke an active and didactic thinking process.

Discrepancies are the buried contradictions inherent in situations and a client's belief system. So, for instance, Mary believed that success came through earning money, yet at the same time she believed that money was the root of all evil. Discrepancies also highlight the polarities of existence: the idea that there are two sides to every experience. Thus what may appear to be a positive experience will also have its negative components. Money for Mary was positive because the more she earned, the more her goals were realized. The negative side, however, was that she got no pleasure in the possession of money per se. She preferred to live like a pauper. Challenging, like the associative interventions, must follow the client's train of thought. There should be no hidden agenda in the way a therapist intervenes, for challenging is asking the client to elucidate and to think more deeply on the material they bring up themselves.

Positive versus negative challenge

The word challenging sounds harsh, but in fact there is a great need for any challenging intervention to be carefully selected and gently handled.

Indiscriminate challenging may distract clients from their issues while too few challenges may create an atmosphere in which clients feel that the therapist is not listening intently enough. Challenging needs to be earned. Before any intervention, the therapist should form an even, if imperfect, framework of the client's world views.

In addition, the therapist must be aware that challenging may be perceived as negative, especially when certain adjectives are used which could damage a client's defences. Clients' rigid views are sometimes essential to their being and premature and negative challenges can create a hostile attitude towards their own behaviour pattern. This in turn may cause guilt and create additional anxiety of anxiety and fear of fear. Ultimately, the most effective way is to make clients aware of their contradictions and allow them to challenge those discrepancies. The following vignette from Sue's case study (see further, Chapter 7) will highlight the complexity of these different types of interventions.

Sue suffered from bulimia nervosa and compulsively binged and then vomited on average fourteen times per day. She realized, soon after her fourth session, that when she physically placed the first piece of chocolate in her mouth she was doing it to avoid feeling the overwhelming anxiety she had about her fear of being rejected. In her terminology, to be 'stodgy', fat, and overweight was to be exiled from her social and family circles. As such she felt an outsider, a loner with very little contact with others and the longer this continued, the more her self-esteem diminished. For Sue her body had to have the exact proportions that were inculcated by her. She was of above average intelligence and it was not difficult for her to challenge herself and to recognize that her value system, from her childhood onwards, centred on her body, family and peers. She came to believe that only when her body was perfect could she find a husband, family and happiness. This was intertwined with her feelings of rejection so that to avoid these unhappy thoughts she turned to the comfort of chocolate. After she had binged, she was so disgusted with herself, so guilty at her bloated body, that she felt compelled to vomit. She hated her body, and at the same time felt enormous guilt every time the cycle was repeated.

However, this realization was not enough. It was only when Sue's attitude towards her bingeing and her beliefs about her body were challenged that she could start to contemplate how they related to her self-concept. She realized that at some point in her life they had given her the positive reassurance which she needed. Rather than actively trying to stop herself, she chose to reflect on the compulsive pattern itself and to clarify her motivations. After asking Sue how she would feel if she weighed more, she began to challenge her value system and to explore other aspects of it. Was there no meaning to her life, apart that is from her body? Could she find happiness, even if she were overweight? As a result of this exploration, she began to be more open about her 'secret' and found the resources to confide in her friends and family. Although her bingeing did not cease completely, it diminished significantly.

The object of challenging is to facilitate clients to clarify and make themselves aware of the contradictions and discrepancies that govern their belief systems. This will enable clients to 'fit' more closely with their experiences and to 'own' them. In the case of Sue there was no negative challenging, there was no need to condemn her bingeing or her beliefs about her self-image. It was more important to point out how she had a vested interest in continuing her patterns, in staying within her familiar and therefore secure environment. Negative challenges might well have exacerbated her feelings of hostility and guilt, while positive challenges enabled Sue to broaden her perspective and challenge her existing value system. Through this she was able to begin to understand that she had other values that she could bring back to her life.

TIME

Time and temporality constantly pervade the therapeutic relationship. In therapy the perception and awareness of time are important for both the therapist and the client. The timing of interventions is also part of the method in this approach. The two wheels shown in Figures 5.5 and 5.6 demonstrate this.

Time, the effects of ending and the temporal aspects of each session are intrinsic elements in the time-limited existential therapeutic approach. Most clients new to therapy will come with a particular agenda, usually that the therapist will give them a strict formula on how to overcome their problems and how to be cured within the shortest possible time. In these cases there is often an issue relating to dependency. This can take various forms, whether dependency on people, dependency on a belief system or dependency on a behaviour pattern. In contrast, one of the aims of time-limited existential therapy is for clients to become independent of their therapist and in so doing to become less reliant on their dependent behaviour pattern.

In this respect a client with whom we worked in open-ended therapy for five years reminds us of the difficulty of ending. The client's dependence and need to continue therapy resulted in working for a long time on the anxiety of separation.

Working within a time-limited structure will affect clients in various ways. The impending termination will be constantly in their minds. For some clients it is a very freeing experience but for others this awareness may put a great deal of pressure on the therapeutic relationship. The therapist, too, may feel the strain and it may trigger his or her desire to cure or to help the client within the time period. For example, in a supervision session a supervisee began by saying that she felt she did not have enough time to work with the client. This declaration in itself points to the effect that the time limitation imposes on the therapist. She felt anguished, despondent and inadequate in helping her clients. These feelings would be picked up by the client and could potentially impede the process. Therefore it was important for the supervisor to understand her supervisee's need to 'help' and at the same time seek to 'bracket' these emotions, allowing the client to reveal and clarify what he felt about the impending ending.

Time is a fundamental notion and the perception of the passage of time always influences therapeutic interactions. The ending will always evoke some kind of emotional response from the client, whether it is expressed as unimportant, as a sense of relief or as a fear of separation. These types of responses relate back to a client's value system, so in many ways confronting the issue of time. An emotional response can be considered as 'the royal road' for clients to identify and connect their value system to their issues. In other words, while the time limitation and the impending separation create feelings of tension and stress, the therapist can employ this as a tool to challenge and make deeper connections. Our perception of the duration of time will constantly vary and be greatly influenced by both the client's and the therapist's emotional state.

Edna, who has already been mentioned in Chapter 4, exemplifies how time and her fear of separation were of paramount significance in her therapy. At the start, everything proceeded smoothly, but as we reached the second half (around the sixth session) Edna was shocked to realize that although she could remember and talk about her childhood experiences and traumas, she was unable to recollect any feelings. She could relate any traumatic event as if indeed it must have been painful, but she could not reactivate the original emotions. Not only was she not able to understand why this was happening, but she also felt totally incompetent. Somehow she had concluded that she had failed herself.

In the same way that Edna could not express or feel her pain, she was also seemingly unaffected by the impending termination of therapy, until the eighth session. After a short time, and without warning, Edna began accusing the therapist of abandoning her and treating her in the same way as both her parents and her boyfriends had treated her in the past. She began to sob vehemently.

Edna was asked to recall and summarize the main points of the previous sessions. In midstream she suddenly shrieked that she had remem-

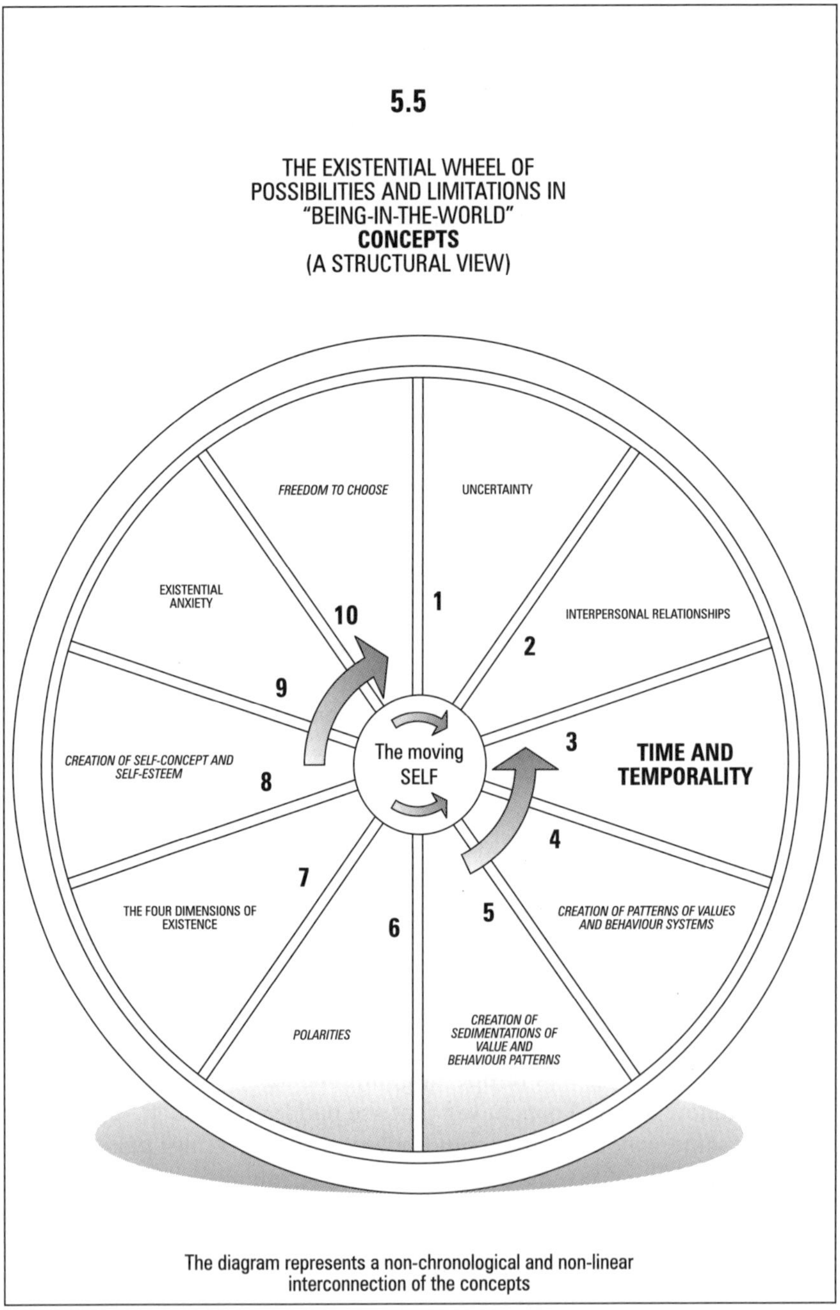
5.5
THE EXISTENTIAL WHEEL OF
POSSIBILITIES AND LIMITATIONS IN
"BEING-IN-THE-WORLD"
CONCEPTS
(A STRUCTURAL VIEW)
FREEDOM TO CHOOSE
UNCERTAINTY
EXISTENTIAL ANXIETY
1
10
INTERPERSONAL RELATIONSHIPS
2
9
3
TIME AND TEMPORALITY
The moving SELF
CREATION OF SELF-CONCEPT AND SELF-ESTEEM
8
4
7
THE FOUR DIMENSIONS OF EXISTENCE
6
5
CREATION OF PATTERNS OF VALUES AND BEHAVIOUR SYSTEMS
POLARITIES
CREATION OF SEDIMENTATIONS OF VALUE AND BEHAVIOUR PATTERNS
The diagram represents a non-chronological and non-linear interconnection of the concepts

Figure 5.5

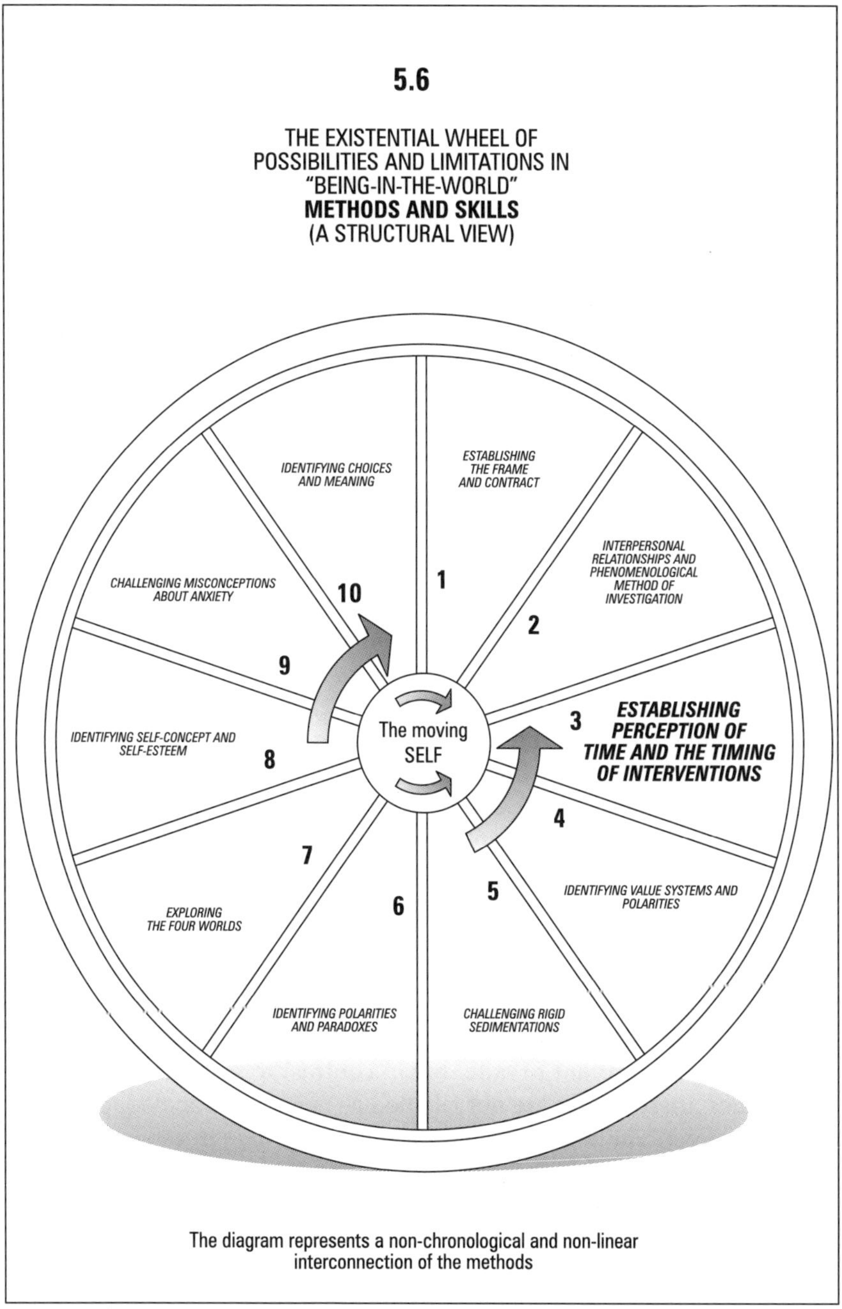
5.6
THE EXISTENTIAL WHEEL OF POSSIBILITIES AND LIMITATIONS IN "BEING-IN-THE-WORLD"
METHODS AND SKILLS
(A STRUCTURAL VIEW)
1
ESTABLISHING THE FRAME AND CONTRACT
2
INTERPERSONAL RELATIONSHIPS AND PHENOMENOLOGICAL METHOD OF INVESTIGATION
3
ESTABLISHING PERCEPTION OF TIME AND THE TIMING OF INTERVENTIONS
4
IDENTIFYING VALUE SYSTEMS AND POLARITIES
5
CHALLENGING RIGID SEDIMENTATIONS
6
IDENTIFYING POLARITIES AND PARADOXES
7
EXPLORING THE FOUR WORLDS
8
IDENTIFYING SELF-CONCEPT AND SELF-ESTEEM
9
CHALLENGING MISCONCEPTIONS ABOUT ANXIETY
10
IDENTIFYING CHOICES AND MEANING
The moving SELF
The diagram represents a non-chronological and non-linear interconnection of the methods

Figure 5.6

bered her first feelings of rejection and abandonment. She had found her mother in bed with a boyfriend. These evoked memories of her past rejections and over the subsequent sessions Edna worked on her feelings as they related to her mother, father, boyfriends and husband. She realized that this fear of rejection had also been inhibiting her desire to write. In the eleventh session she brought a well-written essay about her therapy, and she continued to explore her wish and intention to write.

In this case, the time limit acted as a pressure valve that eventually exploded in the form of extreme anger against the therapist, for abandoning her. It was as if the anger served as a release allowing Edna to remember her early feelings. It is extremely rare for a client not to have some kind of reaction to the impending termination, at some stage during the twelve weeks.

VALUE SYSTEMS

In this section we describe how the awareness of the human propensity to create values and polarities is important in this approach. Indeed one of the functions of the therapist is to prompt and help clients to identify their values, such those represented in Figures 5.7 and 5.8.

Paramount to the underlying theory in this time-limited existential approach are personal values and how these values are not only intrinsic to the client's world view but also the way in which they permeate the therapeutic relationship. It soon becomes apparent that when clients begin to explore their underlying beliefs, they are quite rigid in their way of thinking. Even if a belief is clearly wrong or not working, clients will tenaciously stick to their assumptions. This is not at all surprising, since we have been living and acting on most of our assumptions for many years and they provide part of the security that is craved. However, it is invaluable first for clients to identify their value systems and second to understand why and how those beliefs of sedimented values came into existence. It is important to note that in contrast to some other cognitive approaches, these values are not labelled as negative or maladaptive, but as van Deurzen-Smith says: 'What ultimately matters in existential work is to determine what it is that really matters to the clients, not what ought to matter to them' (1988:116).

Clients need to clarify the distinction between the values that may have been imposed on them by others and the values that they truly cherish as their own. Steven, for example, from adolescence onwards battled with the contradiction between his values and those of his parents until he no longer knew what it was that he genuinely wanted from his life. His parents only valued the 'professions' as a suitable occupation. As a writer, he considered himself an artist, which was a complete anathema to his parents' way of life and their values. During therapy, he realized that he had compromised by remaining a writer and at the same time running his writing as a business with the continued help of his parents. In a roundabout way Steven thought he was keeping his parents happy. I challenged Steven to explore whether these values were 'imposed' by his parents or had he chosen them because of a 'pay-off'.

He began to understand that to keep the business afloat, he was taking on jobs that held no interest for him. Steven simply thought he was keeping his parents happy. Finally he came to the conclusion that as an artist he wanted to be creative and that led him to abandon the business and concentrate on his writing. The irony of this decision was that his parents were in fact relieved that they did not have to keep a continual eye on how the business was doing.

The creation of values is intrinsic to the existence of our being. Van Deurzen-Smith writes that it is bizarre and unrealistic to pretend to be able to abstain from value judgements. In her definition of values can be determined 'whether something is desirable or useful or on the contrary disagreeable and harmful' (1987:238), that is, it is important for the client to determine how much is worth sacrificing for their values.

Values and beliefs vary enormously between clients, but once established it is easy to recognize how these beliefs permeate all aspects of living. People carry with them more than one set of values, but some of them include: modesty, exhibitionism, perfectionism, competence, calmness, bravery, pleasing, loyalty, vulgarity, arrogance, pretension, naturalness, academic laziness, superiority, good judgement, cheating, deceit, tricking, swindling, risk taking, caution, honesty, and dishonesty. These values can be implied or can be explicitly manifested by clients. Clients demonstrate their set of values both in therapeutic encounters and in their everyday activities. It is quite often the case that clients' values will conflict with one's own values, and therefore it is important that therapists 'bracket' their own assumptions.

The next section will demonstrate how these values can become rigid and fixed sedimentations. We will also present a vignette to show how they manifest themselves in therapy.

SEDIMENTATION

Clients' rigid sedimentations of values and behaviour will be the topic of this part of the book. In therapy, the therapist helps clients to challenge their rigid habits and to identify the polarities of their sedimental values.

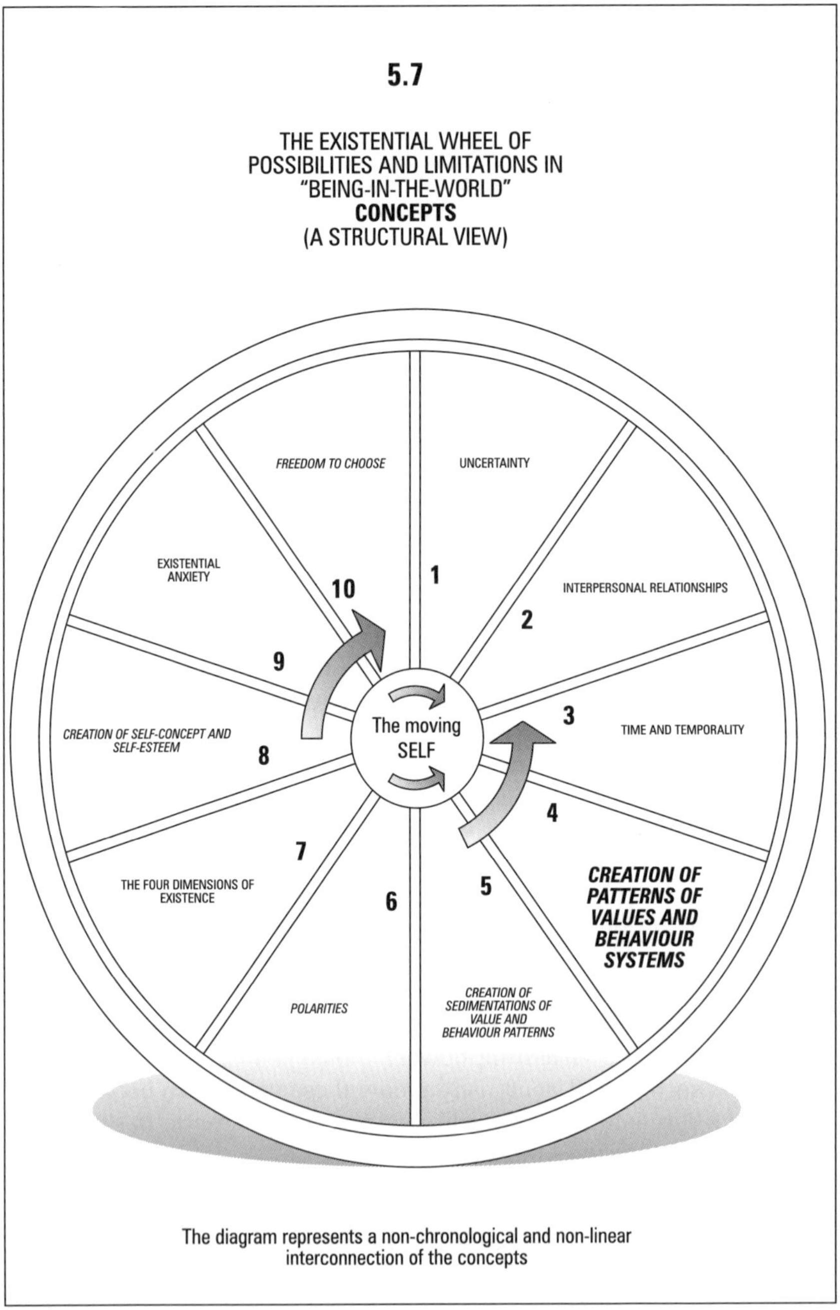
5.7
THE EXISTENTIAL WHEEL OF
POSSIBILITIES AND LIMITATIONS IN
"BEING-IN-THE-WORLD"
CONCEPTS
(A STRUCTURAL VIEW)
The moving SELF
1
UNCERTAINTY
2
INTERPERSONAL RELATIONSHIPS
3
TIME AND TEMPORALITY
4
CREATION OF PATTERNS OF VALUES AND BEHAVIOUR SYSTEMS
5
CREATION OF SEDIMENTATIONS OF VALUE AND BEHAVIOUR PATTERNS
6
POLARITIES
7
THE FOUR DIMENSIONS OF EXISTENCE
8
CREATION OF SELF-CONCEPT AND SELF-ESTEEM
9
EXISTENTIAL ANXIETY
10
FREEDOM TO CHOOSE
The diagram represents a non-chronological and non-linear interconnection of the concepts

Figure 5.7

5.8

THE EXISTENTIAL WHEEL OF
POSSIBILITIES AND LIMITATIONS IN
"BEING-IN-THE-WORLD"
METHODS AND SKILLS
(A STRUCTURAL VIEW)

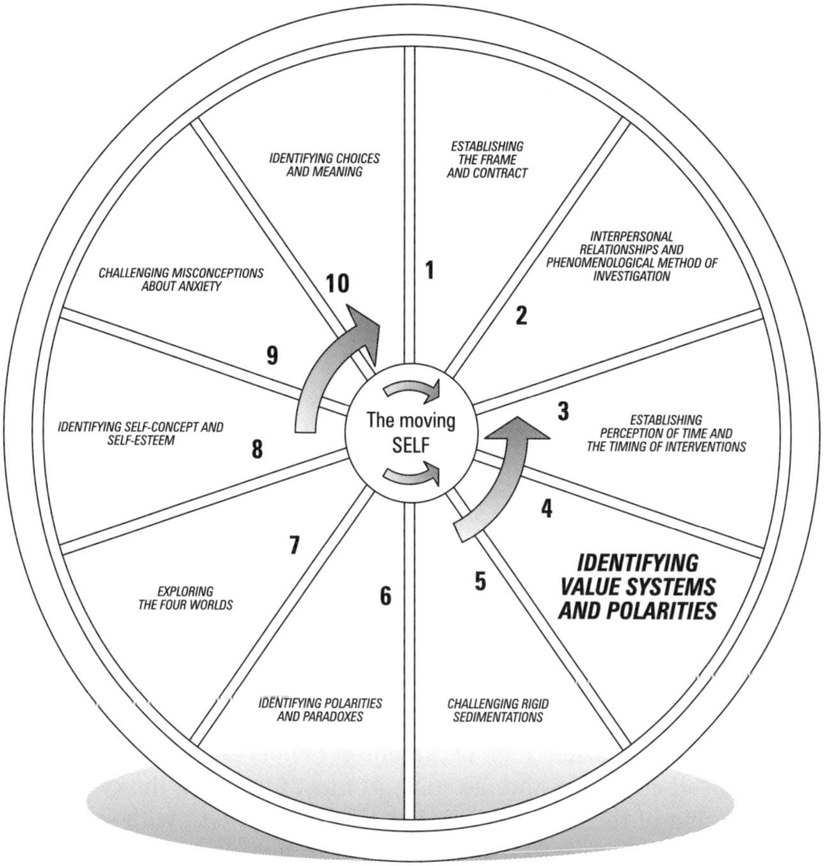

The diagram represents a non-chronological and non-linear
interconnection of the methods

Figure 5.8

The wheels shown in Figures 5.9 and 5.10 demonstrate these, representing a human response to the world's universal 'givens'.

Sedimentation is an unusual word to apply in a therapeutic context. The term 'sediment' is normally used to describe 'the matter that settles at the bottom of a liquid' (*Webster's Third International Dictionary*). Existentialists who have been particularly influenced by phenomenologists such as Merleau-Ponty employ the term to express the experience. Essentially, it is the way human beings become stuck or fixed in certain beliefs and behaviour patterns that deposit themselves deep down in our belief systems in a similar fashion to the sediment that sinks to the bottom of a liquid. These values, assumptions about living and behaviour patterns become integrated to such a degree in the way we operate on a daily basis that they become 'sedimented' and appear immovable. The problem is that they become so enmeshed and intertwined with the way we behave in the everyday world that we are usually totally unaware of their very existence. They are also very difficult to unlearn. Yet, from a phenomenological perspective no sedimented pattern needs to be immovable. Spinelli writes:

> Novelty implies temporality. With the passage of time and, possibly, with the lessening of the anxiety that externally imposed novelties induce, the novelty may become accepted, even highly valued, and itself become part of a new sedimented framework.
>
> (Spinelli, 1989:52)

A significant facet of the therapeutic process is to facilitate clients in becoming aware of their various patterns and sedimentations and then to begin to challenge them. The importance of this exploration is for the client to assess the present usefulness of the sedimented behaviour, for it must be remembered that:

> However restricted, all sedimented beliefs serve to define the self construct and, as such, in most instances, the challenging of these beliefs is highly likely to be met with serious resistance because *a challenge to any part of the self construct also challenges the whole of it*.
>
> (Spinelli, 1994:349)

Indeed, many sedimented behaviour patterns are positive and even those which may, upon reflection, appear negative, have an affirmative and life-enhancing origin. The case of Denise illustrates this. Denise was a 35-

year-old woman who realized that she never truly listened to people. This pattern emerged as a defence against listening to her mother, who continually criticized and demeaned her. As a way of coping, she learned to block out what was unpleasant to her to such an extent that her mother would jump up and down in front of her as if she were performing on a muted television screen. In this way, Denise did not have to listen to her. In therapy, Denise became aware that she was repeating the same habit with people at work, especially those colleagues who might criticize her in some way.

A considerable percentage of our sedimented beliefs originate in cultural attitudes and values imposed on us, such as loyalty, honesty, ambition, perfection and material well-being. These can all be extremely beneficial towards creating successes, achieving goals and maintaining skilful interactions within society. However, when these sedimentations become so rigid and exaggerated that they could almost be considered compulsive, they may truly impede our progress, as was seen in Denise's situation.

Fritz Perls, founder of Gestalt therapy, believed that we develop our belief patterns early on in our developmental stages. Because of our parental and societal conditioning, what we 'must' and 'should' do and what we 'must' value, we become, in Perls' word, 'stuck'. According to Perls these values can be so ingrained in our personalities that we repeat them all our life, irrespective of their beneficial or adverse effects. We are then stuck. Perls inspires therapists to create conditions in therapeutic encounters to re-enact this feeling of 'stuckness':

> So what I do as a therapist is to work as a catalyst both ways: provide situations in which a person can experience this being stuck the unpleasantness and I frustrate his avoidance still further, until he is willing to mobilise his own resources.
>
> (Perls, 1959:56)

While Perls' 'stuckness' has certain similarities to the notion of sedimentation, his method of intervention is still different from the existential approach. If Perls provides a situation and frustrates the client's avoidance, an existential therapist, in divergence to this, would first help the client to identify his or her rigid and dogmatic belief system and would then prompt him or her to explore these from positive and negative angles. From an existential point of view these rigid sedimentations are sometimes so ingrained that we repeat them over and over again, irrespective of their beneficial or adverse effect.

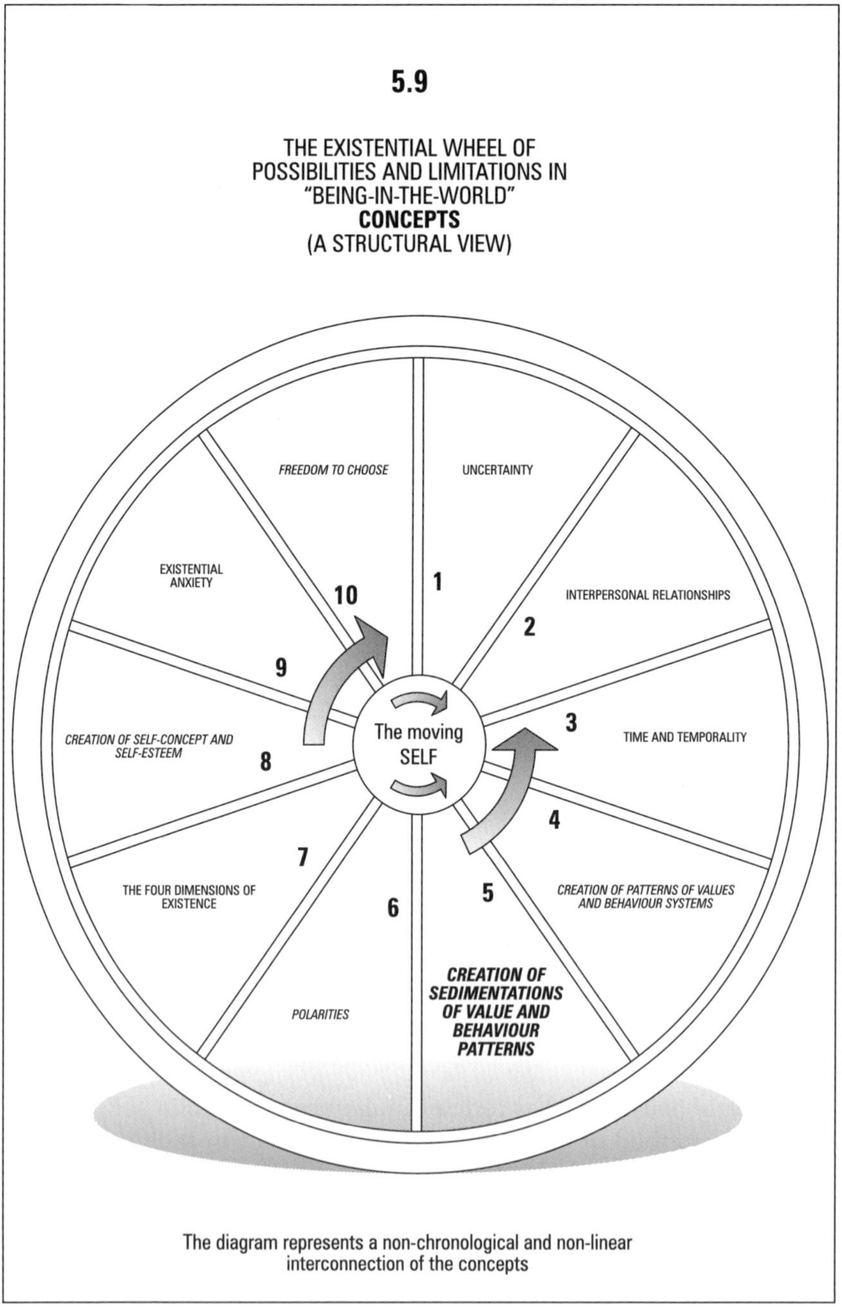
5.9
THE EXISTENTIAL WHEEL OF
POSSIBILITIES AND LIMITATIONS IN
"BEING-IN-THE-WORLD"
CONCEPTS
(A STRUCTURAL VIEW)
FREEDOM TO CHOOSE
UNCERTAINTY
EXISTENTIAL ANXIETY
10
1
INTERPERSONAL RELATIONSHIPS
2
9
The moving SELF
3
TIME AND TEMPORALITY
CREATION OF SELF-CONCEPT AND SELF-ESTEEM
8
4
7
THE FOUR DIMENSIONS OF EXISTENCE
6
5
CREATION OF PATTERNS OF VALUES AND BEHAVIOUR SYSTEMS
POLARITIES
CREATION OF SEDIMENTATIONS OF VALUE AND BEHAVIOUR PATTERNS
The diagram represents a non-chronological and non-linear interconnection of the concepts

Figure 5.9

5.10

THE EXISTENTIAL WHEEL OF POSSIBILITIES AND LIMITATIONS IN "BEING-IN-THE-WORLD"
METHODS AND SKILLS
(A STRUCTURAL VIEW)

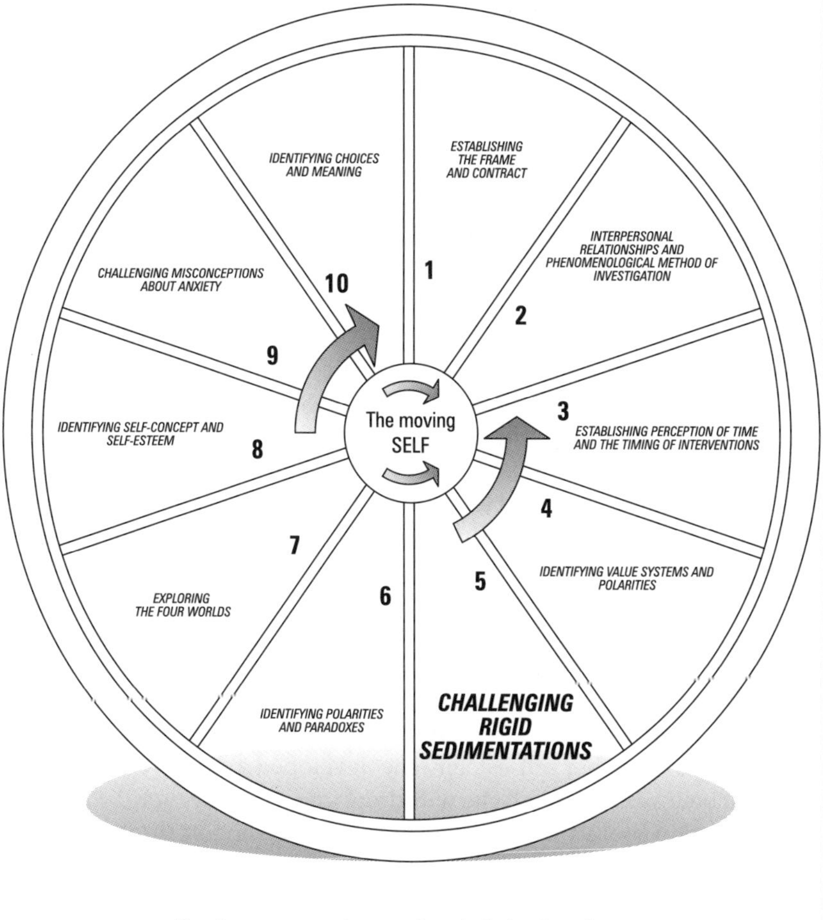

The diagram represents a non-chronological and non-linear interconnection of the methods

Figure 5.10

We can be dogmatic or stuck to such an extent that it is often hard to realize that there might be other ways of viewing the world or other ways of conducting our lives. These rigid, dogmatic tunnel visions are known as 'sedimented' outlooks in phenomenological terminology. We all have a vested interest in defending our old ways of thinking and predictable ways of behaving. After all, we have spent many years building up these patterns to make them work for us. Nevertheless in existential time-limited therapy we assume that however rigid some of the sedimentations have become, there is always a possibility to unlearn them or 'de-sedimentalize' them, although this can sometimes prove very difficult. In order to 'unlearn' sedimentations Merleau-Ponty suggests projecting oneself into the future. Through this method clients could challenge their own value systems and experience insights.

A typical example of sedimentation is a client whose presenting problem was that she experienced difficulty in communicating with people, particularly in groups. During therapy Lynn became aware that one of her sedimented values was that of modesty; to 'show off' was perceived as a deadly sin to such an extent that the slightest manifestation of her immodesty threw her into panic. As a result she withdrew from any communication that might prove dangerous.

As the sessions progressed, Lynn realized that buried deep within herself was a different kind of person; one that was both lively and extrovert. She had vivid memories of a party when she was 5 years old. She recounted how she had joked, danced and sung to entertain both the adults and children present. Her mother, however, stopped her, dragging her from the room, reprimanding her behaviour and shouting at her 'to stop showing off'. Lynn realized that her family, coming from a very restricted, religious Protestant background, condemned any kind of behaviour that could be regarded as flamboyant; it was considered rude and ill mannered. She remembered clearly the devastation she had felt at that moment of being taken out of the room. She had been left feeling demolished and worthless, remaining alone in her bedroom. From this time on, to maintain her self-esteem, she developed a strategy for survival. Instead of being an extrovert, she withdrew into a fantasy world where she found solace in literature and poetry. Each time she felt threatened, she began to withdraw. Indeed, the same pattern existed in the present, where her fear to communicate in groups stemmed from her belief that to state her point of view was the equivalent to 'showing off' and therefore wrong. We can see clearly how Lynn's perception of herself developed from her parents' values, which then became subsumed as her own behaviour.

The driving force behind the sedimentation was her inexorable longing for approval. It meant that she continually pressured herself into pleasing people by remaining modest and unprepossessing. This set off a cycle where she felt lonely, isolated and lacking in self-esteem, not only when she was rebuked but also when she did not achieve her goals because she had not been confident enough about her ideas. This was a 'Catch 22' situation for Lynn.

The question then arises: what is the force behind this ubiquitous, and universal, phenomenon that drives people to these sedimentations? In therapy Lynn's 'showing off' episode with her mother manifested itself as being fundamental to her. It was used as a metaphor to challenge her belief that the only way to function effectively was by maintaining her modesty. Paradoxically, Lynn had originally enjoyed the times that she had 'shown off', as it had attracted people's attention. By dancing and singing to an audience she would gain their approbation and consequently nourish her self-esteem. Her mother had so emphatically and repeatedly shown her disapproval that Lynn's value system underwent a gradual reversal and the positive sides of 'showing off' took on a negative association that by remaining unassuming, she could avoid the disapproval and gain approval. Through these means Lynn's 'self-construct' became limited and contained.

In many ways Lynn's sedimentation represents one of the many paths that we as human beings follow to search for approval and escape disapproval. It is so deeply ingrained in all of us that it is considered a universal 'given'. The need for approval, in whatever form it manifests itself, is prevalent in all avenues of life. For example, Lynn's 'showing off' episode exemplified her need for approval from an audience to satisfy her self-concept. On the other hand, her fear of disapproval was manifesting itself in her fear of public appearances. Lynn's issue was not her sedimented pattern of withdrawal and introversion, for in many ways this model was successful – she became a better student and gained an interest in literature and poetry that might not have occurred if she had remained an extrovert. Nor was her problem due to her sedimentation of gaining approval by her modesty, or her fear of disapproval by 'showing off'. Her true problem was slightly further entrenched in that it stemmed from her fear of criticism, which was synonymous with rejection. Rejection meant loneliness, being an outsider, and unable to join in because of her lack of self-esteem. To avoid these devastating feelings, Lynn began her lifelong quest to gain approval, avoid disapproval and hence maintain her sense of self-esteem.

Although these rigid sedimentations may appear to have started in childhood, there are also others, which may have appeared to have been created in adulthood. The important point is to recognize the sedimentation and attempt to challenge the rigid value system that may precipitate the shift of deep-seated behaviour patterns. In fact, there is no need to search for the so-called sources of sedimentations, as there is always a multitude of events that create, recreate and reinforce those sedimented perceptions.

In therapy, once clients can come to terms with the idea of sedimentation, they can challenge their entrenched beliefs and behaviour systems. Some insights and change of perception may ensue. This was typified in Lynn's situation. In therapy she was able to question her belief, whether her modesty served her always positively, and conversely whether showing off affected her always negatively. Then this challenge set a chain reaction in motion, in which she rapidly began to realize that she possessed the power to choose from her alternative behaviour patterns.

This is also illustrated in Denise's case, where she began to suffer from severe anxiety attacks once she realized that she was completely blocking out her emotional nature. She became aware that she had used her rational thinking as a way of compensating for her lack of feeling. She connected this to her mother, who believed in the ultimate truth. That is, what her mother said was the truth and anything else was meaningless. Denise adopted this sense of the truth and transformed it into what she defined as her sense of reality, which had to be checked and double-checked before she was able to move forward. She started to define 'truth' and to challenge her deep-rooted belief that all truths are absolute. Then she began to listen to people with her whole sense of self. People no longer seemed stupid or inferior as she had felt before. She began to be aware of other people's emotions and found that they also responded differently to her.

POLARITIES AND PARADOXES

The creation of values also produces polarities. In this section we discuss this and the way we prompt clients to identify their polarities. This is exemplified on the wheels shown in Figures 5.11 and 5.12. The moment we create values, a polarity has been established, i.e. values are subject to the universal predicaments of polarities.

Clients will very soon talk about their values, whether it is a belief that to be perfect means working hard or that the only way to be liked by others is to please them. There is an infinite number of possible values available that a person will latch on to at some point in his life, and to a large extent these dictate everyday encounters with people and the decisions made during one's life. Often it is not until the start of therapy that clients will begin to realize how strict their underlying values are.

The interesting aspect of values is that the moment we have created one, we have also created the opposite, or what is known as the polarity. For example, if obedience connotes a positive value for someone, it goes without saying that disobedience denotes a negative meaning for the same individual. This particular ontological characteristic of values is best described by van Deurzen-Smith:

> What stands out as a basic principle is that human existence is a struggle between opposites. There are two sides to every experience. Each argument has a counter argument. Positive aspects turn out to have negative counter parts and vice versa. People always find themselves somewhere on the continuum between life and death, good and bad, positive and negative, active and passive, happiness and sadness. closeness and distance.
>
> (van Deurzen-Smith, 1988:58)

Table 5.1 lists a number of values and their polarities that exemplify how clients may develop a rigid sedimented belief system with positive or negative connotation. The list has been compiled and derived from a long list of our experiences with clients.

Table 5.1 Values and their polarities (*continues on page 100*)

Positive value	*Negative value*
Modesty	Showing off
Monogamy	Promiscuity
Strong	Weak
Tranquillity	Anxiety
Loyalty	Disloyalty
Refinement	Vulgarity
Security	Insecurity
Slim	Fat
Order	Chaos

5.11

THE EXISTENTIAL WHEEL OF
POSSIBILITIES AND LIMITATIONS IN
"BEING-IN-THE-WORLD"
CONCEPTS
(A STRUCTURAL VIEW)

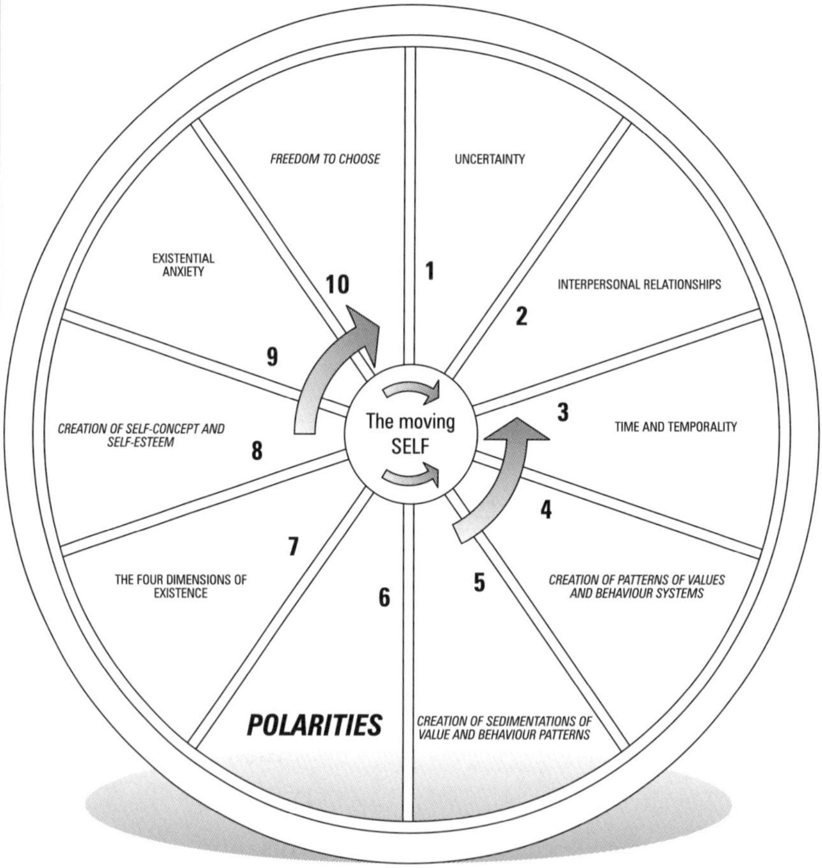

The diagram represents a non-chronological and non-linear interconnection of the concepts

Figure 5.11

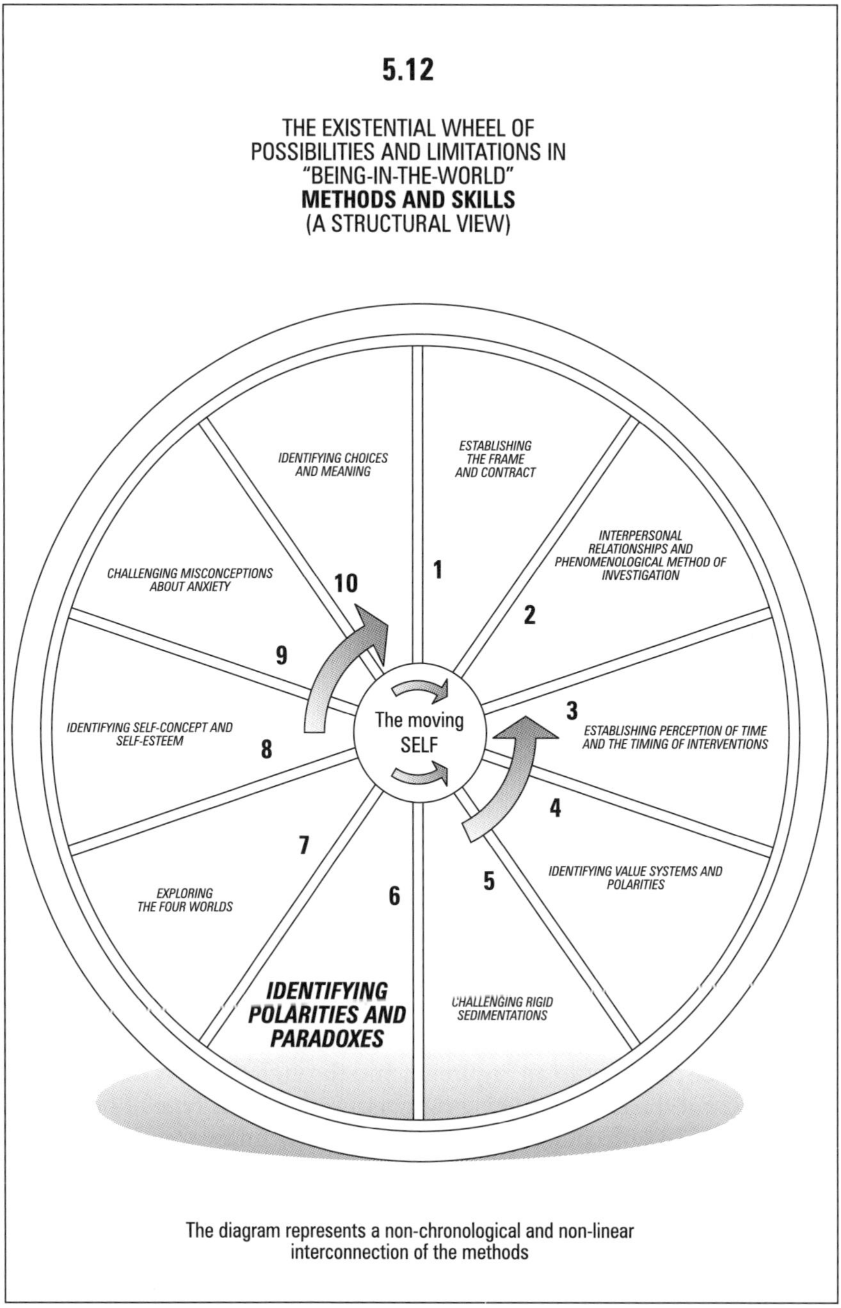
5.12
THE EXISTENTIAL WHEEL OF
POSSIBILITIES AND LIMITATIONS IN
"BEING-IN-THE-WORLD"
METHODS AND SKILLS
(A STRUCTURAL VIEW)
IDENTIFYING CHOICES AND MEANING
ESTABLISHING THE FRAME AND CONTRACT
INTERPERSONAL RELATIONSHIPS AND PHENOMENOLOGICAL METHOD OF INVESTIGATION
CHALLENGING MISCONCEPTIONS ABOUT ANXIETY
10
1
2
9
3
The moving SELF
ESTABLISHING PERCEPTION OF TIME AND THE TIMING OF INTERVENTIONS
IDENTIFYING SELF-CONCEPT AND SELF-ESTEEM
8
4
7
IDENTIFYING VALUE SYSTEMS AND POLARITIES
5
6
EXPLORING THE FOUR WORLDS
IDENTIFYING POLARITIES AND PARADOXES
CHALLENGING RIGID SEDIMENTATIONS
The diagram represents a non-chronological and non-linear interconnection of the methods

Figure 5.12

Table 5.1 continued from page 97

Positive value	*Negative value*
Peace of mind	Agitation
Knowing all	Ignorance
Honesty	Cheating
Natural	Contrived
Intellectual	Intuitive
Superior	Inferior
Good judgement	Bad judgement
To have a real self	Not to have a true self
Make others feel good	Make others feel bad
To please others	To please oneself

For example, Ian found that he had a problem in asking questions. He realized that as a young boy he had been known to possess an extraordinary mental capacity for remembering information. His father enjoyed showing Ian off to his friends and would make Ian 'perform' by asking him questions. One day, he failed to give the right answer to the question, 'What is the capital of Borneo?' He was so shocked by his father's reprimand that he became seriously depressed. As a result of this and other reinforcing events, he gradually developed a belief about himself as someone who had the duty to know everything, and consequently if he did not, he was obviously a 'good-for-nothing'. Every time he did not know an answer he would feel utterly invalidated. He developed the habit of refraining from asking questions. When he really wanted to know something, he automatically stated a fact around the subject, pushing the other person into an argument and through this process he would often find out the answer to his original question. This type of behaviour had become so entrenched that Ian was totally unaware of the convoluted way he had developed of gaining information. In other words, he was doing it compulsively.

Until we begin to explore our underlying value system, we cannot begin to understand the patterns that ensue. As Ian became aware of his compulsive behaviour, that is always to have the correct answers, he began to explore possible alternatives. He began to question whether the only way to be validated was to manifest his knowledge, or whether there were perhaps other ways to maintain his self-esteem. The most important question that he posed was: 'Do I really have to know everything to be accepted by others, and is this at all possible?' Thus, he was able to adopt a value system that was less rigid and more authentic.

THE FOUR WORLDS

In this part we deal with the four dimensions of human existence: physical, public, private and spiritual world. In therapy we prompt clients to explore these dimensions as demonstrated on the two wheels in Figures 5.13 and 5.14. The segment showing the four dimensions of existence is printed in bold as it represents one of the universal 'givens' of the world.

Another way of exploring a client's world view is to clarify how it exists on the four dimensions within which human existence fluctuates. Three of the terms were originally introduced by Ludwig Binswanger and are called the *Umwelt* (physical world), the *Mitwelt* (public world), and the *Eigenwelt* (private world). The last, the *Überwelt* (spiritual world), was added by van Deurzen-Smith. She sees the importance of this kind of exploration as 'providing a map of the different areas through which people travel so as to facilitate their journey through life and encourage expansion into new territory' (1988: 69). The last dimension of the ideal world refers to a person's connection to the abstract and absolute aspect of living. For many people this dimension can be understood to represent the spiritual or religious element.

The *Umwelt* is the physical world, with its predetermined physical and biological dimension. Although one could say that these factors are immutable, there is nevertheless room for flexibility with the way each individual relates to these different factors. For example a person may be tall or short, blond or dark. While the individual has no power to change these facts, he or she can, nevertheless, alter (or not alter) his or her attitude towards them. Existential therapy encourages clients to explore these attitudes. The *Umwelt* also includes the way a person relates to his or her environment, and how the physical body is perceived. People with eating disorders usually have a very distorted view of their size. The way in which they relate to their body shape can bring out a different perspective. One client enjoyed gardening when she felt content with herself; yet when she began to get depressed she would stop watering her plants. She brought out this relationship in therapy and started to use it as an analogy of how she felt towards nurturing both her garden and herself.

The *Mitwelt* is the public world of our relationship to others. It is the world of our attitudes towards social class, race, gender, culture and the general rules of our particular society. It is also the world of our everyday encounters with other people, the way we interact socially with others. Some key points that might emerge are the way that clients cope with other people. Do they automatically take a liking or dislike to people, do they only accept people whom they perceive as having the same views as themselves, do they want to be in control of their relationships or do they prefer to be submissive. These are all aspects of the *Mitwelt* that the therapist can explore with the client in order to clarify his or her attitudes towards these various aspects of society at large.

In the *Mitwelt* there are essentially three ways of relating to other people: dominance over, submission to, or withdrawal from the situation. Every interaction with another person will include one of these modes, although sometimes it changes from moment to moment within one interaction and will vary, too, with interactions with different people. For example, Louise had a professional life as a lawyer where her everyday interactions with colleagues and clients were based in a relatively balanced way within the three modes as described above. However, her home life was a complete contrast in that she was subject to both verbal and physical abuse by her husband. She was largely submissive to his needs in the hope that she could keep their relationship on an even keel. It was not until Louise could recognize the contrast and the imbalance in her relationships, both at the office and at home, that she could begin to work on herself.

The third dimension is that of the *Eigenwelt*, which is the private, intimate world of the client. This is the space of both the intimate relationship that one has with oneself, as well as the relationship one has with significant others. In many ways this is the dimension on which most therapies operate, and from an existential position will take into account the ontological 'givens' such as anxiety, isolation, loneliness and meaninglessness. It will also include the intimate meanings the client has in relation to his or her feelings, thoughts, hopes, and values about life in general. Exploration on this level will reveal how we view and define ourselves and how we interpret our relations with other intimate contacts such as family, close friends and partners.

Most intimate relationships (including the client–therapist dyad) will operate largely in the public world, occasionally moving into the private sphere and acceptance of the inherent differences between two people.

Finally, the *Überwelt*, or the ideal world, is concerned with a person's connection with what may be called spiritual values. This is the world where people and clients create meaning for themselves. Van Deurzen-

Smith writes:

> Understanding the ideal world of a person means grasping how this person makes sense of the world and what it is that she lives for and would be willing to die for. Formulating the values that one lives by is often the first step in the direction of solving problems on the public, private and natural dimension as well.
>
> (van Deurzen-Smith, 1988:98)

The *Überwelt* is the dimension where people have their own beliefs about life and death and what gives them personal meaning. Again, this will encompass different notions for each individual. Even a religious person will take his or her own particular meaning from religious texts, which will be different to someone else of the same religion. Often, the *Überwelt* does not involve religion, but simply personal beliefs about the purpose of life.

In discussing these four dimensions, it must be noted that they are not seen as separate parts of the person but are incorporated in the whole. Each is linked and ideally held in balance in the same fashion, as all existential notions are interconnected. Listening to clients and understanding their relative position on these four dimensions can reveal where possible imbalances lie. Julian, for example, suffered panic attacks that he could describe in detail (the *Umwelt*), and which were related to his relationships in the *Mitwelt*. That is, he began not to want to go out and enjoy himself in case he had a panic attack in public. In his private, intimate world of the *Eigenwelt* he was suffering from a lack of self-confidence, while in his *Überwelt*, he found himself realizing that he was scared of dying. In therapy, all four of these areas were considered as interrelated.

The fourfold world makes it possible for clients and therapists to explore how clients exist on each dimension. This, in turn, may become a powerful tool for clients to delve into and challenge their value system. Some clients may be more preoccupied with one dimension to the virtual exclusion of another. So, for example, if clients are absorbed in their private world (*Eigenwelt*), they may be caught up with their inner conflicts to such an extent that they do not have time to cultivate the other three worlds of the natural (*Umwelt*), the public (*Mitwelt*) and the spiritual (*Überwelt*). The analysis of how clients relate to these worlds and how these worlds are balanced can also interconnect with clients' value systems and behaviour patterns.

John, for example, was overwhelmed by his physical world. He

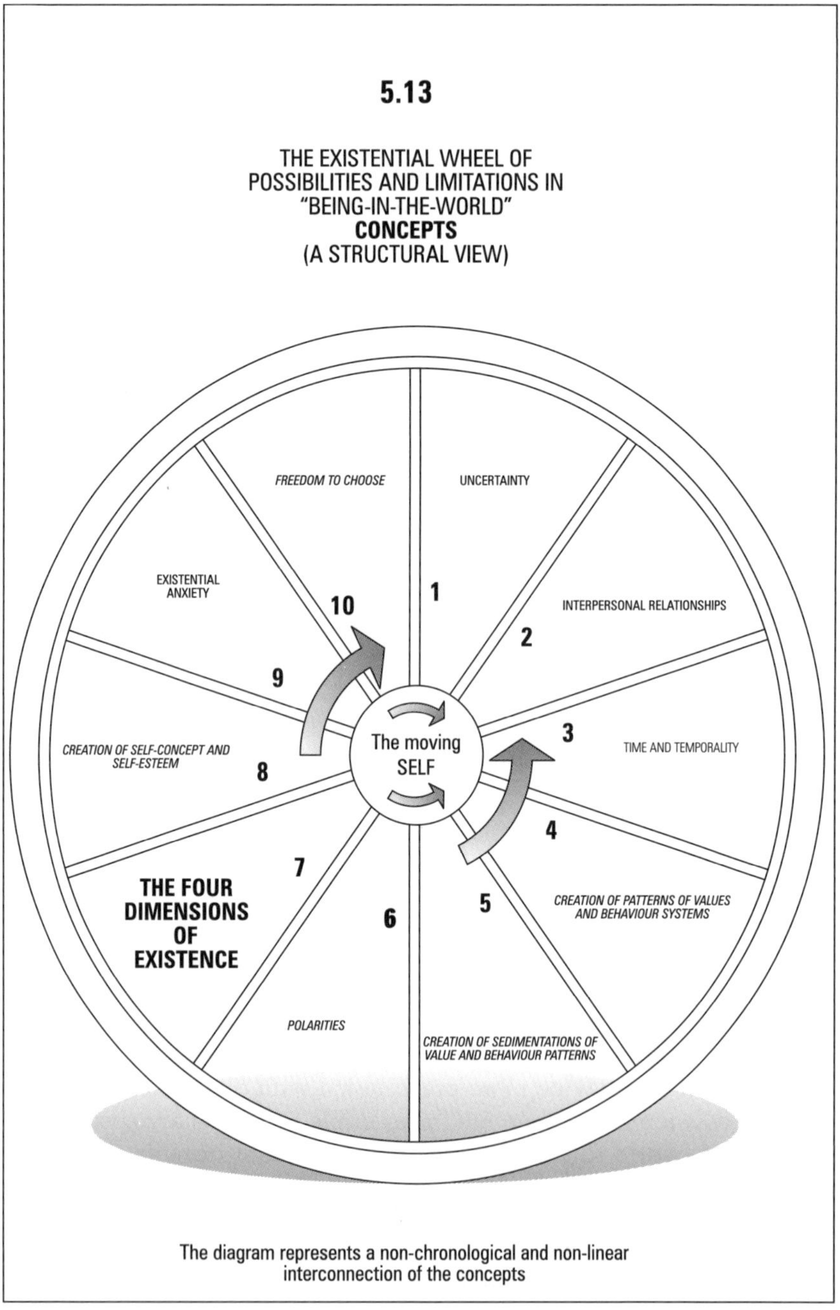
5.13
THE EXISTENTIAL WHEEL OF POSSIBILITIES AND LIMITATIONS IN "BEING-IN-THE-WORLD"
CONCEPTS
(A STRUCTURAL VIEW)
FREEDOM TO CHOOSE
UNCERTAINTY
EXISTENTIAL ANXIETY
INTERPERSONAL RELATIONSHIPS
1
2
3
4
5
6
7
8
9
10
The moving SELF
CREATION OF SELF-CONCEPT AND SELF-ESTEEM
TIME AND TEMPORALITY
CREATION OF PATTERNS OF VALUES AND BEHAVIOUR SYSTEMS
THE FOUR DIMENSIONS OF EXISTENCE
POLARITIES
CREATION OF SEDIMENTATIONS OF VALUE AND BEHAVIOUR PATTERNS
The diagram represents a non-chronological and non-linear interconnection of the concepts

Figure 5.13

5.14

THE EXISTENTIAL WHEEL OF
POSSIBILITIES AND LIMITATIONS IN
"BEING-IN-THE-WORLD"
METHODS AND SKILLS
(A STRUCTURAL VIEW)

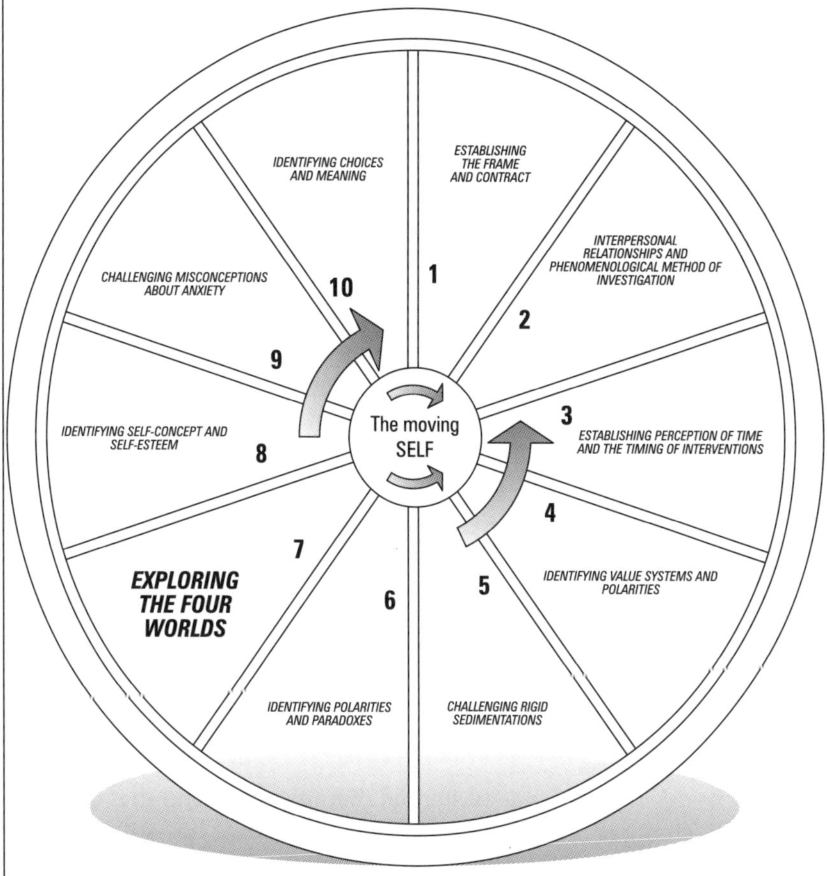

The diagram represents a non-chronological and non-linear interconnection of the methods

Figure 5.14

believed that if his body were fit and healthy he would be able to survive all hardships and adversities of life. His sense of self depended on this ideal of being a 'superman'. In order to maintain this he developed a unique life style which consisted of an ice-cold bath in the morning, a diet of vegetarian food, special toothpaste, all on top of his intense physical regimen. Although his life style was absorbed with maintaining his fitness, he was both embarrassed and ashamed to talk about it. The knock-on effect was that he found it difficult to form close relationships, as he was always anxious that the other person might find out about his 'secret'.

Evidently, although he desired a perfect body, he was also aware that there was something 'wrong' in the way he carried it to the extreme in such an obsessive manner. In therapy John began to realize that he had ignored all other aspects of his life, namely his spiritual, public and to some extent private world. As he was now being challenged he questioned his own fixed belief that the only way to maintain his everyday equilibrium was through some approbation of his physical prowess. John saw that what he was really doing was trying to escape rejection, which would normally throw him into despair.

John is a good example of what can happen if the dimensions are dominated by one of the four worlds. Although it is too much to ask to have an equal balance, if one of the four worlds dominates, it is useful to explore the other three that can open up whole new vistas of viewing one's existence.

CREATION OF SELF-CONSTRUCT

The creation of self-construct and self-esteem are two of the basic human endeavours in therapy. We challenge and prompt clients to explore and identify these. The wheels in Figures 5.15 and 5.16 give a visual presentation of this. Figure 5.15 represents the notion of the creation of self-construct and self-esteem and Figure 5.16 shows the method and application in practice.

As discussed in Chapter 4, existential therapists contend that our 'self' perpetually changes. Every stimulus that we receive has some kind of impact on our self-construct and in turn that affects our concept of self. Other people's opinions are usually at the forefront of how we view ourselves, how we feel about ourselves and how we change our convictions. Generally our self-esteem and self-concept are on a continual 'roller coaster', dependent on the opinions of others.

Our self-concept is intricately entwined with our value system, for how well we conform to our acquired values determines our self-esteem. So, for instance, if our value system is one of needing to please others in order to be accepted and liked, when the pattern works and we are liked our self-esteem is flattered. The opposite is also true: if pleasing others is not successful and we are disliked, our self-esteem takes a battering. Furthermore, we can also say that the formation of our self-concept is not only linked to values but also to our perception of safety, our notion of temporality and with all the other sections represented on the existential wheel.

Lynn, whom we discussed above in the section dealing with 'sedimentation', had a value system which was centred around her experience of modesty. Modesty meant gaining approval, while the opposite, that of 'showing off', denoted disapproval and rejection. Rejection in turn brought on her loneliness and the feeling that she was worthless. Her self-concept suffered and at the same time her low self-concept connected closely with her insecurity, anxiety and total absorption in her private world. As therapy progressed, Lynn's sedimentation was challenged and we examined the possibility of appraising her value system in a different light. In the process she realized that there were other ways of existing. She became aware that it is a very biased judgement continually to deprecate someone who is an extrovert. She began to weigh up the possibility that occasionally to be a 'show-off' could be something positive, and vice versa with modesty: modesty need not be always positive. Thus her values started to change, albeit very slowly, and parallel with this her sense of self-esteem gradually improved. Rather than simply inheriting and adopting the values of her parents, she was able to form her own opinions, which in turn gave her an additional, more realistic self-concept.

EXISTENTIAL ANXIETY

In therapy we often meet with clients who cannot accept that life is unpredictable and that fortitude creates existential anxiety. As therapists we challenge this assumption and prompt clients to explore these misconceptions. The wheels shown in Figures 5.17 and 5.18 illustrate this clearly. Time and temporality create a perennial existential 'angst' that always lurks in the back of the human mind.

In existential psychotherapy anxiety is one of the 'givens', that is to say, it is impossible to live in this world without anxiety. As James Bugental says, 'Existential anxiety, the anxiety of being, is anxiety that cannot be analysed away. It can only be confronted as steadfastly as possible and then incorporated into one's being' (1987: 238). Therefore

5.15

THE EXISTENTIAL WHEEL OF
POSSIBILITIES AND LIMITATIONS IN
"BEING-IN-THE-WORLD"
CONCEPTS
(A STRUCTURAL VIEW)

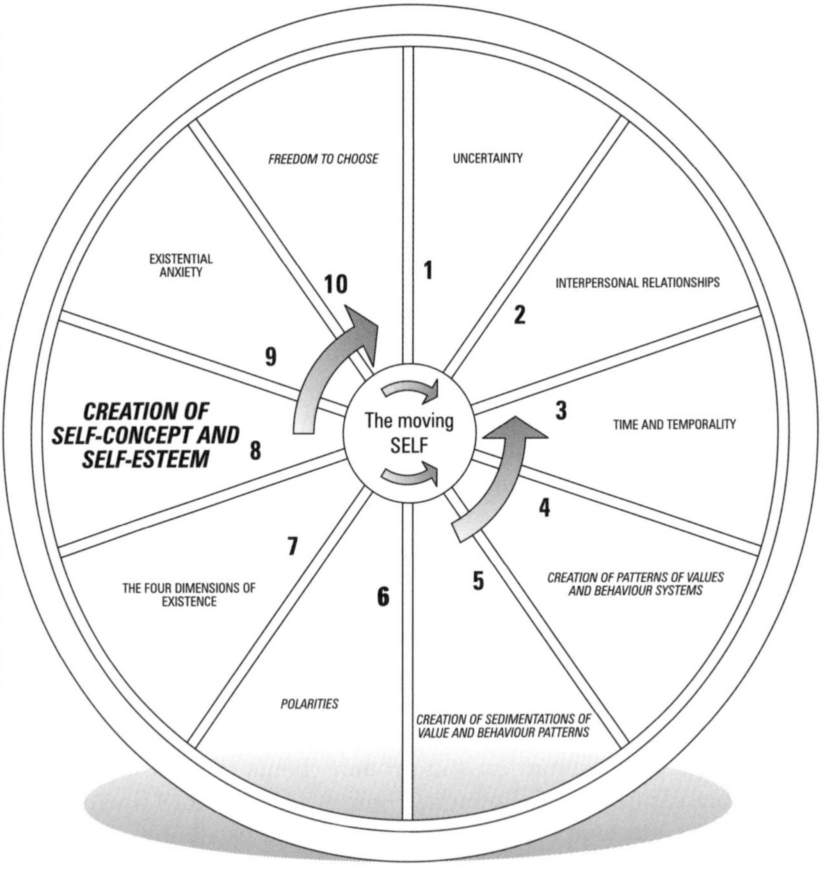

The diagram represents a non-chronological and non-linear interconnection of the concepts

Figure 5.15

5.16

THE EXISTENTIAL WHEEL OF
POSSIBILITIES AND LIMITATIONS IN
"BEING-IN-THE-WORLD"
METHODS AND SKILLS
(A STRUCTURAL VIEW)

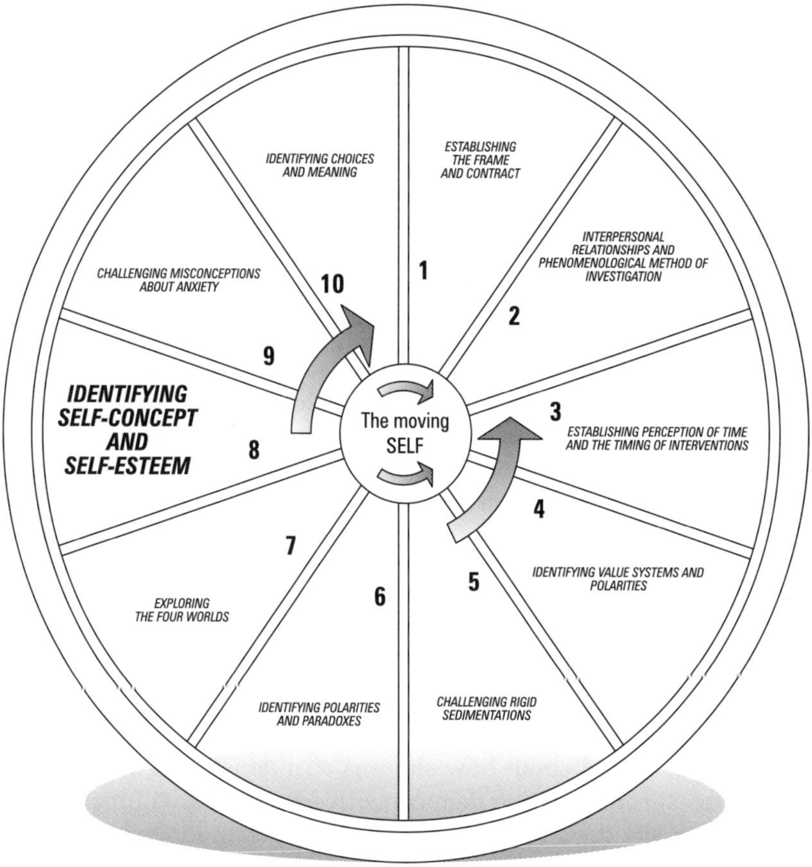

The diagram represents a non-chronological and non-linear interconnection of the methods

Figure 5.16

anxiety needs to be acknowledged as a normal human phenomenon.

Death, anxiety, loneliness and isolation go hand in hand. When we recognize that we are finite, that we must die, we also learn that we are inexorably alone. That our choices are limited is most clearly exemplified in death, which is inevitable for us all. In contrast, existentialists believe that awareness and coming to terms with death gives significance to living. In the same way, rather than trying to eliminate anxieties, the way forward is to understand and to realize that these too can bring meaning to one's life.

Another characteristic of human beings is the ability to think of the future and to contemplate death. This need not be a negative prospect, for the realization of death can provide us with a zest for life and creativity. The denial of death is not only inauthentic but, as Rollo May wrote, one can also become a victim of 'self-alienation' (1961:65). Indeed, from our experiences as therapists, we can say that the proximity of one's own destruction can revitalize personal energy and propel one to start living more intensively.

Death is not the only anxiety that humans have to negotiate, it is just one of several 'givens' of human existence. Anxiety in one form or another lurks continually in everyone's mind. It runs parallel with our emotions, such as fear, confusion, dismay, sorrow, nostalgia, pain, pleasure, joy. Even the emotions that we consider positive, such as happiness, can be connected to anxiety by the realization that happiness cannot last for ever. All emotions and the resulting anxieties can be a useful aid in exploring clients' value systems and behaviour patterns. In fact, one of the shortest routes for a client to recognize his or her way of being is through the clarification of their emotions.

When Edna, for example, became overwhelmed by her fear of the therapy ending, she also recognized that this feeling of angst was similar to the anxiety provoked by her rejection by her mother. She also understood that the feeling of being abandoned was associated with her low self-esteem, her loneliness and the way she felt disconnected from others. As we talked about how she was abandoned, her anxiety level and her fears increased. She then connected this event with her coping strategy that she developed in order to avoid abandonment. She had learnt that by using her body she could attract people and in so doing could stop them from leaving her. Edna's case study can be read in Chapter 6, where we describe in detail how the ending of her therapy course evoked in her a violent fear of rejection. In turn, Edna could then connect her fear of ending of the therapy with her abandonment by her mother. Her mother had forsaken her by 'offering' her body to another man and, paradoxically, Edna developed a coping strategy, to be accepted and validated, that consisted of just that: offering her body to be 'accepted' and not to be 'abandoned'.

Existential anxiety or angst needs to be distinguished from what certain authors would call 'neurotic anxiety'. Neurotic anxiety distorts existential reality. If we accept that existential anxiety is inherent in our being, but is also 'a threat to being', as Paul Tillich described it (1980), then neurotic anxiety would be, in Rollo May's words, 'the reverse of our definition of normal' (1977:188). In other words, it is a threat that is disproportionate to the objective danger. May and Yalom say that neurotic anxiety 'is not appropriate to the situation. For example, parents may be so anxious that their child will be hit by a car that they never let the child go out of the house' (Corsini, 1984:356).

In fact, these two states of anxiety overlap and it is not easy to draw a definite demarcation line. However, Rollo May finds a solution by describing normal anxiety as 'being that which is used for a constructive solution which causes the problem, and neurotic anxiety being that which results in defence from and avoidance of the problem' (May, 1977:399).

Compulsion

Compulsive behaviour habits will not disappear simply by becoming aware of them. This kind of awareness can be described as rational, logical or intellectual, but it has not yet integrated into a client's emotional consciousness; that is, it is not enough for clients cognitively to accept and know what they are doing, they also need emotionally to incorporate this into their very being.

People with eating disorders, for example, realize that the pattern they cling to is both compulsive and abnormal. Sue – as will be seen in Chapter 7 – battled with bulimia nervosa. She could understand intellectually the sedimented pattern that she had established for herself. She recognized that she used her bingeing to assuage her fears of meeting other people and when she failed she would feel totally lacking in self-confidence. In many ways this was an important step, but she still continued to have bingeing sessions and proceed to the vomiting stage. What had become different was her awareness: she knew what she was doing. Although it was still a compulsion, she was able to think about why she needed to binge and then vomit. In this sense she was making a conscious choice to continue.

As Sue's behaviour became more authentic the anxiety gradually subsided. In sessions she began to reveal more of her underlying grief

5-17

THE EXISTENTIAL WHEEL OF POSSIBILITIES AND LIMITATIONS IN "BEING-IN-THE-WORLD"
CONCEPTS
(A STRUCTURAL VIEW)

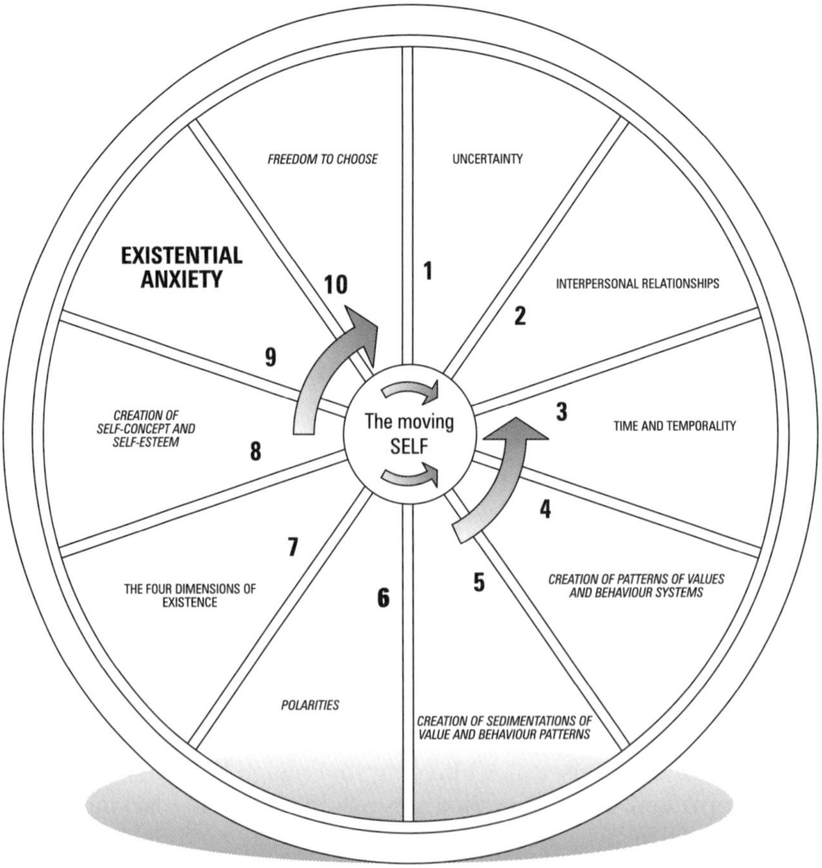

The diagram represents a non-chronological and non-linear interconnection of the concepts

Figure 5.17

5.18

THE EXISTENTIAL WHEEL OF
POSSIBILITIES AND LIMITATIONS IN
"BEING-IN-THE-WORLD"
METHODS AND SKILLS
(A STRUCTURAL VIEW)

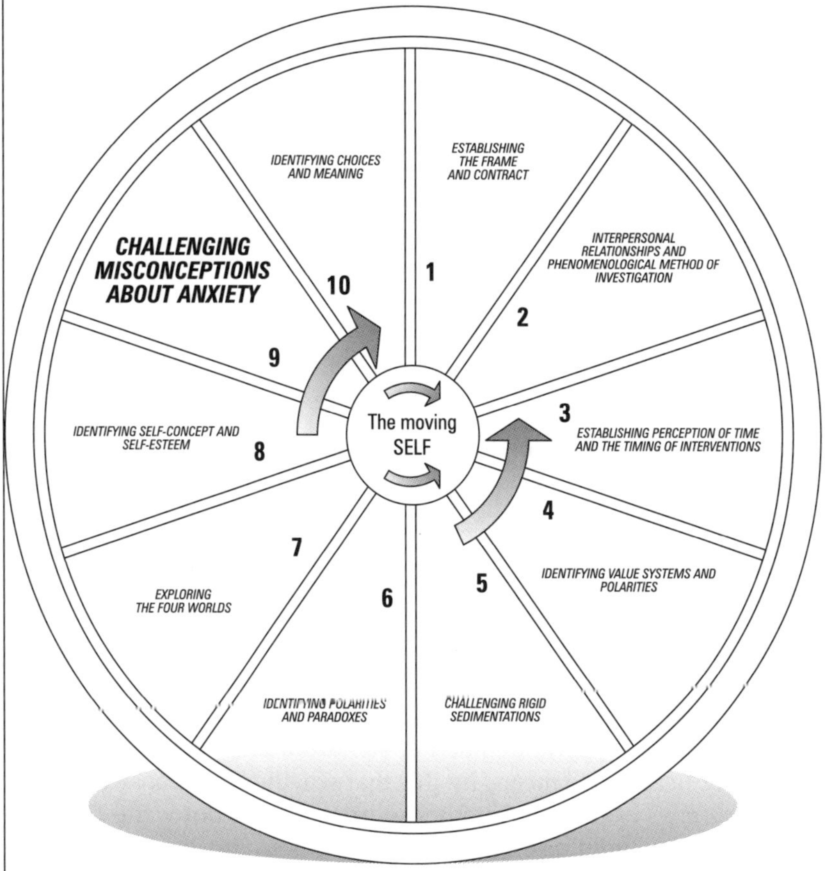

The diagram represents a non-chronological and non-linear interconnection of the methods

Figure 5.18

and was able to disclose her 'secret' to her family and then her friends. Sue moved on to a second module of twelve sessions, where she continued to challenge her compulsion. Many times Sue hit rock bottom. She experienced terrible pain and feelings of loneliness, yet she managed to keep faith that she would survive. This vignette will be discussed in more detail in Chapter 7. Although confronting anxiety is often experienced as hurtful, there are positive aspects to the confrontation of this loneliness. As Rollo May writes:

> When a person has hit bottom, i.e. when he has reached ultimate despair he then can surrender to eternal forces; this is the dynamic of all authentic conversions. I would describe this process as giving up the delusion of false hopes and, thus, acknowledging fully the fact of destiny. Then and only then can this person begin to rebuild himself. It is a superb demonstration of the hypothesis that freedom begins only when we confront destiny.
>
> (May, 1981:236)

One could say, therefore, that joy is the 'other side of the same coin'.

FREEDOM OF CHOICE

This part of the work examines the freedom of choice and meaning that can be created in life. In therapy we prompt clients to identify their choices and meaning. This is exactly what the two wheels represent (see Figures 5.19 and 5.20). Jean-Paul Sartre said, 'The very being of the For-itself which is "condemned to be free" and must forever choose itself – i.e. make itself' (1958:632).

What Sartre means is that, being can be 'being-in-itself' as a non-conscious being and is condemned to stand out from being and choose from him or herself. He means by this that whether we choose or do not choose, we always choose. In other words, if I did not write this sentence, then that would also have been my choice. This is somewhat different to Merleau-Ponty (1962) who believes, in van Deurzen-Smith's words, that 'our freedom is only gained in the way we act. In my actions I show and create my significance and that of others and the world as well' (1987:68).

> Existential counselling is not about providing a comfortable flight from reality, but about reminding people of the impli-

> cations of their situation and of the need to face their own limitations as well as their own strengths.
>
> (van Deurzen-Smith, 1988:58)

The existential position is that we choose to create ourselves and that there are always many possibilities available to choose from. Nevertheless, choices have to be examined within the context of limitations. The nine sections of the wheel that have just been described in this chapter are about such human limitations. We have demonstrated, however, that each of the sections also provides a way of understanding, of achieving a more enlightened awareness and a path to more authentic thinking. As we follow this path, the choices (even within the limitations) become more apparent.

There is an infinite number of possibilities to exert one's freedom of choices. For example, we must accept the fact that we are born tall or short, that we are children of single parents, or that we come from a large family. We can do nothing about whether we are born English or Italian, for example, or the kind of culture that exists around us. Even so, we still have a choice. We have the freedom to choose the kind of attitude we will adopt towards those criteria.

Clients with depression tend to have lost their meaning, yet they too have freedom to choose their meaning. Viktor Frankl, the Viennese psychiatrist, spent two years of grim existence in Auschwitz (1943–5). He devoted his remaining years 'to helping others find their meaning' (1963). He maintained that only because he had found a meaning for his horrific experiences was he able to survive the horrors of the concentration camp and forge an important psychological approach, that of 'Logotherapy'. Frankl found that among his fellow inmates those who could assemble some kind of self-meaning, whether as some form of spirituality or the wish to survive to relate their story, had more chance of surviving than those who could not find meaning. Inmates without a meaning also lost the will to live.

Sue, the client from our previous vignette, also lost her sense of meaning. The more she believed her body to be ugly and fat, the more she was unable to believe in herself. Only when she started to realize that she was a person who could have a meaningful existence without depending on her body image was she able to begin to refrain from her bingeing and vomiting. The next chapter will describe how all these concepts and sections interconnect, and will demonstrate the tools and obstacles of therapy. Case studies will follow in subsequent chapters.

5.19

THE EXISTENTIAL WHEEL OF
POSSIBILITIES AND LIMITATIONS IN
"BEING-IN-THE-WORLD"
CONCEPTS
(A STRUCTURAL VIEW)

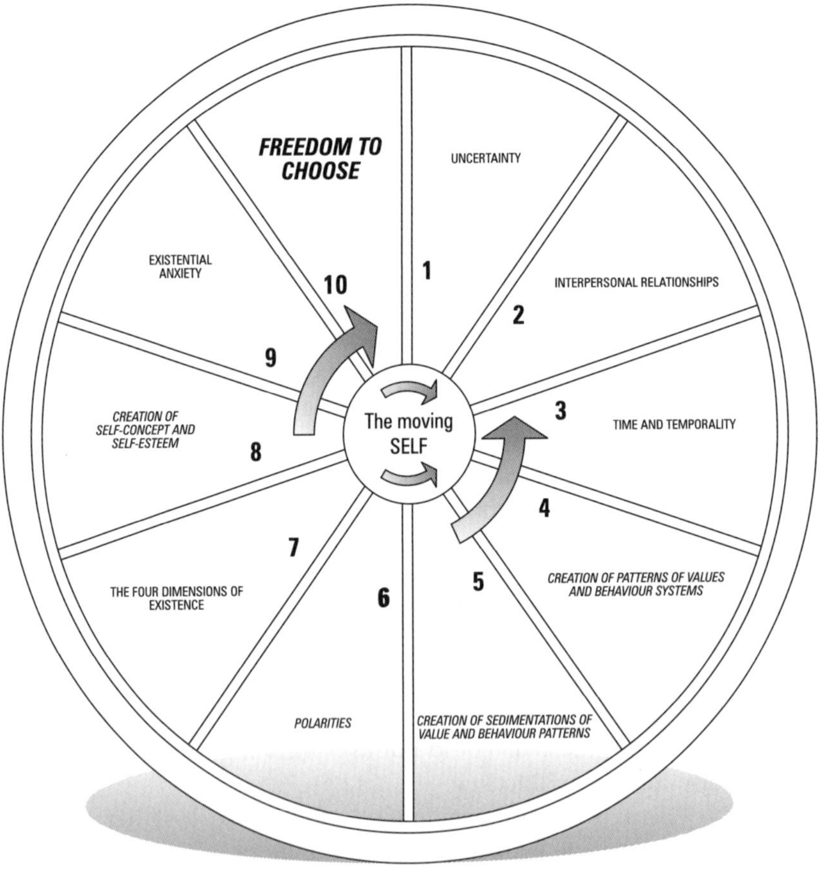

The diagram represents a non-chronological and non-linear interconnection of the concepts

Figure 5.19

5.20

THE EXISTENTIAL WHEEL OF POSSIBILITIES AND LIMITATIONS IN "BEING-IN-THE-WORLD"
METHODS AND SKILLS
(A STRUCTURAL VIEW)

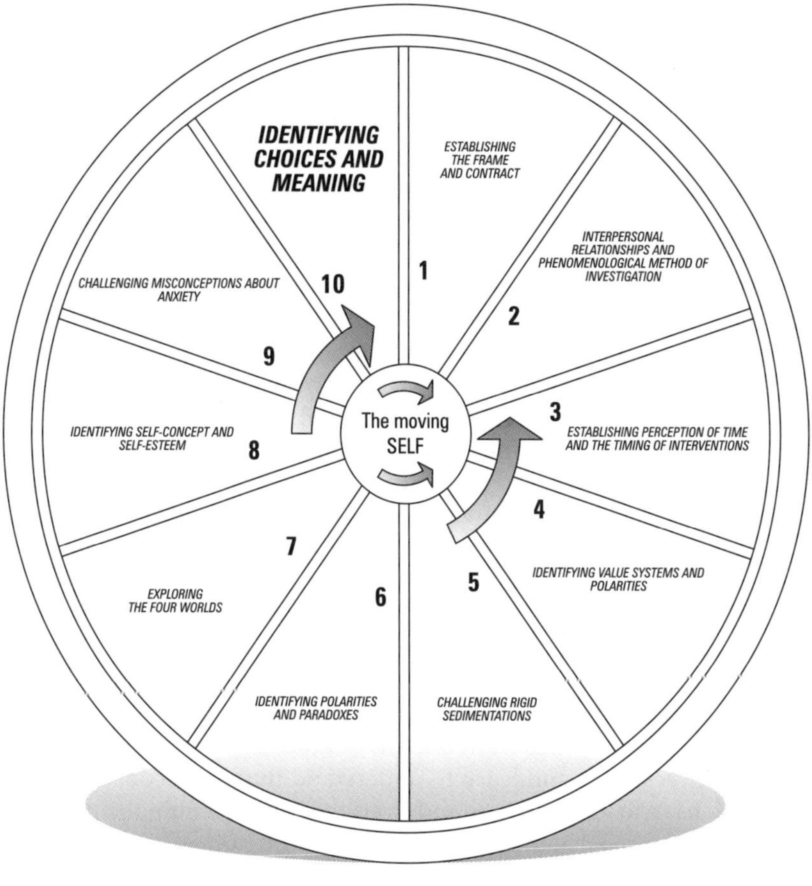

The diagram represents a non-chronological and non-linear interconnection of the methods

Figure 5.20

6

THE MYSTERY OF THE 'INSIGHT'

COMPULSION AND SHIFT OF PERCEPTION

No matter from what therapeutic orientation, one of the main tasks of any therapy is to challenge and facilitate clients' awareness of their rigid behaviour patterns and value beliefs. This process is accompanied by a shift in perception which is often known in psychological jargon as the client 'gaining insight'. In this chapter we will explore this phenomenon and reveal its importance in the existential time-limited paradigm.

As is demonstrated in the case studies, we have found that clients can become aware of their value systems and their behavioural patterns and even understand the contradictions that arise within these sedimentations. However, nine times out of ten, the compulsive behaviour patterns will still exist. In other words, an intellectual, rational understanding is not enough. What is missing is that mélange of emotional and rational ingredients that draws the client into a deeper level of awareness. This kind of awareness or insight will precipitate a shift in perception. These shifts sometimes occur during the therapy session, but are equally likely to occur between sessions and even after therapy has been completed.

In the existential paradigm, we believe that these kinds of insights occur when the therapeutic framework is working at its best. In other words, a climate of trust has been fostered, based around the idea that the therapist and client are in a relationship that allows the client to explore all aspects of their existence. In this environment the therapist facilitates clients to investigate and learn to understand their own constructs and how they have made decisions and lived their lives, within the possibilities and limitations that the world has imposed on human beings.

John, for example, had a fixed sedimented value with regard to his physical appearance. He believed that because he had birthmarks on various places of his body he was a physically inferior person, so he found it hard to relate to people. During one session he announced that he had been listening to one of his songs when it hit him 'like a bolt of lightning, that the intense feelings of shame and humiliation that I have must be related to the appalling acne I suffered in my youth'. From that moment on, John used this incident as a metaphor in therapy. Essentially this insight served as a catalyst for John to recognize and explore these issues further and to change his behaviour pattern.

Shifts of perception can occur in the most unlikely circumstances, for example, while taking a walk, listening to music, playing computer games, listening to other people's conversations – i.e. once the process of therapy has awakened the awareness channels, insights can flow both in and out of therapy.

The therapist too often has these insights which highlight the importance of the relationship between therapist and client. As the therapist enters into the client's world, bracketing his or her assumptions, a clarity of awareness can occur. Kate was in her own words 'fat'. She had started putting on weight around the age of 11; apart from a couple of years in her late teens when she had used dieting pills, she had remained overweight. In speaking of her family background where she was the second youngest with four older brothers and one younger sister, she began talking about childhood in terms of her desperate need for space. There was never even any privacy in the bathroom, where any one of her siblings could barge in and disturb her. She shared a bedroom with her sister and would go to bed early in order to have time on her own. Family meals were also a nightmare; everyone would dive in to get their share of food and unless Kate was quick and forthright she might end up with very little on her plate. As Kate was describing this, she began to 'shrink'. Her body contracted on itself. Looking at her and hearing the words, there was a sudden realization that her size was a statement in itself. She was in some way trying to tell her family something important.

The therapist may have this insight, but the difficulty is in allowing the client to become aware of it. First of all, the therapist might have been totally wrong. The insight might have been misplaced, so it is extremely important to tread carefully and ask open questions such as: 'You have described a situation where it feels as if you had to fight to get your privacy and space and battle for your food. What kind of statement do you think you were trying to make with the size of your body?' In the case of Kate, there was a moment's silence and in a quiet voice she said, 'I need to get attention and it doesn't matter what kind of attention I get, as long as I get it.' This was a turning point in the therapy since, first, she gained the insight herself, and second, she was able to see the benefit of being large.

So, where does this concept of insight come from? Freud used the German term *'freier Einfall'* which in English means literally to free fall; to give the mind free rein to come up with spontaneous thoughts and feelings. Freud used free association to access the world of the unconscious mind. Indeed it is also the pathway for entering our intuitive insight and through this Freud believed that we could precipitate and acknowledge the internal, unconscious conflicts inherent in all humans. Using this insight, the patients eventually could eliminate their complexes. Dreams too for Freud are subject to this free associative insight, as is highlighted by his well-known statement that 'Dreams are the royal road to the unconscious' (1900). The state induced by free association creates the climate for insight to take place. The existential approach uses the Husserlian method of 'bracketing' to provide the necessary conditions for this to occur. The function of bracketing, as described in Chapter 2, is to provide the type of environment in which to observe 'the thing in itself' that intimates an intuitive insight.

In the 1940s and 1950s Fritz Perls, founder of the Gestalt therapy, introduced the term 'AHA' (Eureka). This again referred to the experience of insight. Perls himself had borrowed this word from the Gestalt psychologist Wolfgang Kohler, who used the word 'insight' in his book (Perls, 1947). Kohler, together with Kurt Koffka and Max Wertheimer, launched the Gestalt psychology movement, from which Fritz Perl derived the Gestalt therapeutic approach. Subsequent to this period, all the humanistically oriented therapists and authors engulfed this notion of 'insight' expressing a state of wonder and discovery. 'Insight' and 'AHA experiences' have since become common terms in psychology. 'Insight' is now a also classical psychoanalytical term.

While we can conclude from the above that the inducement of insights is one of the common goals in most therapies, there are significant differences in their approaches, in their methods, their stances and the underlying philosophies of their orientations.

We argue that without the recognition of a preliminary structure, no learning and shifting of perception can take place in therapy. The study of experiential learning processes teaches us that knowledge can be acquired only through an interaction between experience, comprehension and apprehension (insight). Kolb argues that 'apprehensions are the source of validation for comprehension' and that apprehension (which in his terms is 'an immediate grasping of an experience' which we would call an insight experience), 'is the source of validation for comprehension ("thoughts without content are empty"); and comprehensions are the source of guidance in the selection of apprehensions ("intuitions without concepts are blind")' (1984:106).

Thus, an insight cannot be experienced without a structural knowledge, just as a structural knowledge is the sine qua non for an AHA experience. This is best expressed by David Bohm: 'All knowledge is a structure of abstractions, the ultimate test of the validity of which is, however, in the process of coming into contact with the world that takes place in immediate perception' (1965:220).

The function of the therapist is therefore to facilitate a learning process. In other words, clients can learn to absorb through their own explorations in order to challenge their contradictions, to gain 'insight' and to experience a shift of their own perceptions. This will continue even after concluding therapy.

In time-limited existential therapy we constantly place an emphasis on the structure that allows the clients' world views to emerge into the foreground. One of the advantages of having the limited time is that there is an internal pressure for the insight process to be accelerated. Obviously it also occurs in longer term therapy, but the insights tend to take longer to appear and are generally more protracted.

EDNA

It will be demonstrated how through the process of relating experiences, comprehending her world views, Edna gained insight into some of her rigid sedimentations and contradictions. As a result of these she was able to shift her perception and behaviour pattern.

Edna entered into therapy determined to explore 'the world of her inner self'. At the start, she did experience difficulty in disclosing herself but as early as her second session she began to examine her compulsive behaviour patterns.

When she first arrived Edna gave the impression of a well-spoken, intelligent, attractive woman in her early thirties. She was nervous and shy, but that is often the case on first meetings. After an exchange of the usual pleasantries there was a considerable pause and instead of allowing her to take the lead, which is the usual practice, I began to explain that the first session was exploratory in terms of whether we could work together and how this could best be done. We would also examine both our expectations of the outcome and she was free to ask any questions about the process. Edna soon began to talk about her problems.

Frame, contract and the presenting problem

Edna started by describing her excessive anger. She felt angry with everyone and she found it hard to hold back her desire to lash out at anyone who might be in her range of fire. This included her nextdoor neighbour, her mother, her 1-year-old daughter Georgina, her husband Melvin and, principally, herself. When she was alone and angry she sometimes physically harmed herself, although without serious injury. She was obsessively concerned with the upbringing of her daughter and had no confidence in her own knowledge and intuition. She therefore accepted everybody's opinion and advice. This made her very confused and she continuously felt that she was being watched and criticized by others. She suffered from insomnia and allowed her daughter to sleep between herself and her husband which prevented them from having regular sexual intercourse. The first intervention was a question about how she felt when she was criticized and judged. Edna paused and then began exploring this feeling at length. She knew that even the slightest criticism sent her spiralling into a depression which was closely linked to her feelings of being rejected. Further interventions revealed that her depressions were associated with her loneliness and feelings of isolation; the rejection heightened her sense of low self-concept and that she felt rejected.

Edna appeared quite capable and willing to face her compulsive behaviour patterns and to be open to any insights that might occur. We talked about our capacity to work together and at the same time she asked questions about qualifications, marital status, children and how therapy would work. The personal questions were answered and an outline of the process was given, which included the fact that the sessions would be similar to the present one; that she could express herself in safety and security; that the function of a therapist is to prompt and guide her towards expressing and understanding herself from all angles and viewpoints. At this juncture it was also pointed out that she appeared to have the need to please others, which was related back to the opening part of the session where she waited for an invitation to begin talking. This was an area that could be further illuminated in the process of therapy. Edna was given the option to think through whether she wished to continue. She telephoned me the following day and we agreed the time for the next session.

In the next session we discussed and agreed on the frame, which consisted of the duration and frequency of the sessions, which were the twelve weeks with two review sessions spaced at four-weekly intervals. Matters of confidentiality, commitment and fees were also agreed.

The remaining time was used to explore Edna's expectations, which were that she anticipated that all her presenting problems would disappear well before the termination of the twelve weeks. It was interesting that the therapist's expectations were not as specific and were more in line with Edna being able to absorb the therapeutic process and to explore and become aware of her issues from various points of view, a learning process that she would be able to take with her even after the termination of therapy. These differing expectations were not discussed with Edna, essentially because clients usually change their perceptions during the process. It is more important that clients recognize this for themselves, rather than the therapist imposing this view from the outset. During the next few sessions Edna's life story gradually unfolded.

History

In the next three or four sessions Edna expressed her fears, anxieties and insecurities about various aspects of her life. While speaking of her experiences and aspirations she narrated, almost unwittingly, her life story, in a non-chronological order. She was an only child who felt abandoned by her father at the age of 3. Her parents divorced and from that time she rarely saw her father. During her adolescence she met him two or three times, and currently she sees him occasionally. From an early age Edna forged a strong alliance with her mother and together they fought the adversities of life.

As a family they had lived very comfortably, but just the two of them Her mother was forced to fight for their survival and they learnt to live in very difficult circumstances. At one point, while her mother had to work elsewhere, Edna went to live with her 'grandpa', where she found solace, love and care. After an idyllic period of one year Edna changed house again. Her mother moved in with John, who had three children, and Edna went with her. Edna could never get over the hatred she felt for the three children and John's complete lack of care and feeling towards her. The only comfort she experienced during this miserable period was her alliance with her mother, which was their united front on their animosity towards men. She perceived men as tools for her mother's and her own survival, and it came as no surprise when, after two years with John, they moved out, and settled into Paul's home. Paul, in contrast to John, was a considerate and caring person. Many sessions were devoted to exploring Edna's relationship with Paul because it emerged that she did sometimes fantasize about some kind of abuse. Her feelings towards Paul remained very ambiguous. She had recurring dreams where Paul would emerge from her mother's bed with a huge, erect penis. Another time she dreamt that she was making love to her husband, Melvin, but then he metamorphosed into Paul.

The relative calm and safety were soon interrupted. After three years with Paul, her mother met Arthur and both moved yet again into his home. Arthur was a kind but very strict man, who ran his house with a rod of iron. At the age of 15 Edna quarrelled with him and left, with nowhere to go. She ended up in various squats, and in different relationships with men, which she described as her 'promiscuous few years', yet she also managed to keep herself stable enough to study acting. During this time her relationship with her mother was at a low ebb, although it began to improve as she reached her twenties.

Edna met her present husband Melvin while in a relationship with Tom. She left Tom for Melvin, who promised her security and a comfortable home; 'comfortable' being relative, in the sense that Edna's relationship with Melvin was characterized by anger, fear and ambiguities. Her total devotion was to her daughter Georgina and their almost symbiotic union was the subject of much discord with her husband. Characteristically, she was uncertain about her methods and her reading of various books further strengthened her indecisiveness and ambiguities.

THERAPY

The search for Edna's value system

During the first few sessions Edna spoke of her fears, and the feelings of abandonment that she had experienced in her early youth. Yet, when isolated fragments of certain events emerged, Edna had a habit of side-tracking and jumping from one subject to another: 'I cannot feel or remember anything, because it is like a wound plastered up,' she said on many occasions.

Throughout this time, although she often experienced difficulty in expressing her feelings, she was able to discuss her undesirable behaviour patterns towards her husband, daughter, mother and others without inhibition. For instance, she searched for clues and reasons for her submissive behaviour towards her neighbour Sally, recognizing that in reality, she was angry with her. Sally had a child called Gill, of a similar age to Georgina, whom Edna used to look after when Sally went to work. Edna disagreed with Sally's views on feeding babies, but not only was she unable to express her opinion, she was even contemplating accepting Sally's ideas in relation to her own daughter. In therapy she investigated her extreme anger and explored her relationship with Sally. One day she arrived at the session exclaiming, 'I am so angry for allowing myself to be intimidated by Sally. Truly speaking I should not be angry with her since she doesn't have any malevolent intentions towards me.' This was the first significant 'insight' that became the pathway for the remainder of Edna's therapy.

Her past and present relationship with her mother, her ex-stepfathers and Melvin, her present husband, were all talked about. She became aware that one of her exaggerated sedimentations was to place other people on pedestals. Indeed she soon directly related this insight to her relationship with Sally. Edna compulsively perceived Sally as a superior person and was therefore unable to argue with her and instead became angry, redirecting this anger towards Sally.

Another important milestone was analysing the relationship between us. Edna routinely demanded answers and advice. She constantly asked me how to deal with Sally and Arthur; how to deal with her anger; and whether she should be sleeping with her daughter and husband in the same bed. These questions were challenged in view of the original framework (contract), where it was clearly agreed that advice was not part of the process. Edna was asked to put herself in my position and to answer her own questions. As a result she was soon able to do her own linking rather than relying on the therapist's 'superior judgement', which fitted in with her sedimentation that others around her were invested with a superior status. This was quite a shift in terms of the relationship and she also began to dispute and correct some of the statements made by the therapist – sometimes even displaying irritation.

At the fifth session, Edna arrived in a gloomy, depressed state. She related an argument she had had with her husband Melvin about her refusal to go to see a film with him. She had not felt comfortable leaving Georgina with a babysitter. It turned out that she was angry with herself for giving in and going to the cinema, and indeed the evening had not been enjoyable. While she was analysing the event and discussing her feelings, she was challenged to explore Melvin's position to see whether she could imagine his feelings. The fact the therapist was at all 'interested' in Melvin irritated Edna intensely. She felt I was taking sides and ignoring her own pain. Subsequent to exploring this anger I asked whether she could perceive anything positive in the therapeutic relationship between herself and me. She laughed and admitted that 'You are no longer the superior person that you were before and what's more I feel that I can and do express my anger towards you.' This was quite a turning point.

Soon after, Edna began to focus on her feelings of isolation and loneliness. She revealed a dream which involved herself and Paul, her mother's ex-boyfriend. In the dream she had accidentally opened the door of her mother's bedroom and Paul emerged from his bed with an enormously erect penis. She was frightened and in her panic all she could think about was finding her mother. But her mother was not there so she was left feeling totally abandoned and having to fend for herself, which she felt she was not capable of doing. Her own crying woke her up.

Edna began to interpret this dream. She was asked to examine each of the fragments and to explore them from various angles. In summary she felt the dream was saying that 'men are big and powerful and are able to do me a hell of a lot of harm'.

It did not take much prompting for Edna to discover and challenge her value system. Indeed, in her seventh session she realized that her pattern of behaving in her current relationships was similar, if not the same, as the way she related to Paul. All her relationships began with trepidation and anxiety including our therapeutic encounter.

The coping strategy

Also in the seventh session Edna began investigating her need to put people on pedestals. Looking back she saw that it had begun with John, her mother's boyfriend, who had treated her so harshly. This had also been reinforced through her mother, who repeatedly warned her to conform to John's and his children's wishes. Reflecting on the question about what happened when she was disobedient, Edna replied that she was shouted at and sometimes beaten. Her mother never came to the rescue, preferring to keep her own harmony. Her underlying feeling was that if she had defied this 'obedience' prescription, she would have been totally rejected by everyone, including her mother. On further prompting, she revealed that ultimate rejection would be the same as she had felt in the dream, where her mother was not there to protect her from Paul and her feelings of being completely alone. In the remaining fifteen minutes Edna tried to work through her fear of rejection and what it meant to be alone and abandoned. She eventually came to the conclusion that from this time she had learnt to stop falling into the lonely abyss by cowering and obeying the people she deemed to be her superiors. It was an exhausting session, and we both acknowledged how the trust facilitated the achievements that Edna had made.

Self-concept

During the following session Edna endeavoured to recall how she must have felt when she had been attacked by John and his children. She clearly remembered many of the actual events of brutality and the clashes that John and her mother frequently had, yet she was unable to experience the actual feelings. It seemed that Edna was beginning to become obsessed with the notion that if she could grasp these feelings in the present she would find some kind of salvation. It seemed more relevant to explore how Edna felt at this moment, rather than trying to capture some illusory memory. When she was asked to imagine what it would be like for her now to have John shout at her for not complying with his wishes, she replied after a long silence that she would feel discarded, not wanted and in a lot of pain. Pursuing this theme Edna realized that she believed that unless she complied with John, she would be left abandoned, would have no sense of self or self-concept and would have no one to connect with. The final interpretation threaded these strands together and put forward the proposition that Edna complied with people's wishes in order to maintain her self-concept and to feel that in some way she belonged.

Afterwards, reflecting on this session, it seemed that Edna was using the same devices of compliance in the sessions themselves, which may have explained the reason for the 'uncomfortable feelings' of things 'not adding up' that had been noted after the previous session.

Although Edna had gained awareness of her behaviour patterns and was quite clear about how they connected with her value systems, this had not alleviated her way of coping with people and situations. She still put people on pedestals and appeased them by conforming to their needs and wishes. The main difference that emerged was that Edna was now aware of what she was doing and on occasion would express some of her vulnerabilities to her husband. Anger also began to emerge during the sessions or, rather, anger at herself and her inability to shift her behaviour patterns. Instead of dwelling on the negative components, we shifted to exploring the positive aspects of this pattern. She began to realize that there had been times when her compliance had benefited her when she felt liked and loved.

These issues were also related to the impending termination of therapy and her fear of rejection. Edna talked about her fear of being rejected by Melvin and she linked this to the losses of her parents, her various stepfathers and her numerous boyfriends. Indeed, rejection was a major fear to the extent that she often rejected others before they were able to reject her. This was also occurring in the sessions. She began to talk about how she could cope on her own, how she was working on her issues between sessions and was feeling generally more confident about her abilities. Again, the uncomfortable feeling emerged that she was relating all this in order to conform to the process of therapy and in the process please the therapist.

Ending

At the ninth session Edna arrived in quite a happy and lighthearted mood. She spoke of how she felt that she was more confident in communicating with Melvin, although she still had problems relating to her mother. This led her towards further thoughts about how she had been rejected in the past and even linked these ideas to the impending termination of therapy that was scheduled for two weeks' time.

The separation had been a subject for the last few sessions and Edna talked through these ideas in a rational manner, never seeming to manifest any special concern. It was therefore a great surprise when a short while into the session, Edna attacked me, saying that she felt abandoned, that she felt that she was being treated in the same way as she had been in her relationships with her father, her mother's boyfriends and her own relationships with men. As she began to cry, I, too, began to feel distraught and anxious and also to wonder whether in reality Edna would be able to cope with another separation. Would she be attuned enough to work independently, to continue with her own self-exploration?

This brought up issues of the original contract, which had been twelve weeks with two follow-up sessions and no further contract. Therefore a renegotiation of the contract would cause a loss of credibility. Indeed Edna was one the reasons that prompted us to modify the original, rigid twelve-week contract to allow for a more flexible modular approach, as has been described in the previous chapters.

The session continued by making it clear that it was fine for Edna to vent all these feelings and above all her expressiveness was indeed a major progress. For in contrast to her usual pattern of keeping all her emotions locked away, she was quite capable of showing them. Linking some of these feelings to the previous sessions, Edna suddenly shrieked that she remembered the feelings of abandonment and rejection when she saw her mother and boyfriend in bed and moreover they were the same feelings that she felt now about being abandoned in therapy. This recollection evoked the revival of all her rejections, and these were discussed for the remainder of the session.

The last two sessions were concerned with working on her feelings with regard to her mother, father, ex-boyfriends and husband. In the penultimate session Edna revealed that she was convinced that it was her rigid value system that stopped her from exploring her potential to write. Furthermore, her potential was thwarted because of her fear of rejection.

She compared her fear of acting and writing to her fear of men. More specifically her fear of rejection, whether from editors, an audience or significant men related to her fear of losing her self-concept. Hence it was the fear itself that halted her from exploring various areas of her life.

Her self-awareness of interconnecting and relating the various themes or patterns of behaviour were further discussed. Edna was dumbfounded by her realization that her general fears, as well as her fear of interpersonal relationships, her habit of placing people on pedestals, her need to please and submit to others, were all connected to her desperate need for safety, her sedimented value and behaviour system and anxieties. Finally and most importantly, these fears were restricting her possibilities of choice.

DISCUSSION

The most noteworthy feature of working in this existential way is that the clients themselves, to a large extent, make their own revelations. The therapist acts as a catalyst, as a guide, in the sense that he or she will clarify and explore phenomena that emerge from the client; while interventions are kept to either prompting or phenomenologically challenging the client's perceptions. As far as possible, interpretations are kept within the limits of a client's world view, which entails the therapist suspending his or her own assumptions and only intervening when it is in the client's interest. This approach is in harmony with the phenomenological rule of 'epochē' or 'bracketing'.

Therefore it was Edna who was finally able to clarify her values and her world views. She came to the realization that during her early youth she developed a fixed, relatively stagnant view of herself and the world. This distrust of other people and her need to put them on a pedestal affected the first part of the therapy. It was difficult to establish an open and trusting relationship, and only after she had experienced some insight and began to have an inkling that she could understand herself, did the relationship gradually improve.

Following her accusation of desertion, the relationship took on a different mood. Essentially her perception of the therapist's power became irrelevant and Edna's faith in the process and in her capacity to change took precedent. She was then capable of challenging her rigid and cemented values and strategies. This was again pushed to the fore in the ninth session when the realization that the end was nigh took her forward once again. Edna was then able to recognize and challenge her sedimented pattern of elevating others and at the same time putting herself in a subservient position. Spontaneously she showed her anger in the therapy and this brought about the knowledge that anger did not produce the effect that she had anticipated. The therapist was still there for her.

The power of insight was highlighted with Edna, especially when the insight emerges from her. The understanding and euphoria that occurs when the client comes up with his or her own insight can never be underestimated. They experience a true feeling of being in control of their emotions, their behaviour and their self-understanding. It is a truly authentic experience; one where ownership can be expressed and a clearer path to moving forward can be seen. Insight does not occur continuously, but vacillates between clarifying and learning on a more rational level. For instance, when Edna became aware that by putting Sally on a pedestal she had automatically put herself in a submissive position, she realized between sessions that this was only the tip of the iceberg, because she was repeating the same behaviour in all her other relationships. This, in turn, generated further reflections and understanding. She learned how to challenge herself and to understand how her fixed sense of polarities was helping her stay in these behaviour patterns. She also discovered that her sedimented pattern of withdrawing and pleasing others had served her well at times. This process repeated itself in her discovery that she treated me in a subordinate manner. She later had an insight of her general perception of men, namely that they are powerful and can do her a great deal of harm. The circularity of the process – relating to experiences, comprehension, insight and change of perception – continued right through the therapy.

Through the whole process and working through her sense of despair she gradually realized that she did have choices. She could choose how to think about her sense of nothingness or the way she dealt with her relationships.

Although Edna entered therapy expecting an instant cure and explicit advice, she gradually realized that these were unrealistic expectations. Therapy is an initiation into a learning process of self-exploration that is more akin to a journey that does not terminate, but continues long after therapy concludes.

7

THE BODY

In this chapter and those following we shall describe individual case studies. While all of them vary in context and substance, they nevertheless possess essential commonalities. They all exist within the limitations and possibilities that the world imposed upon them and which have been described in previous chapters. The object of this chapter is, thus, to demonstrate how all these cases are linked within the existential structure as it has been presented on the existential wheels. To name but a few features, everyone in the case studies strives for safety and interpersonal relationships; to express themselves freely and honestly. All are heavily influenced by their value systems. All have experienced exaggerated fixed behaviour and value patterns. All suffer from overcharged anxieties, and all have the possibility to choose, even if that means only a choice of attitude. It is also common to all cases that exaggerated compulsive sedimentations, even if they sometimes appeared totally immovable, were always transformable. We shall start with the case study of Sue, whose world view was greatly influenced by her rigid value system, one of them her physical appearance.

SUE

Sue was a 25-year-old unmarried woman who came from a prosperous, middle-class background. It appeared that her family was a loving and well-functioning family; she had an older sister and an older brother. She was studying dentistry and had to pass a number of exams before she would be awarded her degree. In the meantime she was placed in a clinic where she was training.

Sue came down from the north of England to study in London. She lived in her own flat and it seemed that she was supported financially by her family, although she was already earning a salary in the clinic. She gave the impression of a charming, extremely good-looking girl with a perfectly proportioned figure and good body posture. She appeared to be intelligent and a person with whom it is easy to communicate, although I felt that Sue was somehow ashamed of talking about something. It did not occur to me that her issues might also be connected with her body.

While we were establishing our boundaries and contract, I was very aware of the fact that we would need more than one module during the therapy. We agreed all the salient points of the contract. We also negotiated and agreed to begin the therapy with twelve sessions, plus two review sessions with a possibility of further modules.

The presenting problem

Sue was referred to me by word of mouth and I did not ask her to reveal the name of the individual who passed her to me. After our introductions she asked me what she was supposed to do. I outlined to her that the purpose of the first session was primarily to get to know each other. I wanted her to fill me in with the presenting problem, to discuss the process of the therapy and to give space to ask questions. We needed time for us both to make up our minds whether we were suitable to work together.

Sue immediately began to tell me about her complaints. She suffered from insomnia and insecurity, combined with anxiety. Sometimes she experienced palpitations and headaches. She disliked her work and had difficulty with proper communication. While I wanted to know about her expectations of therapy, Sue pleaded for help and advice. She asked how we could improve her situation to enable her to resume work in her everyday life. I explained to her that my role would be to facilitate the clarification of her own issues and that this would involve a great deal of commitment and work for both of us. At this stage it was already completely clear to me that there was much more to Sue's problems than she was prepared to reveal, as will be seen below. For example, she had already admitted to her bulimic state in her third session.

The story

In subsequent sessions little prompting was needed for Sue to tell her story. In fact, I had real difficulty in intervening and focusing on any particular event or episode, as Sue jumped from one subject to another. It took quite a while for Sue to respond to my challenges, to settle on one subject, instead of alternating between subjects with lightning speed. Furthermore, she had a habit of 'side-tracking' as soon as my interventions touched upon an unpleasant subject.

Sue spoke of her poor memory, but certain episodes remained very deeply ingrained in her mind. Her need to express and to narrate her experiences was overwhelming. My intention here is to relate some of Sue's salient experiences, which she described during the first six sessions. These, I believe, were of critical importance in her life and thus necessary to be clarified in therapy and to be connected with her presenting problems.

Sue was brought up in a very close knit family with strong puritanical views. At an early age she became aware of the fact that her parents were much older than the accepted norm in both her extended family and her other circles. The result of this, according to her perception, was that she felt excluded from her playgroup, because the group consisted of children who were generally older then her. Thus, not only did she feel rejected, but she also developed a sense of being an 'outsider'. Indeed, she felt different from her own age group. In the back of her mind always lurked the idea that because she had 'old' parents, she would never be an 'ordinary' child or an 'ordinary' person and would never be accepted in any group.

Sue described her parents as very devoted and loving people. Her father provided everything; whatever she wanted and desired was given to her. Indeed, she gladly and categorically told me that there was never a serious clash between her and her parents, in spite of her parents' conservative views and the prohibitions that were inculcated into her upbringing. I recorded my intuition that there was always an undertone of discomfort in her relationship with her parents and her family. I kept this at the back of my mind all the time.

Another episode that is significant in understanding Sue's story was her loss of confidence during a holiday abroad. Sue was travelling with her mother and father when suddenly her father suffered a heart attack. Sue, at the age of 14, collapsed and felt she would lose her father. Although fortunately her father recovered, this feeling of fear and uncertainty constantly accompanied her in all her relationships and activities in life. When I questioned her about how she would have felt if, by misfortune, her father had actually died, she recounted her fantasy that she would have sat on the street pavement, completely abandoned and without any resources to continue ordinary life.

Important and relevant to this study is Sue's perception of her mental relationship with her body image. She spoke about her experiences during her childhood when between the ages of 7 and 13 she saw herself as a girl who was coined 'stodgy', 'podgy' and 'squinting'. Due to this she felt ugly and not only excluded from her peer group, but also ridiculed. This need is also to be seen from the perspective of her family ethos: being fat meant being revolting while being slim was the only way to exist successfully.

Sue chose to study dentistry, after a long and conscious deliberation. Her original choice was psychology, a subject she liked and found easy to study. In spite of this she chose dentistry because she and her family felt that it would provide material security and other benefits in her life.

Sue struggled excessively with her study of dentistry, dreading exams. She had to retake almost every one, in spite of the great effort she put into studying. Indeed, studying and fear of exams were part of her presenting problems. In spite of her struggles she was determined to get through her exams, since, failure 'would mean total insecurity in her life'.

The therapy: first module

In the first two sessions Sue was visibly concealing something which I felt was of great significance to her. At the beginning I also challenged Sue for being 'all over the place' and about her difficulty in focusing and finishing one subject. She was very receptive and began to explore her feelings in her relationship with me. She found that she felt insecure in her therapy but she could not express it and had no 'inkling' what she was insecure about. Sue was soon able to connect her insecurity within the therapy with her general feeling of insecurity in life. She related her cravings for safety to her fear about her parents and particularly her father. From childhood onwards she had always felt that, much as her parents loved her and offered her everything she wanted, she was totally insecure; this was due largely to her father's age. Sue mentioned the incident of her father's heart attack. I prompted her to explore the occasion fully. This was a very emotional moment for Sue. She re-experienced her feelings of abandonment and loneliness as she recounted the event. Somehow this episode served as a metaphor for her in the therapy and her explanation of her insecurity. It was interesting how it led Sue to look into her past and see the way it influenced every aspect of her life. For example, she chose to become a dentist as she had always been convinced that she needed to acquire qualifications in order to feel economically safe. This choice was made in spite of her real desire to study either art or psychology. Dentistry for Sue in some way represented economic security, whereas in her perception psychology or art were subjects that she could enjoy but would not be viable economic propositions. Concerning the period between the ages of 7 and 13, Sue spoke of a very unhappy time when she felt that she was ostracized from her peer group, not only because of her older parents but also due to her fat and 'ugly' appearance. These were the moments in the session when

Sue became aware of and revealed her extreme pain in her loneliness and low self-concept.

In fact, that was her perception and accompanied her throughout her life. In pursuing this theme, in the third session I challenged Sue as to what she did to escape the feeling of being ostracized and feeling lonely. She gradually disclosed that she suffered from bulimia nervosa. I say gradually, since at first Sue simply mentioned casually that she had binged the night before.

It took this session and the fourth for Sue to open up and tell me that for the previous two years she was not only bingeing every day, but she also suffered from compulsive vomiting. She was so ashamed of her bingeing and vomiting that she concealed it from everyone; she was even surprised that she managed to disclose it in our sessions. As a result of this admission, I knew for certain that Sue would need additional modules in her therapy and I was glad that the frame and the contract incorporated a contingency for them. As I browse through my notes on Sue's case, even now I am fascinated by the process of her revelations. Namely, it took Sue one full module and part of another before she admitted that she had compulsively vomited and binged for years, as much as fourteen times per day. As if this were not enough, Sue disclosed, only towards the end of the second module, at the time when she had already practically stopped vomiting and bingeing, that she had never been totally honest about the true extent of her compulsion. Yes, for Sue the shame was too deep; in fact she had vomited and binged regularly for more then three years, fourteen times per day.

Sue was a girl of good looks, good posture and extremely intelligent. She had loving parents, a brother and a sister. She had a reasonable time in her studies and training, a great number of friends, good sexual relationships with sexual satisfaction. What then was making Sue so compulsive and depressive?

Value system, coping strategy and structure

We returned to the 'stodgy', 'squinty' period (between the ages of 7 and 13). Sue established a very rigid sedimented value system in her life. We have already seen from the previous sessions that for Sue material security was a vital ingredient in life, without which she perceived life as unbearable. In addition, Sue acquired an equally rigid sedimentation about her body image. Without these two attributes she felt completely devoid of any self-concept and as such she fell into regular depressions when she felt disconnected from others.

In the ensuing sessions, we worked on Sue's existing coping strategies;

namely, what did she do so as not to fall into this depression and awful state of nothingness and loneliness. As soon as she realized that she had formed very rigid sedimented behaviour patterns for her survival, the structure of Sue's world views emerged. For example, choosing her profession in order to gain economic security and slimming to keep herself physically immaculate belonged to her strategic behaviour patterns to keep depression and loneliness at bay. In my mind I fitted Sue's structure of her world view (hypothetically) into the existential wheel.

- **Safety**. Sue yearned for safety and security. Indeed, to acquire it she studied dentistry. This in her perception would provide her with financial safety.
- **Interpersonal relationship**. Sue craved to express herself in an honest interpersonal relationship. She chose to come to therapy because she needed to conceal her shame from others, as well as express herself freely.
- **Time and temporality**. Sue's existence both outside and inside therapy was governed by temporality. She was 25 years old and believed she was ruining her life. There was no time to rectify what she had lost during her years of compulsive behaviour. She constantly felt guilty that she was not doing enough to fulfil her potential. In therapy she was concerned at each session that the course of therapy would end prematurely. Towards the ending of each module, as will be described further, she became very much aware of our impending separation.
- **Value system**. Sue developed rigid assumptions from an early age that were difficult to change. To conform with her values she acquired behaviour patterns to cope with these assumptions and most of the time these sedimented behaviour patterns served her well. Her choice of dentistry provided her, in a limited way, with security. Her preservation of her body image helped her to socialize and communicate and to become at times the centre of attention. Nevertheless, she paid a heavy price for these. She binged and vomited and lived in a deceptive mode. She needed to pretend, because she could not be open – she was ashamed of too much.
- **The four worlds**. As for the four worlds, Sue's life centred on her body and how others perceived it. She neglected her relationship with the spiritual and other worlds.
- **Anxiety**. Sue's anxiety when she experienced situations whereby her value system could not be fulfilled was devastating and drove her into

depression. This was not limited to an existential anxiety only, but was an exaggerated fear of rejection and abandonment.

- **Self-concept**. Sue's aspirations, values, behaviours, anxieties and her choices were closely linked with her self-concept. In other words, her world view was dependent on her self-concept.
- **Free will**. As for freedom of choice, in my mind, Sue had many possibilities. She could, for example, challenge her values. Is the body the only thing that counts? Could the body image sometimes be positive as much as negative? Is the chase for economic security always positive? Can it on occasion have negative connotations? Furthermore, to what degree was the acquirement of security important to Sue?

Having formulated these assumptions and placed them in my mental image of the existential wheel, my therapeutic relationship with Sue changed. While I suspended my desire to use this structure in my interventions, it provided me with a base, an anchor, from which we both worked in relative security. As soon as Sue became aware of what her values were, how she behaved to maintain her self-concept, she was able to become more open, to challenge herself more freely and gradually to be less ashamed of herself.

Sue's story unfolded itself rapidly through the next few sessions. Between the ages of 9 and 13 she had struggled to lose weight and to reach her body image: slim, beautiful, immaculate in her wardrobe and make-up. As she could not achieve these aims, she felt almost constantly depressed. Yet, Sue recounted, she had two bright spots. Denise and Claire were two friends who accepted her as she was and the relationship worked reciprocally. They had fun and developed a true interpersonal relationship until the age of 14.

Then something vital happened in Sue's life. She was 14 years old when she was invited to a party. As usual, she arrived and placed herself in an inconspicuous corner. Then, out of the blue, an adult approached her and complimented her on her pretty dress, her good figure and her attractiveness. For some reason, this incident was repeated many times during the same evening. Everyone who approached her looked at her in astonishment, repeating how beautiful, elegant and slim she had become. Sue returned home in wonder and her self-concept and confidence grew rapidly. She looked at herself in the mirror from all angles and, yes, she saw herself, for the first time, as a changed person; a slim, graceful creature with beautiful features. A new chapter in Sue's life ensued. As she progressively gained confidence, so did she start to become a party-goer and a party-giver. As she developed her social skills, she became the centre of attention at parties. She felt beautiful, well dressed and able to entertain and keep the interest of her guests. She always had a great number of male followers and used to choose, as she would say, the 'best' of them.

In the background, however, was Sue's problem with her studies. She had chosen dentistry for security reasons, but it was a struggle since she did not enjoy her subject. She would have much preferred art or psychology, and she had in fact experimented with psychology for two years. She soon realized, however, that because 'psychology was not a vocational discipline which can secure material security' she needed to continue studying dentistry. There were two opposing forces within Sue: on the one hand was her massive will to do anything to achieve security; on the other she hated dentistry and loved psychology, but this, she believed, would throw her into insecurity.

In addition to this discomfort about her education, in her personal life she found that the happiness and confidence in her body was not so easily maintained. It was important for Sue to be slim, able to entertain others and remain at the centre of attention. This was not an easy task to achieve. She had to maintain a permanently jolly countenance and project a body image that conformed with her picture of a slim, beautiful person who would attract people. It was extremely hard for her to sustain the body image, requiring dieting and a constant vigilance of her weight and, in her words, she also needed a permanent pretence to keep up her social image.

In this phase of the therapy, namely the fifth and sixth sessions, she also spoke of John. She had fallen in love with him and for over eighteen months they had enjoyed what she called a 'blissful relationship'. They were deeply involved in a trusting, loving relationship and had planned their wedding day when she discovered that John had betrayed her constantly. He had had affairs with various girls, including her own girlfriends.

The trust that she had invested in John could never be recovered. She felt rejected, devastated and her self-concept sank to the same low level as in her adolescence. She felt alone and unable to turn to anyone. Her two real true friends, Denise and Claire, were no longer available in the same intimate manner as before.

Sue then realized that as she became popular and the centre of attention at parties, she had neglected her friendship with her two best friends. This episode was discussed in the seventh and eighth sessions. Sue challenged her own behaviour and described this period as her 'abandoning her only two intimate friends, when something better came along'. She felt guilty. It was dramatic for Sue to consider that, as a result of this, she believed others would similarly abandon her if something or someone better came along.

John's betrayal triggered off a great crisis in Sue's life. She left him, failed her exams, gave up her studies and returned home where she spent a miserable six months. She then put on weight, and started to binge and vomit in secret. She felt depressed and lost all meaning in life. In spite of all this, after six months her ambition and strong will prevailed and drove her back to university. She finished her degree, even though she had to retake many exams and despite great difficulties in studying and much trepidation at exam time.

Following her degree she moved to London, to train to complete her qualifications. She was in the middle of socializing, with lots of boyfriends and everyday bingeing and vomiting, when all this made her feel depressed and hopeless. She decided that she needed help, and thus was referred to me.

Following the sixth session, Sue gradually recognized how her rigid value system about her body image influenced her behaviour pattern. She became aware of the fact that her compulsive partying and changing of boyfriends was her coping strategy for maintaining her self-concept; that without constant approval from men she would sink into depression. She needed male approval and when this was not forthcoming she compulsively binged in order not to fall into depression. Bingeing became an obsession and, at the same time, because she needed to maintain her body image to remain slim, she compulsively vomited. The vomiting fuelled her guilt and triggered off the same cycle. It was better to go to parties and see men than to become depressed. The everlasting cycle continued. While Sue recognized these cycles and patterns, she nevertheless continued with her compulsive behaviour. Despite this, some changes in her bingeing and vomiting habits occurred. Sue gradually became aware that she had a great many choices within her value and behaviour systems. Our relationship changed, namely, she focused on her issues, accepted challenges easily and had faith that something positive would happen to her, without too much effort and intent on being hostile with herself.

Compulsion

In July Sue became increasingly anxious about her impending qualifying exam that was scheduled for September. She began to explore all aspects of her studies. If she were to fail her exams, this would confirm to her that she was a 'good for nothing'. A blow of this sort would devastate her father so much that he might not survive. If, on the other hand, she passed her exams, so she deliberated, she would be the happiest person in the world. She would have security, make a great deal of money and could pursue the activities that she really enjoyed. Yet, as she explored this possibility she became aware that something else was needed to fulfil her. Somehow she felt that even her qualifying degree would not give her economic security and the trust in herself that she needed to establish a single meaningful relationship.

Her behaviour during this period alternated between regular bingeing, vomiting, and dressing up to go out with men. In addition she was hard at work. It was a period of total compulsion. Sue's nervous system was at its lowest ebb and she was desperate. She knew that her physiological state was deteriorating. Her teeth began to decay from the constant vomiting and she feared that her digestive system was also suffering. She was angry and hostile with every part of herself. She fought desperately to stop bingeing. Sometimes at night she felt like scraping wallpaper off the walls.

We explored at length what were the triggering factors for Sue when she placed a piece of chocolate in her mouth. By now, it was not difficult for her to work out that any thoughts of failing exams or the slightest hint of rejection would throw her into depression. Bingeing and going out were for Sue the only survival strategy. The metaphor which we used was that she felt like that fat, squinting girl who had been ostracized by her peer group. It was better to binge or be hugged by anybody than to fall back to this state of oblivion.

Insights

Despite this Sue succeeded in reducing her bingeing considerably. Indeed, the knowledge that she had a choice in bingeing reminded her that she could stop because she was doing it only to escape from her low self-concept. There were sessions when she came in gleefully and reported how she had stopped herself bingeing and discovered that despite her loneliness she had still survived.

The time approached for her exam, which coincided with the ending of the twelve sessions. Sue became extremely anxious about her bingeing and vomiting. One night she went to a party where she met Leslie, one of her ex-lovers. She wanted to vindicate the humiliation that she had experienced with him. First she ignored him, then flirted ostentatiously in front of him. Towards the end of the evening, she accepted an invitation for dinner the following night.

When she arrived at the session following the dinner appointment, she appeared dishevelled and depressed and said she felt totally humiliated by Leslie. She related how he called her a loose and uncaring woman. All this happened just a few days before her exam. She said she had never been so belittled in such a crude way, and she felt suicidal. Sue believed that Leslie was correct when he told her that she was a worthless creature. I let her examine what 'worthless creature' meant to her and what were those features in herself that she was so hostile about.

Following Sue's exploration of her behaviour patterns, such as deception and her pretension in her communications with others, together with her compulsive craving for security, I challenged her to investigate the positive side of her values and behaviour patterns. As a result of this, she realized that all these values that she judged as negatives had also served her in some positive way to become the person she was. Namely, through her ambition to achieve security, she had already gained her first degree in science, and that was certainly not negative. She also found positive aspects of her strong bonding to her family. Through her pretensions in company she managed to acquire a large circle of friends. These all carried a positive aspect. Admittedly, she also had to pay a price for her exaggerated ingrained value and behaviour system. At this session I felt that she managed not only to challenge herself, but also to perceive things that made her less hostile to herself, diminishing the impact of Leslie's encounter. I expected a shift of perception, generally, of her masochistic tendencies toward herself.

Nevertheless, the following week she spoke of her previous week's activities and how she had spent almost every night with different boyfriends. Only towards the end of the session did she mention desperately that she could not stop bingeing and the only substitute was, yet again, to date men. So, she alternated between going out, bingeing and vomiting. It was also difficult to do this and to conceal the bingeing and vomiting. She felt very low at this session. She thought of herself as fat, ugly, stupid and worthless.

At the next session Sue's account was of a horrendous week. She had not stepped out of her house except to take her exam. She passed the main subjects of her qualifying exams, but had to retake seven subjects in six months' time. Despite this she managed, amazingly, to stop bingeing and vomiting during that week.

We had two sessions and two more review sessions left in this module. Sue wanted to come to an agreement at this meeting that we would have a follow-up module which would be part of our contract. While I was convinced that Sue needed some further support, I managed to postpone the decision until the review sessions. I felt that this would give Sue the maximum incentive to work on herself between sessions.

We then reassessed Sue's progress in her therapy in depth. While she felt despondent about the intensity of her compulsion, she nevertheless relished the fact that she could reduce her bingeing and vomiting cycle considerably. In fact, this was the first time that she had been able to stop bingeing for a complete week.

During the last few sessions we worked on how Sue would really feel if she were grossly overweight – 16 stone, for example. At first she said that she would be suicidal, but then, something dawned on her. She remembered that although between the ages of 7 and 13 she had been very fat and in her words 'miserable', she had spent some noteworthy times with Claire and Denise. Maybe she could find some other purpose in life than her own body which would give meaning to her. I challenged her to think about the fact that through her compulsion to please others with her body, she was at their mercy. In other words she was a servant of others.

Sue discussed the possibility, in this and the next few sessions, of trying to stop vomiting, even if it meant that she would put on weight. We had four weeks' break before the two review sessions. While her bingeing and vomiting pattern changed, in a way she became more authentic about it, knowing that she had a choice. We agreed on another module within six weeks.

Second module

The second module was characterized by Sue's knowledge of her structure. She knew exactly what she was doing, how she was doing it, and that she was doing it compulsively. She knew that her emphasis on her body and security was illogical and that she was driven by an inconceivable force to satisfy her original value system. Yet, the compulsion to go out or binge still persisted. Admittedly, bingeing fourteen time per day, every day diminished considerably, but from time to time it reoccurred with a vengeance.

This module was also marked by dreams. Dreams became a very important metaphor for Sue and they possibly clarified many aspects of her aspirations. At this time she was still working in a placement to practice dentistry as well as preparing for her final exams. Sue started the second module speaking very little about her compulsive eating. She began to hate going out to parties and felt in a way hostile to men and to the whole social environment to which she belonged. At the same time her hostility extended to food. She challenged the contradiction that she hated food and still binged and vomited, albeit less.

During this period Sue was preparing for her final exams. Every time she spoke about it, she drove herself into a frenzy, that it would mean the end of her very being if she failed them. While challenging her attitude towards this, she investigated the possibility of changing profession to either art, music, or psychology. I also challenged her conviction that if she passed her exams then bliss would ensue. Many times during the therapy she had a clear inspiration that only a shift of attitude in her belief system about the importance of her body image and the approval of others would give her relief and a more satisfactory life style.

For many sessions Sue was preoccupied with her dreams and I helped her to find her 'meaning' herself. As we went along, her dreams became more and more lucid and meaningful and produced more and more insight for her.

DREAMS

In subsequent sessions dreams were plentiful. In some of her sessions Sue reconstructed more than two dreams, while at other times we stayed with one dream for more than two sessions. All the dreams were very significant for Sue and they always related to the same subjects.

In this section we will relate three dreams, the last of which, 'Animal Farm', was the most explicit and remained the most important metaphor for Sue's further development.

'Marriage'

Sue was getting married in a church. She was beautifully dressed in white, her father in black. The groom was by her side and they walked all together, the three of them, towards the altar. As the ceremony progressed, Sue suddenly became conscious that she simply did not want to marry this man, who had been her father's favourite choice. She refused to continue with the celebration, which infuriated her father.

As a sequel to this Sue found herself in heaven, facing God, in utter trepidation. She felt guilty and in a panic when she asked God whether she would pass her exams. God would not give her a straight answer. In fact, Sue got the impression that God did not know; she woke up frightened and bewildered.

Her interpretation of this dream was that she always needed to behave according to her parents' values. However, she argued, the omnipotence of this force might not be unbreakable.

'The door with the yellow light'

Haley was the only friend who did not belong to the crowd of 'dressing up party-goers' and whose values were different to those of Sue's surroundings. In this dream Sue stood with Haley in front of a large door with a yellow light on top. Each time Haley passed the door the yellow light flickered, the door opened and a real heaven appeared. Yet when Sue passed the door the yellow light did not flicker, thus, she could not experience heaven. Haley encouraged her to try again and the door opened. Sue entered heaven and met God. God told her that all would be well with her and that she would pass her exams. Yet, when she asked God, 'How do you know, have you looked up my file?', God said, 'No, but if you fail, that will be your destiny and this will give you a new perception.' While she was furious that God contradicted himself, which suggested to her that even God did not know whether she would pass or not, God made love to her. That made her even more unhappy in that God made her promiscuous.

We explored the dream. When I asked her, at the end of the session, to summarize in a few sentences her meaning about the dream, she said, 'Haley, who for me exemplifies a person who is not driven by money, expensive clothes and has a very good relationship with her partner, can show me the way to another world. Yet, if I arrive at this new world, my uncertainties and insecurities will not disappear. It might be a better world, but there is no ideal one.'

During this period, while preoccupied with her studies and work, Sue binged and vomited intermittently. There were weeks when she stopped completely, weeks when she binged once or twice a week, and times when total compulsion took over.

'Animal Farm'

At the tenth session, while we were frantically analysing what the body meant to Sue and why her life was totally subservient to her body, she started to narrate her dream of the animal farm. It was based on Orwell's book *Animal Farm* and became a very important metaphor in our future sessions.

The dream was about her being imprisoned in a space where pigs were the governing notables. The other animals were subservient and submitted themselves to them. Her mother, her father, John and all her family belonged to the ruling class.

Sue was struggling hard to escape from the farm that was surrounded and fortified by high walls. Her father and mother quarrelled intensely at the farm and the ruling pigs were beating and punishing the other animals. Sue's whole purpose, in this animal farm, was to escape. She devised many plots, one of which was to climb over the high walls and to abscond. Indeed, on one occasion she managed to bribe the guard, but as soon as she was halfway over the steep wall, she was pulled back by her legs. She was severely punished, locked up, and beaten. When she woke up she was terrified.

The dream was very significant for future sessions. From then on, Sue continued to relate dreams that she consequently worked on. Curiously, however, all her dreams followed the same theme, namely transcending from one side of the fence, which characterized hardship and torture, to another territory that epitomized for her bliss and heaven. She felt that the animal farm for her meant the world of pretence and deception: having a slim body, covering it with beautiful dresses, always smiling to charm other people; these were all deceptions to attract attention and to survive. The other side of the fence was heaven, where she could be honest and would not have to deceive others and herself. Yet, she knew from the previous dream that even heaven was not heaven.

As we have said, this was the tenth session in the second module. By now Sue understood her world completely. She knew that her behaviour pattern to seek security was not all bad, and that if she were to succeed in climbing over the wall to her other world, she needed to maintain her strong will and ambition to reach security. She also knew that she had to let go of some of her pretensions if she wanted to progress and develop meaningful interpersonal relationships. The same applied to her body image; she wanted to maintain some of it, but lose the compulsion element.

Sue's exams were scheduled for the week between the tenth and eleventh sessions. Her anxiety peaked to a climax. Nevertheless, she managed to keep bingeing down to twice a week. We discussed this phenomenon and, amid trepidation and anxiety about her exams, we managed to celebrate the fact that she had reduced her regular bingeing from fourteen times per day to twice per week, two weeks before her exams. This was a significant achievement.

At the eleventh session she reported that she had passed her qualifying exam. Her happiness at this session is hard to describe. She radiated joy and we discussed her future. She also reported that that week she had not binged or vomited. Yet when we spoke of ending the therapy she felt shaky. I also felt that Sue would need some more support in the future before being left entirely to her own resources. We decided that we would leave the discussion of the contract for the next module to the last review session.

During the period between the twelfth session and the review sessions Sue found a good job and moved home, but felt very unsure of herself. She binged and vomited three times. Her insecurity and meaninglessness returned from time to time. She acknowledged that her compulsion had not disappeared as, in a way, she already predicted before her final exam. We agreed to start a third module and celebrated that in spite of everything, she had indeed moved on from the time when she was bingeing and vomiting fourteen times per day.

The third module

The twelve sessions in the third module signified for Sue a continuing struggle to move from the animal farm to another world. She wanted to break ties with her social and family circle that represented for her ambition for wealth, expensive clothes and pretension. She contemplated taking up music, studying the flute, art or, what was nearest to her heart, returning to psychology. For a long time in this period Sue managed to withhold bingeing and vomiting by keeping busy all the time. When she found herself alone at home her compulsion to binge sometimes reappeared. Thus, she worked long hours and went out in the evenings, as it was better for her to occupy herself than to be alone. Her sexual libido returned and she reverted, in her words to 'promiscuity'. While the bingeing and vomiting subsided, the compulsion element still persisted. It manifested itself in that instead of bingeing Sue always had to be occupied in order to take her mind off her habit.

In the middle of this module she was invited by her mother to take a week's holiday abroad. A great dilemma presented itself: during this holiday week there would be nothing to do but spend time with her mother, so that her desire to binge would be irresistible. How would she keep her 'great secret' that nobody knew of? In the session Sue questioned herself as to the consequence of telling her mother about the bulimia. At first she thought she would be ostracized by her family and 'the whole world would know about her shame'.

I challenged her again and again to explore what it meant for her to be 'ashamed', 'rejected' and 'lonely'. What was she defending with such a massive force? Was it really so horrible to be an outsider as the 'podgy', 'stodgy', 'squinty', abandoned little girl? Sue argued with herself that maybe it was not as horrible as all that. She had, after all, her two faithful friends, Claire and Denise, with whom she had a noteworthy relationship. At this session Sue was still undecided about whether to disclose her problems to her mother.

In the next session Sue reported joyfully that on holiday she had had a premonition that she would tell her mother all her secrets, about bingeing and compulsion. Miraculously, when told, her mother was most understanding and helpful. In fact she felt very relieved, as she had always been afraid that Sue suffered from a mental depression. According to her mother this would be much worse than Sue's present condition.

Meaning

This episode marked another cornerstone in Sue's therapy. Gradually, she was able to disclose her sensitive issues, first to Haley and then to other close friends, and the shame mattered much less. At this time Sue was able to stop vomiting completely, but the bingeing continued to some extent. Admittedly, it was not as extensive, but from time to time it was compulsive. Towards the end of the therapy, she moved away from the area where her family and close friends lived. She felt ready to move out from the 'animal farm'.

By the end of the review session she had decided to take a part-time psychology course, while continuing her job as a dentist. Her relationship with her family became less symbiotic but she still maintained a good relationship with them. At that time she was still searching for a good relationship with a man, but her drive to go out every night subsided considerably. Sue thought that she could now manage on her own, although we agreed that if she felt the need for support in the future, she would contact me – even if only for one session.

By the end of the therapy, both her bingeing and vomiting had stopped completely.

DISCUSSION

Sue's case exemplified the way an intelligent individual grasped the basic structure of her existence in a very short time. She had no difficulties in challenging herself and became aware by the middle of the first module that she behaved compulsively and how these behaviour patterns were underpinned by her rigid value and coping systems.

It has been illustrated in this study that feelings, cognition and insight go hand in hand. Structural cognition of Sue's values had initiated insight; insight triggered off further insight, until slowly shifts of perceptions became an almost imperceptible part of the therapy. At an early stage, in the middle of the first module, Sue's world views emerged. From then on my work consisted of nothing more than to facilitate Sue to explore phenomenologically the contradictions and discrepancies in her world views. This in turn opened the door for her to make attitudinal and behavioural choices. All these were linked with the aspects of the existential structure, as represented by the wheels. I had to trust the situation and prompt Sue that through 'insight' she would gain faith in her capacity to change her perception. This can happen before, during sessions, before or after therapy. We did not know how Sue would fare in life. Yet we knew that she had acquired a skill – a learning process by which she would be able, somewhat better than before, to deal with her problematic issues. The therapeutic method that I followed was as presented on the wheel in Figure 4.2.

Safety

The fixing and maintenance of the boundaries of contract and framework kept the therapeutic situation safe from the first session onwards. Sue maintained her commitment to the therapy right through to the end.

I tried empathically to distance myself from Sue's distress and agony, so as to be able to point out on occasions her contradictions. It was not difficult to do this, because she soon had the capacity to challenge her own contradictions. Thus I facilitated Sue to examine through phenomenological exploration every single issue from all angles.

Perception of time

Sue was constantly aware of the time limitations of sessions, as of the therapy as a whole. It had been important for me to monitor my own motivations and suspend premature interventions, which would have served my own end; namely to produce a result in the shortest possible time. This on the other hand would have impeded the therapeutic process.

Identifying values and coping behaviour patterns

Sue was able to identify her rigid assumptions about her body and security in the first part of the therapy. As soon as she became aware of her compulsive behaviour patterns, she started to challenge her basic assumptions.

Challenging polarities

Sue's values, by the nature of all values, incorporate polarities. For example, one of her rigid sedimentations centred round her material insecurity. While her rigid attitude towards it generated a great deal of pain, anguish, undesirable behaviour and insecurity, it had also produced positive effects. For example, her ambition to complete her university course could be perceived as a positive achievement, yet it stemmed from Sue's drive to attain security. It was an important part of the therapy to challenge and investigate both poles of her values.

Exploration of the four dimensions of existence

Sue had analysed her lack of interest in her spiritual and other worlds. We challenged her assumption that her whole attention had to be focused on material security, while to centre only on her inner world was to the detriment of her other dimensions.

Challenging the misconception about the givens

A part of Sue's therapy focused upon her assumption that fear and anxiety would and could be eliminated totally through therapy. It was an important factor for Sue to accept the limitations of the 'givens' within which Sue could reconstruct her world view.

Identifying possibilities and the challenge to choose

While Sue became aware already in the early part of the therapy that some of her behaviours were of compulsive nature, it took her a long time and a series of 'insights' until she was able gradually to change some of her rigid sedimentations. Needless to say, some of the issues have remained and new issues will probably emerge. Nevertheless we both hope that she has gained some fundamental insight and acquired a learning process to deal with these issues on her own.

As has been described earlier, the success of the therapy depends partly on a working paradigm, on the therapist's ability to 'bracket' the client's structure and keep it in the background. Although I had vaguely formulated Sue's structure of her world view very early on in the therapy, I believe that I was also able to keep it totally in the back of my mind. Thus, I hope it did not become a disturbing technique, but a starting point that grounded us both and provided us imperceptibly with a direction in the therapy. Through this process Sue succeeded in shifting little by little her perception about her basic assumption which brought changes in her behaviour pattern. In view of the gravity of Sue's predicament the therapy was relatively short. Nevertheless, the second and third modules appeared for both of us a protracted process, as changes of perception took place almost imperceptibly. Yet we both trusted that through the process she would gain insights which would change her perception and her behaviour patterns. We also knew that these changes would happen not only during sessions, but also after the therapy.

EPILOGUE (WRITTEN BY SUE)

During the therapy I continually contemplated that it could be beneficial to convey my inhuman struggle and suffering to those individuals who might be entrapped in this horrendous human cultural value judgement about the 'body image'. In doing this, I felt that I may possibly contribute something positive that came out of my agonies and distress.

When I first glanced through Freddie's draft outline of my case in his consulting room I became first numb and then it was as if it had no effect on me. However, I could not wait to read it again at home. When I did that, at first I began to cry and then I continued to read – I am not sure how many times. I saw myself in a mirror. An immense sadness overtook me. The enormity of my predicament overwhelmed me. Images appeared in my mind.

I remember the first time I really binged and vomited. It was during my final year at university. I was very desperate and afraid. I was losing control of my life in every way and no one seemed to have any answers. I was deeply unhappy. It began one afternoon while I was studying, I began to eat All Bran and milk, really shoving the food into my mouth and forgetting all my worries at that moment – the only actual feeling I had was the hand to mouth action. One plate after another until I munched a whole box of Kellogg's All Bran, plus two pints of milk.

This is when the feeling of guilt and shame engulfed me – I felt worthless, fat and a failure. I felt so bloated that the only way to relieve the cramp in my bowels was by vomiting, which was easy, as I already felt sick. This continued for the following two weeks.

By the time I sat my exams, all my fellow classmates commented on how great I looked. Was that the perfect solution? Weight control and dieting? When my exams were over it would all end. I only craved for food when I was down, and interestingly when I felt well had no need to eat in excess. After my exams – I had finally qualified – something I never thought capable of achieving – I felt my life started to fall into place. I was quite attractive, I had my friends and people liked me. I had a good job where I was treated with respect and was at last financially secure. Yet the bingeing and vomiting were getting worse. I was going through the routine six to ten times a day, all day: all my working hours. This 'thing' was taking over my life. A phone call was an interruption, washing and simply brushing my teeth took too much time. Some nights I would sleep on the bathroom floor unable to move to my bedroom and then I would wake up and the cycle would begin again.

When I realized I had a problem that was not going to go away by passing my exams, that was when I finally owned up to Freddie. I was at my lowest, I knew I could not feel any worse; in some ways I couldn't feel at all. I wanted to die, only I did not have the will or the energy to take my life into my own hands. When I look back at the turning point in my life, when I decided to seek therapy, I was in a state of desperation and depression. Now, while I am reading this, I feel sad, insecure and shaky, as if walking on very unfamiliar wobbly ground; and this is in spite of the fact that I hope that the compulsive bingeing and vomiting is behind me. New mental images return to me: in the nursery school one of my peers would only play with me if I gave her some crisps or chocolates. I felt always excluded, even at high school, and I was terrified by this separation, even from my parents. I was ashamed that I had to buy myself out of this shameful failure. First I had to give crisps or chocolates, later I had to become outstanding in all that I was doing. I had to be chatty, rebellious and rude to teachers. By these means I had become popular with my peer group. I had to be like a performing monkey to be accepted.

At this time I feel isolated and lonely, but I have not binged or vomited for many months, and most of the time I enjoy being alone. The day of my 'coming out' to Freddie and later to my mother and my closest friend was the day my recovery began.

That time in my life – admitting to others what I was doing – was the first time I really admitted it all to myself. Now I am in a new flat and looking forward to enrolling on my new course. I feel that I moved out from the 'Animal Farm' with some attributes still with me. These may be good ones. A few days ago I felt shaky and miserable. I had no reason for this. I have a good job, a beautiful flat, a support group such as my mother and a few good friends, and I am looking forward to the new university course. Yet I was in crisis.

The other day I re-read my case again and I suddenly began to sob loudly and what seemed to be incessantly as never before, and then slowly I felt 'lighter'. I also started to think what we discussed so many times in the therapy sessions, that I have faith and trust in my own intuitions, which will take me out of this state, as happened so often before. I have left behind my coping mechanisms at the 'Animal Farm': the bingeing, the vomiting, the boys and the performing monkey are all in the past. Yet everything feels very uncertain, although I now feel tranquil and calm. Although this state is very unfamiliar for me, I nonetheless found that I can be on my own and have 'ME' home, not having to escape to food. I actually like to be alone occasionally. I am learning to like myself, to know and get to know myself. While I am not ready yet to share myself with anyone else (until I have finished getting to know myself better), I now trust that this will happen.

8

THE 'GIVENS'

This chapter will describe two cases: 'The curse of perfection' and 'Couple therapy'. While they both appear to be of a totally different nature, they unite in that all the participants react to the fear of rejection and abandonment which throws them into a state of loss of self-concept and loneliness. Nevertheless they each develop individual and very different coping mechanisms to survive.

THE CURSE OF PERFECTION

We present this case to demonstrate how exaggerated and rigid value systems, even if they are ethically accepted and honourable, may influence an individual's life in a destructive manner. All sedimentations have their positive and negative attributes, but when they become rigid and deeply ingrained in someone's world view, they may ruin that person's life.

Simona presented her problem simply. She suffered from a compulsion that prevented her getting up in the morning. This was a great impediment because she was thus incapable of spending sufficient time on her studies and frequently missed morning lectures. Simona was reading psychology and was absolutely determined to finish her studies in London. Her further complaint was, in her words an 'obsessional rage' that was uncontrollable and usually directed towards her boyfriend. The reason for this was his over-attentive and constant presence during her studies.

The story

Simona came from a foreign aristocratic family. She lived in a palatial abode, with her father, mother and two older sisters in the centre of a town. In spite of this Simona felt even at a young age that something was wrong, since her parents had constant financial worries and difficulties even in obtaining elementary commodities. When Simona was 5 years old her two sisters moved to live with their aunt and when she was 8 her father left home for good. Her mother had to go out to work and Simona was left to her own devices. She walked on her own to school and when she was picked up by her mother Simona was compelled to listen to her repeated complaints.

Simona's mother had to fend for herself and her children. She owned some very valuable property, yet she and her daughters were left to lead a poverty-stricken life. The valuable furniture, with the exception of essentials, was sold. Simona and her mother lived in dire poverty and even had difficulty in acquiring essential food and clothing.

Despite all their problems Simona had to maintain an image of wealth in her school and in her social interaction within her peer group. It was immensely difficult for her as she was sometimes even hungry at school, but was ashamed to ask for food. Her father lived with another woman in a different town. He was described by her family as a 'good-for-nothing spendthrift'. He not only squandered the family fortune but was incapable of leading a normal domestic life. An important feature in her family history was that her uncle, the brother of her father, lived in similar circumstances. Simona thus feared that she might inherit the 'mad gene' from her father's family.

At the age of 11 her father returned and said that he was suffering from terminal cancer. He needed care and attention. With very limited resources now stretched even further they did their best for six months, until they discovered that the disease was a pretence. Her father left again. When Simona was 14 she and her family experienced another trauma when her mother found out that her boyfriend was having an affair with Simona's eldest sister. Shortly after this, her mother succeeded in sending Simona to boarding school. Although she remembered happy days in this school, by the time she was 16 Simona had a nervous breakdown. She was taken to a psychiatrist who treated her with medication. She returned home and just got through her secondary schooling. In the meantime her mother had found a permanent boyfriend. Through the courts her mother succeeded in acquiring part of the palace where they lived. The family's fortunes changed drastically from poverty to considerable comfort.

Simona in the meantime met her present boyfriend Carl, who became her permanent companion. Although Carl was married, he was prepared to divorce. Simona started university in another town after which she decided to move to London. Carl regularly visited her in London, at the time when Simona had started her therapy.

Therapy

In the first session we covered all the preliminary boundary questions and negotiated our contract. We agreed on all salient points of framework. We also set the time limit for twelve sessions plus two review sessions, with the proviso that, if we felt that this was insufficient, we would negotiate an additional module.

The first six sessions

The first five to six sessions consisted of establishing our relationship and trust. I had also facilitated Simona to explore her stagnated world view and questioned what motivated her value system.

Simona was similar to many other clients and brought to therapy a conglomeration of issues. She jumped from one subject to another without exploring a single one, despite my many interventions. As the essence of our paradigm was that all issues are interconnected anyway, I listened to every topic until we came to her relationship with her mother, which Simona had wanted to explore more thoroughly. She spoke of her resentment that her mother relied on her all her life and that she, Simona, was the recipient of all her complaints since childhood. She felt that she was really the mother of her own mother, with much of the responsibility falling on her shoulders. When her father and two sisters had left, Simona was still very young, but despite this her mother's only way to express her anger was to unburden all her grievances and pain on Simona. We investigated this situation from all angles. Simona discovered that as a result of this she felt not only that she needed to control every situation, but also felt guilty if she could not control. As the ultimate example of this she felt guilt because of her parents' separation.

Simona also became aware of her state of desperation whenever she could not help her mother or when she thought she had lost control of a situation at school, especially when they discovered her 'state of poverty'. These moments of desperation were so painful that she felt that her self-concept had completely disappeared and that she was totally abandoned by everybody. To avoid this, Simona had to perform every act to perfection and always be in total control of every situation. Only by being perfect in every way could she expect approval from others and herself. It had not taken long for Simona to connect these issues to others and to her presenting problems.

She had to help to 'control' her boyfriend to find a job. This she did, although Carl had substantial financial backing. Simona felt that if he remained without a steady job she could not stay with him and marry him. Without a job their life would be insecure, and she believed that precisely this type of existence had influenced her father's waywardness. She looked for a first-class degree followed by a first-class job for security and the same applied to Carl. It was thus not surprising that Simona so often felt desperate and her feeling of insecurity was an almost permanent feature of her life.

Following the sixth session, during which we had explored Simona's compulsive late sleeping, she arrived at the session and spoke of the following discovery: 'Yesterday after midday, I struggled and fought my compulsion not to continue to stay in bed for longer. In my endeavour to get up, I started to analyse my problems. First, I felt that there was nothing to get up for. My belief was that to get up and do something would be a meaningless exercise for me. As for my studies I know that whatever I do I will not get a first degree and if I apply for a job it is far too remote a hope to find one that would give me some security. Should I press Carl to get a job it will only lead to a quarrel. Wherever I look life is full of insecurities, therefore I'd rather stay in bed and sleep. On the other hand whenever I do not do something like studying or looking for a job I feel guilty. Guilt, however, makes me feel even more insecure, thus, I stay in bed and the cycle perpetuates itself.'

This insight had constituted a significant discovery for Simona because it had made her aware that her behavioural pattern was nothing else but a coping strategy. In other words Simona had realized that to maintain her 'security' she needed to control her own performance to total perfection. She also had to control others to perform according to her own standards. If others were unable to fulfil her high ideals she fell into depression. After a while we began to challenge her belief system that 'I must always control every situation and perform perfectly, to be somebody'.

Simona delved into this question of control and perfection thoroughly. She investigated how her strong belief system influenced each relationship. Indeed, she now discovered that most of the time her controlling attitude impeded her relationship with Carl and it proved equally counterproductive with her mother and others. Her drive to be perfect in her studies, paradoxically, had also proved a failure. She could not study properly because she could not make herself get up in the morning and feel 'alive'. Her own low self-concept and guilt had made her devoid of any meaning in life. She argued that this vicious circle would continue compulsively until a radical change took place.

It was not difficult for Simona to deduce from all these things that she had in her power to choose not only her attitude towards control and perfection, but also that she could alter her behaviour. She could, for example, have made an attitudinal change in her perception concerning her degree; a second-class degree from an English university could be seen as a considerable achievement, as opposed to arousing feelings of guilt.

She could also have made changes in her behaviour pattern. She could have respected Carl's efforts to find a permanent job rather than be miserable about his failure. Simona realized that she could have chosen between lethargically staying in bed or being aware of the process and choosing authentically between getting up or staying there. Slowly Simona's world view emerged and I could clearly see in my mind how it fitted in and interconnected with all aspects of the existential wheel.

Safety and security

Simona had a strong sedimentation that she could reach a state of total security. She aimed to achieve this by being perfect and in control of her affairs; obtaining the best degree; her boyfriend aspiring to get the best job; her mother and her sisters behaving in the way she thought they ought to behave. She even had difficulty in contemplating the possibility that the existing world does not provide total security. All her relationships were influenced by searching for security. Her feeling of insecurity was compounded by her anxiety about her existential angst, which resulted in 'neurotic anxiety'.

Interpersonal relationship

While I tried to identify myself empathically with Simona's distress, I also distanced myself from her agony. I further distanced myself in order to be able to point out contradictions. It was not difficult to do this, because Simona soon had the capacity to challenge in her own defence. Thus I facilitated Simona to examine through phenomenological exploration every issue from all angles.

Time and temporality

As with everyone else, Simona's existence both outside and inside therapy was governed by temporality. She was 25 years old and she thought that she should already have a first-class degree and a permanent job. She constantly felt guilty that at her age she was not doing enough to fulfil her potential.

In therapy she was concerned at each session that she did not work hard enough. Nearing half-time of her therapy course, Simona was also concerned that she had still not achieved her expectations, namely her behaviour pattern had not yet changed materially. As we approached the ending – as will be described below – she became very much aware of our impending separation, which helped to connect the issue of separation with other issues.

As described in Chapter 3, time is a factor that needs to be addressed constantly in time-limited therapy. I had to be careful in Simona's case not to be affected by her impatience to achieve results within the shortest possible time. Whenever I felt that my interventions were driven by my desire to help and accelerate the process of therapy, I had to stop and try to suspend this desire. Instead I needed to explore whether the intended intervention would be in the client's long-term interest or if it was only to satisfy our desire to succeed. This aspect of therapy, namely the therapist's strong motivation to cure the client in the shortest possible time, is described in Chapter 3 under Time and temporality.

Value and behaviour pattern

Simona's world view in therapy centred on her exaggerated sedimentation of control and perfection. No doubt she had many other values, but these were the ones she focused on; all other issues were interconnected. As we have already shown, when Simona was not capable of performing, she either fell into depression and remained in bed or she became angry with her boyfriend. These were her two obvious strategies for survival.

The four worlds

Simona was so preoccupied with her natural world (sleeping, getting up) and her inner life that she hardly had time to observe herself from a practical perspective. She was missing approval and until she came to therapy her private world (the exploration of her inner perception) was totally unexplored.

Self-concept and anxiety

All Simona's behaviour problems were subjugated to her self-concept: to maintain it and not to fall into that 'no-man's world'. She would rather sleep and stay in an oblivious state than experience that depression. She would also be angry with her boyfriend in such a way that would 'make him inferior', allowing Simona to feel superior.

Anxiety

Anxiety was a companion for Simona with every change, fear or aspiration. It began with the anxiety of time limitation of sessions, to the angst of ending and separation; from Simona's expressions of all her emotions to her aspirations to achieve a shift of perception.

Possibilities and freedom of choice

It did not take Simona too long to discover that she could have a choice of many possibilities: to choose her behaviour pattern and modify her value system. The time she took to put this into practice was, however, much longer. Nonetheless we could say that already by Simona's so-called cognitive recognition of her motivation and world view, that her behaviour became more authentic. Cognitive awareness within itself carries emotional elements, which altogether facilitate insight and shift of perception.

It took a relatively brief period for Simona to argue, challenge and then work out her world view. Nevertheless, it took the majority of the second part of the therapy for her to go through the process of transforming this awareness to insights that produced almost impalpably some changes in her perceptions of her world view. At the beginning of the second half of the course, Simona renegotiated the boundaries insofar as she wanted to change the time of her therapy sessions. Instead of 4 pm to 5 pm, Simona wanted to attend between 10 am and 12 pm. She hoped this arrangement would compel her to get up, at least for the therapy, at a reasonable hour. We agreed on suitable dates and Simona, indeed, arrived punctually throughout the therapy.

Simona hoped for a first-class degree but received only a second-class one. While she resented that, she was able to challenge her compulsion to feel a failure. Before the end of the therapy she returned home for a week, after which she announced that she had decided to marry Carl. She had already found a place in her home country to study for her MSc degree course.

The two review sessions were uneventful, but at the last session we had an emotional farewell.

DISCUSSION

Simona was able to work, challenge and become aware of her world view in a relatively short time. Almost the whole of the rest of the therapy was spent in integrating her knowledge about her inner perception into insights. Through this process Simona managed to shift her perception bit by bit regarding her basic assumptions, which brought changes in her behaviour pattern. The therapeutic method that I followed was as presented on the existential wheel in Figure 4.2.

Safety

The fixing of contract and framework, from the first session on, kept the therapeutic perimeter safe, in spite of Simona's compulsion to deviate from her own boundaries (being late or not appearing at all for lectures). She managed consistently to keep her commitment to the therapy until the end.

Perception of time

Simona was constantly aware of the time limitations in sessions, as in the therapy as a whole. It was important for me to monitor my own motivations and suspend premature interventions, which would have served my own end, namely to produce a result in the shortest possible time.

Identifying values and coping behaviour patterns

Simona was able to identify her rigid assumptions about control and perfection in the first part of the therapy. As soon as she became aware that her compulsive sleeping-in was connected with her failure to perform and control events perfectly, she started to challenge her basic assumptions.

Challenging polarities

Simona's values, by their very nature, incorporated polarities. That Simona could not have attempted life without perfection and without control, in turn put a negative connotation on imperfection and on situations that were out of her control. It was an important part of the therapy to challenge and investigate both poles of these values.

Exploration of the four dimensions of existence

Simona analysed her lack of interest in her spiritual and social world. She challenged her assumption that her whole attention had to be focused on Carl and her studies.

Challenging the misconception about the givens

A very large part of Simona's therapy was centred on her assumption that fear and anxiety would be totally eliminated. It was an important factor in Simona's therapy that she was able to investigate her assumption that for her anxiety was something that could be eliminated through therapy.

Ending

Near the end of the therapy Simona worked on her fear of finishing it because she felt that it was just the time when she would need most support. She felt lonely and she was indecisive with her boyfriend. She practically forced a separation with him to be able to study and to be alone. She was also afraid that she would either fail her examinations or receive a low-grade degree. Although she applied for jobs, she was incapable of completing an application form. At the age of 27 she felt too old for job applications, still carrying the 'scars' of her younger university years. During this period her self-concept fluctuated. She was able, however, to get up at a normal time and arrive at her sessions at 10 am.

We explored all the possibilities of introducing another module after the review sessions, as well as the option of ending according to the schedule. In this respect Simona explored what was her expectation of the therapy, what she thought she would take away from it and how she would exist without the support.

The main emphasis during these last few sessions, however, was on her compulsive 'perfectionist' tendencies. This behaviour pattern manifested itself in her desire that all issues should be properly 'analysed' in therapy before the ending. This was even though she knew what this rigid belief meant to her. She worked and explored whether or not she could accept a 'good enough' therapy. Furthermore, she investigated whether she could trust herself that she had now acquired some confidence that she would be able to deal with her own issues.

The same applied to her boyfriend. Could she accept things as they were and trust that they could work out their issues mutually? At the twelfth session, Simona was still playing with the idea of the introduction of another six- to twelve-session module. As it was, in the intervals between the twelfth session and the first review session she went home (overseas), where she met her fiancé.

She returned exactly on time for her last two sessions. She reported that she had received a second-class degree – not quite what she expected. She also explained that she and Carl had decided to get together again and that she would work at their differences and try to accept him as he was.

COUPLE THERAPY

In this section we give an example of how time-limited existential therapy can also be applied to couples. The same principles, namely those of exploring patterns that emerge in response to the universal limitations and possibilities, can be applied to working with two people. As we have mentioned before, while the world's limitations and possibilities are universal, the particular way we react and respond to them is unique. In couples, these patterns and responses appear in various ways. First, each person will have their own beliefs; second, the couple as a unit will have developed their own values and beliefs as a duo. Again, the process of therapy is to explore their contradictory responses to the limitations and uncertainties.

The couple

Edward was 42 and June 36 years old. They had been married for eighteen years and now seemed to be on the verge of divorce. As soon as they arrived at the first session June began her story. However, before she could get properly started Edward interrupted her and quite vehemently, albeit in a low voice, contradicted her. I suggested that to begin with it might be easier for them both to be able to relate their stories and to express their feelings without interruption, and to use the therapist as the person to relate to. It was also important that they should each recount their stories while the other listened.

June started by saying that three years before she had accidentally discovered that Edward was in the midst of an affair with a mutual acquaintance. While Edward first denied and then defended himself, he finally admitted to the affair, but said that it was in the past and had ended some time ago. Despite this, June found she was unable to forgive Edward to the extent that since that time she had been unable to have a sexual relationship with him.

Edward's interpretation of the story was slightly different. He spoke flippantly of the affair and angrily about June's version and her ensuing behaviour. He said that he was still fond of her and he was worried about how the divorce would damage their 13-year-old son and 15-year-old daughter. Nevertheless, June's non-communication was driving him away. Divorce seemed a better option for all the family than staying together and pretending that nothing was wrong.

After listening, prompting and sometimes challenging their contradictions, I told them that while I would be happy to work with them, they would have to decide whether they felt that I was the best therapist for them. I then proposed that they ask me any questions they felt relevant. They wanted to know about my marital status and whether I had any children. As a matter of principle, I felt it was only right to disclose what was deemed pertinent to them, before the frame and the contract were agreed. Later we discussed my neutrality and other points regarding the frame. I explained that I would facilitate them to explore their own issues and through this process they would be able to obtain insight not only in terms of their own vulnerability but also to feel and acknowledge their partner's weakness, fears and aspirations. We agreed to have two sessions on a one-to-one basis seeing June and Edward separately, to be followed by one joint session. We would then repeat the pattern, making a total of seven sessions, after which we would agree a new module if necessary.

Edward arrived at his first session, keen and punctual. He was well dressed and appeared younger than his age. He had difficulty expressing himself in English, as it was not his first language, and I needed to prompt him regularly to tell his story. I was reminded how eloquent, open and to the point June had been during the first session. I could immediately see his reluctance to tell me his story fluidly, although it emerged that he felt that in order to be accepted by others he needed to express himself well. I tentatively constructed in my mind some of Edward's world view. I hypothesized that if he were prevented or not able to communicate he would feel worthless. Needless to say, I bracketed these thoughts.

It took Edward both of his one-to-one sessions to recount his story. Everything he had done in his life so far had been 'right'. He was brought up in a community with other children, his parents living close by, up until the age of 11, experiencing love and care from both of his parents and the community. He had excelled in sports and was also an academic achiever, being treated like a prince by most people. Out of the blue, when he was 11, an event occurred that changed his life. His father came to him one evening and very gently explained that he and Edward's mother were going to separate. Edward could not understand the 'whys' and 'wherefores', but he perceived it as something shameful. His greatest fear was that if others were to find out he would be ostracized by the community and his friends.

This incident was a turning point and although the separation was probably not the cause of his problems, it certainly was a pivot in terms of his consideration of what was important in his life – in other words, the formation of one of his intrinsic value systems.

Challenging Edward about what it meant to be ostracized, to feel excluded and what his feelings might be if I rejected him, were the initial kinds of questions. Several times he relived the moment when he had been told of his parents' impending separation, and the sense of abandonment when his parents finally divorced. Edward began to connect his suffering and his sense of loneliness not only to these initial events, but also to other situations that occurred later.

Following this, the probing began to centre around what Edward did in order to escape from re-experiencing the painful feelings of abandonment and loneliness. It was not difficult for him to realize and acknowledge that his behaviour pattern was characterized by the fear of revealing his shame which was that of being an outsider, or rather a person different to his peers. Experiencing this sense of shame would immediately make him relive this sense of desperation. It was no wonder therefore that Edward found himself increasingly unable to express himself and instead concentrated on sport, where physical prowess and not verbal or written communication was the only requirement. Likening these past events to the present possibility that June might leave him, Edward started to cry and talked about his fears of being abandoned again.

June unfolded her story easily. She was articulate and extremely skilful in venting her feelings. Her thoughts about divorce had been carefully considered. She felt humiliated by Edward, not only by his initial betrayal but also by the continuing lies, and thought that marriage without sexual contact was a complete farce. Even Edward's argument that his unfaithfulness had been a meaningless transgression could not placate her.

On prompting, June began to explore what it meant for her to be betrayed in her marriage, but then continued to speak of her sense of devastation and the ruination of her own family when her father had left when she was young. She had never been able to reconcile herself entirely with his leaving, and while still on speaking terms with him, the wound and the pain had still not healed. Late adolescence had been based around her need to find a fulfilling, lifelong relationship. In Edward, she believed she had found what she wanted and worked hard to keep the family together. She admitted that they had both struggled financially and emotionally to build up the family, and this had taken a good deal of effort and teamwork. The dedication to this made his betrayal even more harrowing, which was why she could not forgive him for what he had done.

She realized that Edward's betrayal was the reason that she was now uninterested in sex, even though she understood his need for affection and a sexual relationship. Previously they had enjoyed an excellent sex life and indeed spoke proudly of Edward's masculinity, calling him 'a good lover'. When I asked her what she thought Edward did about his libido, she just looked at me with sadness and did not answer.

Gradually June herself started to investigate her own assumptions about her desire for eternal faithfulness and loyalty, exploring from various angles how her value judgements affected these two qualities. June admitted that she had always enjoyed flirting, although she saw this as very different from the eighteen months of betrayal initiated by Edward. She became aware that there were similarities between her recent feelings of betrayal and sense of abandonment with those when her father left. There was a great sense of humiliation and belittlement. Further questions around how she escaped from these feelings revealed that by rejecting Edward physically, she was in fact belittling him. By punishing him, June had to some degree taken the upper hand. She was very much affected by this discovery and became quite melancholic. She began to rationalize her difficulty in initiating a physical relationship with Edward.

The two ensuing couple sessions that took place alternately between each individual session were marked by a conciliatory atmosphere. They were both working together on their issues and expressing their feelings through me and at the same time trying to understand each other's vulnerabilities. To enhance this process, June was asked to imagine that she was Edward and express what she thought Edward might say about his pain in coming to a decision. Edward was asked, too, to imagine that he was June. During the second couple session it became apparent that they both intended to give the marriage another try. After each session the mood was subdued, more forgiving and peaceable, even serene, but also sad.

We began to discuss our ending and considered the various alternatives. The choices were:

- to have another module of the mixed six sessions (without the first introductory one);
- to finish with the third couple session and for them to come to some sort of arrangement between themselves.

It transpired that the last session of the module was that of an agreement to try to keep the family together. Their physical relationship had begun to improve and Edward was able to express his love to June. We parted and agreed that if they needed any further support they could contact me.

Afterthought

Although June and Edward's therapy may not be considered typical of couple therapy in that a reconciliation was achieved relatively painlessly and in a short period of time, it is indeed a rewarding story. Obviously, working with couples may take a longer time span, whether in terms of the amount of weeks each module incorporates or the amount of modules required.

It had been nine months since Edward and June completed their therapy and in order to get their permission for inclusion in this book, it was necessary to contact them. Edward answered the phone and immediately recognized my voice. He was friendly and pleasant, and discussed the children, happily saying that everyone was doing well. He certainly had no doubts about being included in the book, but felt it necessary to speak to June. Within an hour Edward rang back confirming that both of them would be delighted to co-operate.

As with all the other cases, this one demonstrates how their issues still centre around the existential givens as shown on the wheel. In the case of Edward and June, we have two people with their individual belief systems which have a profound effect on the way they communicate and understand each other as a couple.

In Edward's case his fear of uncertainty and sense of shame was connected to his loss of security by the dissolution of his family. His rigid value system was so connected with his family and sense of self that his shame caused him to believe he was a worthless, disconnected individual. In order to avoid the shame, he concealed the 'evidence' from others. To survive in the long term he developed a strategy of withdrawing from anything that required verbal communication and focused instead on physical activity. In this respect he was very successful, but the price he paid was in losing real communication with others, particularly his wife. Edward's world view was therefore connected with security, interpersonal relationships, a value system and anxiety. Within these existential givens Edward had many possibilities from which to choose, the major one being to change his attitude towards his behaviour and value patterns. By exploring these givens, Edward was able to understand the effect that he had on other people and also to see and feel June's vulnerability. This in itself changed his attitude towards himself and towards June.

Sedimented values and behaviour patterns were also part of June, who had developed a very rigid belief about family loyalty. This belief was sacrosanct and any deviation caused her enormous distress. Her only defence was total physical withdrawal. She placed all the blame on others and through non-communication felt she was maintaining her dignity. Indeed, June became aware that through this behaviour she was able to maintain her superiority and avoid depression and loss of self-concept.

As soon as both realized and understood each other's vulnerability, they became more open and embarked on a firm endeavour of reconciliation.

In a way one could say that this case gives an impression of a straightforward and almost oversimplified study. Yet, in all respects it reflects the immense complications and diversities of human responses to the threat of uncertainty and the vicissitudes of existing in this world. Indeed, each person has his or her own way of dealing with and reacting to the whimsical uncertainties of the world. This case study shows how two different belief systems can block the flow of communication between two people. At the same time, however, it also demonstrates the universality of 'givens' to which we humans generically respond.

EDWARD'S COMMENTS

I knew that my marriage was in difficulties but wanted it to survive. I had strong feelings for my wife but felt guilty and lacked the ability to express my emotions. It took me a long time to realize that we needed outside help and even longer to gather the courage to approach a counsellor.

I found Freddie comfortable to be with, and even though it took me a while to begin to express myself I was pleased to have begun the process. The sessions were very useful both in helping me to express my feelings and realizing that it was necessary for me to do so with my wife. I recognized that I withdrew from situations where I felt inadequate but that this only increased the problem. It also helped me to see the situation from my wife's point of view and as a result to start the process of reconciliation.

As a result of the sessions, although of fairly short duration, I feel I have changed quite significantly. I am opening up much more to people and am aware of the difference in their response to me.

JUNE'S COMMENTS

The point at which Edward and I came to Freddie was in itself an important step. I had been very hurt and angry by the discovery of the affair and needed to understand what this meant for Edward and to see if our marriage could survive. This was extremely difficult. Edward seemed unwilling to explore what had led to the affair. He seemed unwilling to discuss anything at all. He still wanted a physical relationship with me but I felt increasingly frustrated and my sense of hurt and anger intensified. We arrived at a point where the subject could no longer be raised, yet nothing had been resolved. I began to withdraw physically and emotionally from Edward.

It became an issue on my part that if the marriage was to have any chance of surviving we needed to seek outside help. Edward was extremely reluctant to take this step but when it became increasingly apparent that I was seriously considering a separation he initiated our meeting with Freddie.

For me this was significant. Although I was uncertain what the outcome might be I was acutely aware that for Edward to discuss his feelings would be very difficult. The fact that he was willing to do so came as something of a relief as I felt we were both locked into a situation we did not have the tools to deal with.

Our individual and combined meetings with Freddie were extremely helpful. On my part I began to realize that the break up of my parent's marriage when I was very young and my difficulty in coming to terms with this had made it vital to me that my own marriage should 'succeed'. My parents had both had affairs that had made me feel ashamed and guilty. Fidelity in my own marriage was essential. As Edward, too, had been very hurt when his parents broke up I thought fidelity was equally important to him. I trusted him implicitly in this and the devastation I felt was total.

From Edward's first meeting with Freddie there was a perceptible change. He began tentatively to discuss aspects of our relationship. In turn I tried to be less rigid and judgemental. We were able to move on.

Today we are still rebuilding. There are times when I feel angry and hurt. There are areas where Edward has undoubtedly felt resentment at my behaviour. But we have turned a corner. Edward has become far more open, not only with me but with other people in general. It is as if he feels it safer to let go. We have a far better forum for discussing problems. There has been a change in the balance of our relationship.

9

'CONNECTEDNESS'

We have described the significance of the relationship between therapist and client in previous chapters and what emerges in the process of therapy is how the therapist's own unresolved issues may well impede the process. This means that therapists have to be continually aware of the possibility that a client may bring up an old or even a new issue that may touch on them. Since the concept of our 'self' is always changing, it is impossible to have reached a full understanding of ourselves. Therefore therapy is a learning process for the therapist as well as the client. Obviously, if the issue is too great for the therapist and he or she is unable to bracket, then this must be further examined either in supervision or with the therapist's therapist.

This is a continual process, for every client will have an issue which will connect to some degree with that of the therapist. Sometimes it is important for this to be bracketed but at other times this is how the therapist identifies with the client's world, how he or she can 'tune in' to the client's pain and joy. Indeed, without this connectedness, therapists could not comprehend the clients' world view and fully understand their process of living. It is as if each human being comprises the seed of each other person's being and it is through this experience that clients gain their insight.

ECSTASY AND THE FEAR OF DEATH: MARK

This is what occurred in the case of Mark, where the sudden revelation that he was mortal, that he was going to die, was too much for him to cope with. Death, or anxiety about death, is one of the existential givens and as such was also an important issue for the therapist. Generally speaking, people force these anxieties to the back of the mind until something triggers the thoughts to come to the surface. These triggers can include the death or illness of someone else, becoming sick oneself, or activities such as flying, driving, getting stuck in lifts, and so on.

Mark was 26 years old, single and still living at home, with a close relationship to both parents. He enjoyed playing golf, had a steady job as a manager in a paint factory and felt it was time for him to settle down, get married and have children.

Presenting problem

Mark was referred by an ex-client, in quite a state of agitation. He had been experiencing dizzy spells and severe anxiety attacks since taking the drug Ecstasy – waking up in the middle of the night with heart palpitations, sweating and having nightmares of being flung across rooms. He was no longer going out with friends and was taking time off work. His parents had taken him to see various doctors. He had had blood tests to see whether the paint fumes had physically affected him, had psychiatric tests and been given relaxation exercises to help him through the attacks. Essentially, none of these tactics had had much effect.

Mark was not at all sure what therapy might be able to offer him. He had been referred by a friend who had assured him that it would help. His main concern was to get over his panic attacks and to start a life again. We agreed to twelve weeks, with the review sessions and a possible further module.

The story

Several months before presenting himself for therapy, Mark had started socializing with a crowd of people who until that point had only been on the periphery of his social scene. At weekends they would go to Ecstasy parties and for the first couple of months he had thoroughly enjoyed the experience. This surprised him because until then he had been totally against drugs and although he drank the occasional beer, he had never drunk to excess. He strongly felt that his dizziness and palpitations were from the effects of taking Ecstasy, even though doctors had assured him that this was extremely unlikely.

The therapy

In the first session, it quickly emerged that Mark had stopped going to these parties after a weekend when a girl who had also taken the drug was dancing close to him and had suddenly collapsed on the floor and died. Immediately I had a strong image that the death of this girl and his subsequent anxiety attacks were somehow linked. Knowing that it was much more important for Mark to make this association, I bracketed the idea and instead began to explore with him his life and his sense of being.

A few months before he had started going to these parties, Mark had broken off an engagement to get married. He said that one of his concerns was that he had always thought he would be married by the age of 28 and now this was looking more and more remote. He had also changed jobs and was now in a more responsible, managerial position which is what he felt he needed to start 'growing up'. Around this time, too, he decided to stop being the child at home and helped his parents out with the housework such as tidying his room, mowing the lawn and generally taking a more active role. He wanted this responsibility, but it was also alien to him.

Moving on to how Mark felt when he took Ecstasy, he said it was 'fantastic', he felt loose and free, able to talk and to be whoever he wanted. He did not have to be in any responsible role. He could escape into another world where he did not have to address his fears about being alone and unmarried. He was very quick to add that this was the first time in his life that he had done anything like this. Before, he had always been 'good' and was very much against taking drugs. Ironically it was the 'escape' itself that confronted him with his own worst fear – that of dying. This abrupt confrontation with reality shook him literally to the core. A couple of weeks later he began to experience anxiety attacks. However, his rationalization was that the cause was the drug and he had been a 'bad boy' to partake.

Initially, Mark found it difficult even to talk about death. His first encounter had been when he was 10 years old; his grandfather, to whom he had been very close, had died. He remembered not being allowed to go the funeral, but that was all. This brought up a strong memory for me, when watching a close friend of the family, a woman who had spent many patient moments indulging my fantasies as a small girl, suffer through a wasting cancerous death. I, too, at the age of 12 had not been allowed to visit her in hospital or go to her funeral. I remember a morbid sense of curiosity about her illness and death which was both frightening in the sense of my own mortality and fascinating in how the body can crumble and waste away. Although this was an issue that I had discussed in my own therapy, the image was still very strong, especially since there remains a great sense of anxiety and uncertainty surrounding my own death and that of loved ones.

It was with this bracketed image in mind that I set about trying to explore with Mark his own fears around death and how using the drug

Ecstasy had in some way been an escape from the realities of life, from the responsibilities he had taken on and from the fears of being alone. In fact, as Mark started talking about what it felt like to be out of control when he had his anxiety attacks, his sense of panic was evident. He didn't want to be bad, he did not want to spend his life alone. He enjoyed the security of his parents' love and their life style and had been cushioned from taking the plunge into life's uncertainties; yet these were now emerging and he was frightened. The panic attacks were when he felt his worse. Mark was sure that he was going to die. He felt so out of control and so alone. Even his parents could not alleviate his fears and he so much wanted to be the good son.

The picture was emerging of a jumbled-up sense of his fear of dying, his fear of being out of control and of being alone, as well as a very clear sense of what he should be doing with his life in order to gain what he thought his parents would respect. The 'givens' on the wheel had begun to come to life.

Value system

Mark had always been good. He had never been particularly badly behaved at school and although he had concentrated on the sporting side of school life, ignoring his academic side which had not been in tune with his parents' wishes, he was pleased with the job he was now doing. In recent months he had decided to become more responsible, so rather than leaving his room untidy, or ignoring the fact that the lawn needed to be mowed, he began to do these jobs to please his parents.

He compared his values to those of his parents, believing that drugs, smoking and drinking to excess were certain ways to kill oneself. In fact he could not remember ever disobeying them, apart from a few small incidents at school. He had always had a chatty relationship with his mother, and although he had felt estranged from his father during his adolescence, he put this down to a stage in his life which had now been rectified. The picture Mark painted was of a happy childhood. His parents were happily married. They both worked hard in the professions and it was important for Mark to live a life that slotted in with this picture. In other words, he too wanted a happy marriage with someone he could share and talk about things that mattered to them both.

These family values contrasted sharply with his experience of taking Ecstasy. He was now the bad boy and his parents had been proved right. Ecstasy must have damaged his brain. It occurred to me as I was listening to how he needed to be good to maintain his parents' approval that coming to see me was a necessary juncture in returning to his obedient state. He certainly had his parents' blessing and had even discussed with them the issues we had been talking about. In addition, he was also a model client. He was very punctual and at the only session to which he arrived a few minutes late, due to unforeseen traffic conditions, he was most apologetic. What would happen if he was disobedient? Mark's answer was that something terrible would happen, such as dying through taking Ecstasy.

Coping strategies

Control of his life and destiny featured strongly in Mark's story. He would plan and imagine anything that he was about to embark on, whether it was work or pleasure related. So for instance, he was going on a weekend golfing jaunt with his father and a couple of close friends. He had been to the golf course previously and had even stayed in the same house. Several days before the planned trip, he began a process of running the two days' events through his head. He felt safe doing this. He was going with people that were safe and known and he could even safely anticipate the entire weekend. This added to his excitement and the knowledge that he was going to enjoy the weekend, which indeed he did.

Shopping was another example. If Mark knew exactly what he was going to buy, he had no problems entering shopping malls. He could anticipate the event a week in advance, get excited about the prospect and be extremely happy about his purchase. However, going to a shopping centre with only a vague idea immediately brought on a dizzy spell. His life plan was one of controlling events, by anticipating their outcome. Even the taking of Ecstasy, after the first weekend, was initially predictable – he knew that he would feel good and have a good time until, of course, the unpredictable occurred and someone died.

Challenging Mark to look at what it meant when he was not safe was taken slowly. When we first started talking about it, he would complain of feeling dizzy which he likened to various occasions. For instance, at work, if the phone rang as he was trying to complete something else, he would begin to feel stressed and start getting dizzy. He also described a scene when he ventured out with some friends and just as he was beginning to enjoy himself, he started to think about how he should not be enjoying himself. He started to get dizzy and so left. Every day was becoming uncertain and he began to lose confidence in everything he did. He took leave of absence from his new job because he felt that the work was making him too stressed and he stopped going out unless it was with old friends. In other words anxiety, loss of control, lack of confidence and certain interrelationships were all connected.

What was it that made Mark even venture into the unknown in the first place? His answer was that at some level he wanted excitement, he wanted to be 'naughty'. He had taken on a new, more responsible job, he thought it was time he grew up, and yet at the same time he wanted something different, something exciting. However, it was this venturing out that also made him rapidly retreat. The paradox was occurring. In order not to experience the anxiety of growing up, the possibility that he might not find a partner and would have to face adulthood and impending death on his own, Mark decided to escape into the fantasy of drugs. Yet it was this action that made him confront these very same fears, so Mark withdrew to the safety of his family, which was known and predictable. But unfortunately, this time, he could not escape far enough, and instead of feeling safe and secure, he was reminded continually of his mortality through his anxiety attacks.

Talking about his fear of the unpredictable, Mark realized that he did also enjoy being with one of his male friends, precisely because he was unpredictable. Indeed this friend liked going out with Mark because he felt that he was often spontaneous, deciding to change what they had planned to do on the spur of the moment. So another picture was being painted, in direct contrast to his need for a predictable and reliable outcome.

Anxiety

When Mark first started talking about his anxiety attacks, his only concern was his strong desire to get rid of them. He did not want to think about what his thoughts and feelings might be when he woke up in the midst of his panic. Eventually I asked him what he thought he might be avoiding by not wanting to think about what was happening to him. After a long silence, he said that he was very scared that he might die. It also emerged that a few years before he had had a minor version of his panic, when he had been flying through a storm and had been convinced that his end was nigh. He was also a careful driver, rarely exceeding the speed limit, and would never drive if he had been drinking.

Caution, control and the panic attacks themselves were all coping mechanisms for Mark, that he did not have to face anything associated with the idea of death or oblivion.

Instead of avoiding his anxiety attacks, in the third session I asked Mark to live through them. This meant looking at his thoughts and his feelings as they were happening. In the following session, Mark described how darkness was the word that sprang to mind. Challenging him to go further, he said he was frightened of being out of control because there was nothing at the end of it. He also described a shadowy dream where something black was being thrown at him and he kept having to duck to avoid it. Asking Mark to think of himself as the black object, he paused and said it was like having death flung in his face, but he would do anything to avoid it. He had finally made the connection himself. He had achieved his insight.

The first thing that Mark stated on his arrival at the fifth session was that he was not going to die – well, anyway, not while he was having one of his panic attacks. The attacks themselves began to get shorter, finally ceasing around the seventh session. Mark returned to work and although he occasionally felt dizzy when he felt overloaded, he would stay with his sense of anxiety. Instead of trying to avoid his anxieties, he was now acknowledging them as part of himself, rather than something alien to his sense of being.

Safety

Mark felt safe within the frame that we set up, which was the twelve weeks, plus the follow-up sessions, with the option of a further module. He had already decided before completing the first twelve weeks that he wished to continue. He was creating his own safety within the boundaries of the contract. By predicting how he would continue, he was again, to a certain extent, trying to gain control of his outcome.

This was a dilemma for me. I could see that Mark needed more time to gain further insights into his need for control against his anxieties, yet at the same time the original contract was providing his safety. In other words, he was dismissing, or rather ignoring the process of ending. Trying to challenge him to examine the imminent end revealed that he felt he had learned so much about himself, he no longer had the panic attacks, so would be quite content to finish. After the two follow-up sessions, he said he wished to continue because he was experiencing and enjoying a new way of thinking. In hindsight, I might contemplate the idea that his compliments were flattering, so rather than challenging Mark regarding his feelings about ending, we agreed to a second module.

Interpersonal relationship

Mark's relationship to both his parents was very important. He was proud of the fact that his Dad was the only father that came along and blended in with his friends when playing golf. He would also spend time chatting with his mother. He was not afraid of expressing his care and love for other people, and was easily moved to tears. This was also true of our relationship.

Throughout I had to restrain myself from making interpretations, especially around his avoidance of thinking about death. I knew it was much more beneficial for Mark to realize this insight himself. There was certainly no 'eureka' when he made the link, for it was a gradual process of piecing together various aspects of his anxieties, before he began to consider the impact of dying, his need to control these thoughts and his fears of being alone.

The question mark still remains in my mind as to how much our relationship was related to his need to control against his immediate fear of dying. As his anxiety attacks decreased, his sense of urgency about confronting these major issues also diminished. He terminated therapy when he found the woman whom he felt would be his life partner. Was she a substitute for his fears?

Time and temporality

Mark's need to stay in control manifested itself in imagining future events. That is, he gained his safety by using the future as a crutch. Living in the present represented uncertainty and anxiety, although ultimately it was by staying in the present that he managed to eliminate his anxiety attacks. At the end of the first module, Mark was certain that he wanted a second one. We discussed this in terms of his need to feel secure. Although there were times when he found it hard work, I had become part of his internal dialogue and in that sense ending was too severe.

Self-concept

The onset of Mark's own confrontation with mortality had a profound effect on his self-concept. He thought he would never be able to live a normal life again. This thought in itself would literally send him into a spin. His realization of his own mortality as one of the human limitations threw Mark into a lonely, isolated place, without self-concept and where he felt disconnected from what he considered his normal position. He had become aware that as soon as his self-concept was threatened, he needed to defend himself by returning to this 'place'. The whole spiral of feelings and thoughts was such an uncomfortable experience that even the panic attacks and falling into oblivion were better then returning to the experience of nothingness. Yet, the irony was that the anxiety attacks themselves created fear of further panic attacks, creating a vicious spiral of fear of fears.

However, it must be noted that the anxiety attacks themselves were not considered a cause of any problem but were used as a metaphor to allow Mark to explore his own attitude towards the existential 'givens'. Therefore as therapy progressed, Mark began to understand how he avoided confronting his fears of being alone, his sense of being out of control in not achieving his plans, and how these affected his self-esteem. He had failed himself and it was this sense of failure that was partly related to his anxieties. As he became more aware of his anxieties, his self-concept changed. He began to socialize with his friends again and met a woman whom he strongly felt was his future partner. He could talk to her about his anxieties. He began to have fun and they planned to move in together with the intention of getting married.

Free will

Although Mark's presenting problem, his anxiety attacks, was almost completely eliminated well before the end of the first module, he felt that he wanted to continue for another twelve weeks. He said he was enjoying the process so much and for the first time he was thinking about himself from a different perspective.

Yet after the third session of the second module, he rang to say that he did not want to continue. We agreed on one last ending session. Essentially Mark felt that now that he had met someone with whom he wanted to share his life, he also wanted to share his thoughts and feelings with her. He had learned so much from being in therapy and he wanted to continue the process himself. He understood now that life was a roller coaster and although there would be difficult times ahead, but he felt that he could cope and wanted to prove that he could. He had exercised his free will.

DISCUSSION

This case exemplified the significance of the therapist connecting with the client. Through this inter-subjective mode of 'being' with the client, Mark was facilitated to challenge his behaviour patterns, comprehend his world view, and to experience all these as a process of living. Thus Mark was able to bring new insights into his day-to-day experiences and to shift his perceptions to allow for the uncertainties of living. Many believe that the therapist's own issues may be detrimental to the therapy. Contrary to this view, Mark's case has demonstrated that the themes were catalytic for the therapist to connect, understand and tune into the client's perceptual mind. Admittedly, this case highlighted the importance of bracketing my own assumptions about anxiety, control, death and loneliness. But the bracketing of these issues served to consider interventions that would serve my own purposes and to consider what was in the client's interest, as well as facilitating my tuning into the client's pain.

Mark's own values and beliefs around what constituted being a good person had an impact on his anxieties about being in control. Not living up to his values of being a good person meant that he was a bad person and out of control. This manifested itself physically in his dizzy spells and anxiety attacks, so until he could become less rigid about his beliefs around 'good' and 'bad', 'being in control' and 'out of control', he was stuck in a merry-go-round of his own choosing. By exercising a different perspective, Mark was able to be less rigid and therefore more able to understand and accept his anxieties.

Issues around death have implications for everyone and this, of course, includes me as a therapist. Many times, I had to search hard to understand how I, too, avoided this confrontation and perhaps by allowing Mark to go forward to a second module was a way for both him and me to avoid the inevitable ending.

This case also demonstrates how the process of 'becoming' is continual and that there is no such thing as a completely successful therapy. Mark walked out 'cured' of his anxiety attacks and ready to face life and responsibilities with a new partner and a changed concept of 'self'. He was happy with his progress, had learnt new ways of addressing himself and was also aware that new and old issues may emerge and re-emerge. Yet he has also gained trust that he will be able to address these issues on his own. For my part it must be added that it was also a learning process that reinforced my belief of my changed and forever changing perception as a human being and a therapist.

10

THE TYRANNY OF HIGH MORALITY

THE DOUBLE OUTSIDER: JAMES

The most honourable and precious of human values, if over-emphasized, can wreck people's lives. Exaggerated efforts to be loyal, selfless, to live in harmony and to help people may turn into a disastrous human enterprise. James exemplified these characteristics and had to pay a high price for his rigid sedimentations.

James was a university lecturer in psychotherapy. He was 40 years old and was on six months' sick leave because of his depression. He had a pleasant appearance, was tall and spoke in a deliberate manner – very modest but always to the point. He lived with a friend in a provincial town.

Presenting problem

James suffered, in his words, from being 'purposeless and devoid of hope and meaning'. He had been in therapy for a long time and had a great deal of experience of being both a client and a therapist.

The story

The child of a working-class family, James was forced by his very puritanical parents to conform with their strict values and moral principles. He had a particularly close relationship with his mother, whom he put on such a high pedestal that he could not even contemplate challenging her views or orders. At a very early age he was already aware that his feelings and emotions were somewhat in contradiction with those values which he had learned were sacrosanct.

At the age of 15 he fell in love with one of his male friends. Nothing developed beyond his romantic feelings, but as a result of the experience he was left with all his emotions entombed within himself. At 19 he had his first real homosexual relationship. During his high-school years James was driven by a massive ambition to extricate himself from whatever his 'working-class' background signified for him. He put all his efforts into his studies and was accepted at university with ease. University was an egression for James, which introduced him to people with diverse backgrounds and values. He enjoyed his studies and his years there were a period for him of lively intellectual debates, pleasure in reading and studies, together with an opportunity to forge lasting friendships. Following his graduation, James decided to stay within the academic sphere by teaching and lecturing.

After fifteen years of teaching, lecturing and writing, James found himself in an untenable position with one of his students. He lost his temper, which resulted in disciplinary action. As a consequence of this he became depressed and decided to ask for sick leave. James had two significant relationships in all that time. Adam was the first, with whom the relationship lasted twelve years. Adam came from a similar background to James, but educationally he remained far behind him. Nevertheless, Adam was a clever and 'streetwise' person, who was able to attract and entertain people from all circles.

James and Adam experienced some very pleasant and idyllic times together. Yet there were great gaps in their relationship. James was serious, contemplative, and self-reflective, while Adam was a flippant, pleasure-seeking and materialistic person. Towards the end of their relationship Adam stayed away on many nights. James then found out that Adam was involved with someone else. It was finally Adam who broke off the relationship and left James for the other man. This caused James great pain and he did not recover for some time.

Some years later James met Stewart. The relationship between them developed in the same vein as it had with Adam. Stewart had left school at an early age. He had developed good social skills, which came easily to him because of his good looks. Stewart and James stayed together for some years, but Stewart was unfaithful and left James. Again, James was left alone and felt abandoned.

After many months James accidentally met Adam again. He found him in a dire state; he had contracted an incurable disease, was penniless and lived in miserable conditions. James could not but take pity on him and 'rescue' him. He took him home and nursed him. At the time of the therapy they were still together.

The therapy

When James arrived for his first session, without prompting he began to tell me his story and present problems. His voice was quiet and he told his tale lucidly and concisely. He chose to tell only that part of his life which was relevant to his issues in therapy. Already at this stage of the session I pointed out certain discrepancies and contradictions in James' world view. He took this very seriously and started to explore his issues in a very open-minded manner. I told him that the purpose of the first visit was only to acquaint ourselves with one another and to see if we could work together. I urged him to ask any questions that he felt were important or relevant to him. In return, I described how I envisaged our co-operation and framework. I stated categorically that I would work with him, but it depended on him whether he wanted to enter into this commitment. I asked him not to make any premature decisions; indeed he could go home and consider it.

Despite this we agreed there and then to twelve sessions, plus two review sessions, on a once a week, one-hourly basis. I also spoke of the possibility of another module, should he feel it necessary after the termination of the first.

Value system

We still had time within this first session to revert to his story and I prompted James to explore some of his assumptions. He mentioned that as a result of his previous therapy he had found solace and quietude in his loneliness. He found extreme pleasure in solitary sailing. He had decided to withdraw from social activities and to remain alone. He also spoke of his relationship with Adam that was based purely on his (James') guilt and compulsion to help him, devoid of any real sexual or other relations. At the end of the session James had reflected on his own assumptions:

- that he had to be always and totally loyal to one partner for the rest of his days;
- that loneliness implied a solitary state, which for him was always a positive attribute.

When I had time to reflect and look at my notes on this first session, I knew that I would have trouble with my own issues concerning this client. I realized how impressed I was with his way of relating his story and his capacity for self-reflection. I knew that I liked him and could easily become highjacked by my desire to help him quickly. I also knew how unproductive this could prove for James' therapy. In addition I realized that for the sake of the therapy I had to bracket all my emotions and perceived ideas in the session so as not to make premature and biased interventions.

In subsequent sessions James brought up the subject of his relationship with his mother. He related an early incident when she had had an angry outburst at James, who apparently had committed some 'misdemeanour'. In spite of the fact that he had not felt guilty, he had felt the need to withhold his anger and remain silent. When I urged him to hypothesize what would have happened if he had retaliated, James recounted many incidents when his mother had disapproved of him. Her emotionally powerful counterblows, in turn, meant the possibility of dishonour and total separation for James. This immense loss was soon connected with similar losses, one of them being Stewart's departure. This is what James wrote in his commentary:

> Seven months prior to commencing therapy, my partner, Stewart, left me for someone else. It still felt as if it were yesterday. The emptiness and devastation were almost unbearable. Somewhat to my surprise I felt no anger towards Stewart. For some years I had been aware that my tiredness and lack of vitality acted as a brake in our relationship yet I felt powerless to do anything about it. I attributed my feeling of tiredness to age and, to some extent, a heavy workload. Stewart and I also ceased to enjoy a physically intimate relationship two years previously and this left me feeling undesired and valued only for the kind of love that a good older brother might supply.

We pursued this line of argument, and James became aware of a deep fear of rejection that would bring him pain, loneliness, isolation, loss of self-concept and total dissociation from the world. This led to the subject of sexuality. The struggle within himself arose because of his conflict in his mind between his sexual propensities and his orthodox value judgement. James' natural tendency towards his own sex threw him, thus, into a permanent belief of being an outsider.

From all these sessions James was able to extrapolate his very rigid value sedimentations: putting such an exaggerated positive value on loyalty, harmony and sexual conformity.

Coping strategies

To remain 'inside' (in other words not an outsider) James had to avoid all conflicts, because harmony became a sacrosanct value for him. So, in order for him to remain a person with some modicum of self-concept he had put his mother on a pedestal and kept harmony. In James' view, if he allowed himself to vent his anger, this would have become a selfish act. He would be 'acting in his own interests' and it would cause dissension. Similarly, he allowed Stewart to be unfaithful to him and he, James, knew that he was not a suitable partner for him. Yet he remained with him until Stewart left him. Thus, James realized in the therapy that for the sake of loyalty and harmony he needed to sacrifice his own needs.

James' coping strategy was exemplified further in a session when he pursued this topic and explored how this theme related to his relationship with Adam. He had already mentioned in previous sessions that he was angry at Adam and at himself for keeping Adam in his house in spite of the lack of a proper interpersonal relationship. I prompted James to examine this connection from all angles; I asked him to delve into both the positive and negative aspects of their relationship. While James found many beautiful and exhilarating moments in his previous partnership with Adam, he found the present situation irritating and soul destroying. There was not a single subject that they had in common and Adam's total lack of interest in James' intellectual activities was painful to bear. Yet he stayed with Adam. This is how James saw his relationship with Adam:

> Shortly before I began my psychotherapy with Freddie a further sadness had intensified. For some years my first partner, Adam, had known he had a terminal illness. Adam and I had lived together throughout the 1970s. He no longer had a home of his own and was living in temporary accommodation. His health was deteriorating rapidly. Our friendship still meant a great deal to both of us and I invited him to move into my house so that he could be looked after. Shortly after he moved in he had a serious attack of pneumonia but recovered to a reasonably stable state of health after about a month. Living under the same roof as Adam after a separation of sixteen years was not always easy. The differences between us that had led to our separation many years earlier had not, of course, evaporated. My own depression meant sometimes I was irritable and this contributed to the uneasy peace that existed between the two of us. At the beginning of the therapy I also felt that I had no choice but to continue to provide Adam with a home even though I wanted to move house in the future. It

> seemed to me that it would be unforgivably callous to even raise the issue of Adam needing to find a new home. This undoubtedly contributed to my feeling of being hopelessly stuck and without a future that I could shape or determine.

At about this time I invited James to explore what was happening in our therapeutic relationship. If he put his mother on a pedestal, and harmony was so vital for him, I challenged him as to whether he could express his anger towards me. 'No,' he replied, 'that would be a selfish act.' James explored and we both challenged what was selfishness and what was altruism.

From this point on, it did not take long for James to challenge his own behaviour patterns. What was it that made him repeatedly choose partners with a lower intellectual capacity? What made him so compulsive to rescue and help others? James soon became aware that he chose 'inferior partners' so as to be in a controlling and unchallenged position. From this standpoint he could maintain harmony: James had to do everything to maintain harmony and consensus. If that were broken and if, for example, he would get Adam to leave, his guilt would have thrown him into a state of loneliness and disconnectedness, which he had experienced so many times before. Therefore James had to do everything to avoid this state.

In time the structure of James' world view emerged clearly and with the existential structural view it could be defined in the following form.

Safety

For James, the search for safety and security, as for all of us, was inherent in his world view. Yet, as has been described in previous chapters, each individual has his or her own personal strategy for achieving these. James found safety in harmony and dreaded dissension, for fear of losing his 'security'.

Interpersonal relationship

James's purpose in life was to establish a 'real' permanent relationship. He experienced difficulty in forming a relationship with someone his equal, afraid that he would experience dissension. For example, he realized that he had refused Abe's invitation, (see penultimate section of this chapter, under the heading 'Free will') because he was afraid of being ashamed, of his 'narrow experience, his emptiness' and of being, in his words, 'a double outsider'.

Time and temporality

The limitation of time in therapy played a vital role in the intensity of James' desire to achieve something. Indeed, his remark: 'I have had many therapies and this one must succeed, otherwise . . . ' exemplified this. On the other hand I had to bracket my wishes and each intervention of mine was driven by my overwhelming desire to help in the shortest possible time. The temporality of our existence and the insecurity that this produced outside and inside the therapy were the subjects of many sessions.

Value system and coping strategies

James challenged his rigid value system from the beginning of the therapy. His belief in loyalty and keeping a relationship going at all costs meant that he remained far too long in unsuitable relationships. He also felt that he had to be selfless to be somebody. To survive James had to use strategies that would maintain his self-concept; strategies that would keep him away from the concept of self that made him feel disconnected from others. One of his survival strategies, for example, was his sedimented behaviour pattern to strive to help people. This not only manifested itself in his relationships, but also in his choice of profession (helping others). To maintain harmony in all situations was another coping mechanism for James. Dissension meant rejection, which in turn meant depression – a depression that deprived him of his self-concept and all that accompanied it.

The four worlds

James' life centred on his private inner and natural world. This made his relation to the world somewhat unbalanced. He neglected his relationship with his social world and left untended his own spirituality.

Anxiety

Anxiety was present in all James' sedimented behaviour patterns. For instance, his compulsive withdrawal from any dissension was the result of his fear of rejection and abandonment, resulting in depression.

Self-concept

Self-concept was connected with all James' behaviour patterns. James was rescuing others, keeping harmony, withdrawing from society, all in order to elicit approval that would maintain his self-concept.

Free will

James had many choices within the limitations of the 'givens'. Some were beyond his scope, such as his financial situation, or his social background, but he could certainly change many of his attitudes toward them. Indeed, James confronted his basic belief system: he was able to challenge his assumption that loyalty must always be absolute and always good, that he must under all circumstances maintain harmony. He went as far as acting upon that, and asked Adam how he would feel if he had to move out. While the structure of James' world view emerged in a relatively short time, I had to be very careful not to use it as a technique in therapy, but to allow it to remain in the back of my mind. Nonetheless, I felt that it somehow served as an anchor in therapy to maintain the safe environment.

James arrived at his next session, in his words, 'without an agenda'. However, he wanted to relate his discussion with Adam. He managed to disclose to Adam that he would feel happier if they were to separate. To his greatest surprise Adam was not averse to this and said that he would be quite happy to move to a home nearer a hospital that he knew could cater for his needs. James was pleased with this insight and his courage, and we celebrated the event.

James casually mentioned that an old acquaintance of his, Abe, had invited him to dinner in London. He refused to go because it would have been too much effort. He spoke of Abe as a very respected literary individual who was known as a raconteur, author and producer. James liked him and held him in high esteem. I challenged James with a remark that, 'You like him, he holds you in esteem and yet you chose not to accept the opportunity to see him again.'

James felt that if he accepted the invitation he would have to match Abe's intellectual capacity, which would have been too stressful for him. This was inconsistent, I pointed out, with the fact that Adam (who in James' perception was intellectually inferior) was also invited. Consequently, James challenged his own motivation for refusing the invitation. He realized that he feared the encounter with Abe because he would have had to expose some aspects of himself that he was ashamed of. In fact, James became aware of how much he felt inferior to Abe, whose rejection would push James into his familiar depression.

This brought James to conclude that his motivation to choose 'inferior' partners was his desire for superiority, where he would feel safe. I challenged his assumption of Abe's greater intelligence and asked him whether he could detect any vulnerability in his character.

Following this discussion, James told me that he was invited to an alumni gathering of his university colleagues. He spoke of his reluctance to accept the invitation, due to the effort that this would involve, and we related this to the issue regarding himself and Abe. Indeed, James took the opportunity to challenge his sedimentation about his feelings of inferiority. This sentiment was also connected with his necessity to please others and with his fundamental belief that the slightest disagreement would involve a fear of dissension and disharmony. In fact, all these sedimentations manifested themselves not only regarding Abe and others but also in our therapeutic situation.

More recently, James brought up his issue of perfection and how this prevented him, or made it difficult for him, to write articles and books. In the process of these dialectics I challenged him to explore all the positive and negative aspects of the possibility of putting into words his therapy. As a result of this the remaining sessions were spent on just this topic.

DISCUSSION

James, due to his life experiences and his sensitivity, was able to grasp in a very short time the way he existed in the world: the sedimentations, value and behavioural rigidities that together underpinned his world view. The moment he became aware of the process of the therapy in illuminating his world view, my work consisted of nothing more than to 'be' with him and to facilitate him to explore phenomenologically the contradictions and discrepancies in his perceptions. In my relationship with James I needed to suspend all my biases, my agenda and especially the structure expressed on the wheel. Indeed, our interventions must never become a 'technique'. It was necessary not to employ a method or a technique that could impede the therapy. This in turn opened the door for James to make attitudinal and behavioural choices.

JAMES' COMMENTS

When I first began therapy with Freddie I was at an extremely low ebb. It seemed to me that the two major sources of happiness and satisfaction in my life had disappeared. In short my life had become purposeless, and devoid of hope and meaning.

Two events seemed to have brought me to this point, the first being the departure of my partner, Stewart, the pain of which has already been recounted above. The second major loss was what seemed like a complete collapse of my professional life. I had become exasperated with a student whom I felt was making excessive demands and I lost my temper. Although I had only raised my voice, the extent of the student's distress was such that the University, in its wisdom, chose to invoke a formal disciplinary procedure. This resulted in a written warning that I interpreted as a devastating verdict on an otherwise unblemished career going back twenty-seven years. Not only did I feel overwhelmed by shame and embarrassment but it also felt as if I had lost forever the stimulation and fascination my work provided. Ironically, I was regarded as somewhat 'laid back' and urbane by many of my colleagues and, prior to this one incident, students assessed my approach in tutorials as supportive and patient. Inside, however, I knew these descriptions to be roles or masks I adopted in order to appear 'professional'. My real feelings often included anxiety and panic. The anxiety was about doing 'well enough' to satisfy the stringent appraisals which lecturers were subject to. The panic arose from the continual dread that I would not have work completed by the increasingly demanding deadlines. The rapidly growing administrative and research demands that characterized life in British universities during the 1990s also contributed to my feeling of insecurity and inadequacy.

So when I first arrived on Freddie's doorstep I felt as if the two most precious things in my life had been taken away from me. Worse still was the feeling that nothing would replace the void left inside me. I also felt I had committed my life to the care of an old friend and yet I had profoundly ambivalent feelings about the consequences of this. In short I felt empty and powerless to change my life.

During my first meeting with Freddie I was impressed by the way in which my life experiences and beliefs were valued. At the same time I gradually became aware of the gentle way in which some of my beliefs and values were questioned. This was well illustrated in the way the concept of loyalty was dealt with. In the early sessions I felt that I had an inescapable commitment to

Adam. I was 'my brother's keeper' was a belief I had always treasured. In practice I believed this meant that it was my duty to share my home with Adam and care for him without help and for an indefinite period of time. I was only dimly aware of the personal cost this commitment entailed. I knew that I was unhappy about the magnitude of what I had undertaken but I kept telling myself that it would be inhumane to indicate that I had separate and incompatible needs. Adam's need for a home and carer were to take precedence over everything else, including any needs I might have.

I knew at some level that I didn't want to share the rest of my life with Adam and yet to say this to him seemed unthinkable and would have resulted in unbearable guilt. Slowly Freddie challenged the absolute nature of this belief or value system. Without feeling the slightest sense of threat or attack I gradually allowed myself to see that I did indeed have needs and that these could not be submerged forever. More than this I came to see that my own happiness was intimately bound up with the need to take some control over my life. If I failed to do so I would continue to feel stuck and hopeless. The central structure of the challenging process seemed to involve an acknowledgement of the value of a belief, or of a value. It also involved the unravelling of the two polarities each value seems inevitably to imply. The process of change seemed to me to rely on an appraisal of the personal costs and consequences of an overly strict adherence to one pole of the belief or value system. In my case I was helped to see that loyalty and care for others was a virtue. The implied polarity for me would be selfishness and 'self before others'. Many of my difficulties seemed to be due to an excessive adherence to the 'others before self' end of the polarity. This led to denial of my needs and resentments inevitably followed. These became all the more acute because I also seemed to believe that 'loyal friends don't resent what they do for their friends'! This is almost like a feedback loop that continuously increases in error each time the loop is repeated.

With Freddie I also became aware of the central role of paradox. It became clear that values such as loyalty are inherently paradoxical (or is it that they can become paradoxical?) in the sense that they imply positive and valuable ways of being, yet, at the same time, they can become severely limiting when over-rigidly applied. I came to appreciate the paradoxical nature of my own value system and in consequence I felt able to be less 'demanding' of myself. I came, at last, to see than I owed it to myself to be honest about my needs and that if I wasn't there would be very little psychological future for me. Of course, with this realization the feeling of guilt lightened considerably.

After our second or third session a surprising event occurred. I finally summoned up the courage to tell Adam that I could not undertake to provide a home for him indefinitely and that I might in the future want to move to another part of the country. His response came as an enormous relief. He said that he, too, thought that separate homes would be good for both of us and he had already started the process of seeking one through a housing association! This was not what I expected but I was enormously relieved to discover that my belief about how he would react to my having separate needs was quite erroneous. This clearly validated the idea that I had grossly exaggerated his 'neediness' in my own mind. I could see that it was possible to be a loyal friend and be true to my own needs. The one did not necessarily negate, or exclude, the other.

A little later on in therapy I became aware of the way I had exaggerated the need for harmony in my life. Conflict and argument had always been an area of difficulty for me. In my personal relationship I felt disharmony would inevitably lead to rupture of any bond I enjoyed with anyone I was close to. I can recall from childhood numerous occasions in which arguments between my parents, or between them and either myself, my brother or sister, would be linked with threats of desertion. There was a good deal of disharmony and it always made me feel alone. Worse still was the violence between my father and my older brother and my mother. This somehow left me feeling that the difference between oneself and those one loved was necessarily problematic and likely to lead to the ending of relationships.

Interestingly this feeling only seemed to apply to loved ones. At school, and later at university, I experienced no such inhibitions when it came to expressing ideas forcibly and with conviction. It was with those that I loved that disharmony had to be avoided. When it came to seeking a partner I felt afraid of those with convictions that I might disagree with. Yet I had plenty of my own! I sought to establish close relationships with young men who had little or no formal education beyond the age of 15 or 16 and who, like me at a deep level, felt confused and bewildered by the complexity of life.

Only once was there an exception to this pattern. At university I formed a very close relationship with a fellow student a few years older than my self. He was someone who was deeply immersed in left-wing politics, serious music, art and literature. He had a profound influence on my thinking and was in many ways my mentor. This friend was a unique individual in my experience. He offered a new vision of the world and was extremely able in arguing the case for the brand of Marxism in which he passionately believed. Uniquely he also managed to debate issues in a spirit of friendship and comradeship. Somehow this made all the difference, and debate ceased to be a threat and became almost a pleasure. We enjoyed a very valuable relationship over two or three years but lost contact with one another when we left university.

It was Freddie who pointed out the link between my wish to avoid disharmony and my choice of partners. I remember one session in which Freddie pointed out that there is a profound value in disharmony. The training in Marxism I had received during university days allowed me to appreciate this at an intellectual level. I was quite happy with the idea of the dialectical method but failed to apply this to my own personal life. It was as if I carried a child's fear of argument and discord into adulthood. At an emotional level I just accepted that differences made me feel very uneasy and I avoided those who 'made' me feel this way. Both Adam and Stewart had little or no interest in politics, or contentious issues of any kind, so it was easy for me to feel free of the threat which discord implied. I also recall that one session focused on the ways I felt drawn to those who, in some sense, could be rescued.

Adam did not enjoy perfect health even when I first met him in 1970. When I discovered the nature of the illness he then immediately felt I would stay with him for a very long time. This was a very vivid memory and one that I have recalled many times over the years. Stewart was very young when we met and certainly had a 'little boy lost' look that I found irresistible. I suppose I always wanted to rescue him, too. I'm not sure what from exactly, but perhaps it was just from being lost.

Freddie remarked that even my political beliefs could, at one level, be interpreted as a wish to rescue the world! I didn't feel that he was pathologizing my beliefs because he acknowledged that this was only true at a certain level of abstraction. In fact, I remember laughing at the idea, or more precisely, at myself really. The importance of the pattern of rescuing behaviour did not escape me however. It formed the basis of a number of extremely valuable reflections. In the weeks that followed this insight I saw how in trying to 'save' others I had neglected my own needs. I remember when Freddie and I discussed this I said rescuing others seemed to be one end of the polarity and the other end seemed to be about selfishly pursuing one's own wants and needs. Freddie said that there was, of course, a certain value in the latter pole in that it was linked to preservation of self and survival. I could see the point he was making and recalled a phrase a former colleague of mine used. I said 'Ah, you mean healthy, narcissistic buoyancy.' We both laughed at that but the real significance of the shift of meaning was shared by us both, I think.

I have begun to envisage living in ways that I would be kinder to myself but less of a rescuing hero. I can see that it is no longer a case of 'either/or', but a question of getting the balance right. This continues to be a struggle, but at least now I know what the struggle is about and I have 'permission' to explore ways of resolving dilemmas that previously I would never have allowed myself to consider. I guess this struggle will continue throughout my life but I am indeed very grateful to be freed of the absolutist way of thinking I previously adhered to.

Throughout my therapy with Freddie I felt he offered me an open and honest relationship. There was no sense of a person hiding behind a professional facade. I felt we really engaged with each other and he felt able to share his view of the world. This was particularly important for me because part of the therapeutic work involved acknowledging the universality of the dilemmas I was confronting. I had got stuck in a particular set of rigid assumptions but the issues were not unique to me. There continues to be great comfort in knowing that questions like: 'what are the limits of friendship?' or 'how can I survive in an unsafe world?' pose dilemmas for all of us. Our own temporary and changing ways of responding to these dilemmas leave us more or less able to deal effectively with our lives. With Freddie's invaluable help I feel, for the time being at least, more able to live.

11

CONCLUSION

We hope that the case studies described in the last few chapters have clarified how we approach therapy from a time-limited existential angle. The particular way that we practise existential therapy has emerged from our direct work with clients, and as such changes continually. This is not to say that the existential and phenomenological philosophies and existing therapies have not given us a theoretical grounding, but in the final analysis it is the experiential work with clients and the nature of the relationship formed with them that has taken us forward in our thinking and practice. The outstanding feature for us is in how many ways the numerous similarities between the existential concerns of the clients manifest themselves.

Naturally, their stories, their life histories, their cultural and family heritage, their language, their personalities, etc. are all quite different. Yet in some way, beneath all these outer trappings, we find that generally people have similar responses to the existential 'givens' of existence. For instance, Sue and James both reacted strongly and rigidly to the necessity for an interpersonal relationship and to establish a safe environment. Sue experienced amidst her issues, because of her perceived physical appearance, a violent rejection from her peer group and her family. This required her to develop a strategy for survival.

On the other hand James felt that he was being rejected because of his ambiguous sexuality that in turn made his interpersonal relationships questionable. They both responded with a fixed sedimented value and behaviour pattern, yet both defended themselves in their particular, individual manner. To be valued and to be 'somebody', Sue believed that she had to develop her body to a certain standard. To this end she needed to have the best body and to take up the role of an entertainer – in her own words to be a 'performing monkey'. James' strategy for his survival was withdrawal and to restrict himself to a lonely existence.

The similarities we are talking about are based on the fact that humans have the inevitable propensity to respond to the various limitations of the world in remarkably analogous ways.

The case histories demonstrate, too, how the structure that we outline in the existential wheels corresponds with the limitations and possibilities highlighted by the clients themselves. There is a definite convergence around these 'givens' in clients' responses, such as their insecurities and inconsistencies of being in the world, how they struggle with their value and coping systems, how they form and deal with their sedimentations, self-concepts, anxieties and their possibilities.

So although on many levels the similarities converge around the general human concerns of just living in this world, there are also numerous differences that emerge from the case studies. Each client, each person, has a wealth of different attitudes and his or her own particular way of dealing with predicaments. Therefore in this respect there are no similarities between clients. As much as clients' issues converge around the macrocosm of the 'givens', they equally diverge in their behaviours and their attitudes toward these 'givens' within the microcosm.

In addition, the case studies show how all the segments or concepts of the wheels are interconnected. The structure is a learning implement for the therapist to understand how the 'givens' are part of the whole. Each section represents an area worth exploring with clients to help them understand how they perceive their world. The wheel is not there as an absolute or concrete tool, but as a basis for listening and asking questions which relate to the client's existential possibilities and limitations.

Developing the structure and the existential wheels was the major leap forward. Although initially formulated to give us therapists a basis for working within the time-limited frame, we also recognize that they serve as a framework for longer term or as we now say, time-aware therapy. Time is of such significance in our lives that it is also of great importance in any therapeutic situation. An understanding of a client's perception of time can relate immediately to his or her particular view of the world and can also highlight elements of dependency and non-dependency issues in relationships both in and out of therapy.

The concept of time, in terms of having an ending, we also found to be effective. As the case studies show, there is usually a realization anywhere from the eighth to the eleventh session that the end is nigh. The manner in which the client relates to this ending is again very much a reflection of previous farewells, whether they be of losses and rejections, or relief at parting. Some clients will avoid the subject altogether, some may even miss sessions as a delaying tactic, to gain more time. Sometimes the emotion is expressed as anger, sometimes as fear or grief; while on other occasions, it can be vented as happiness or awareness that they are ready to face the world. As a therapist it is important to relate what happens in the session to the client's real-life situations.

This also highlights the significance we attribute to the relationship formed between therapist and client. Apart from the importance and need to build up trust, through empathy, (for without trust, the client is unlikely to begin the process of self-exploration) the relationship again is a microcosm of what happens in client's other relationships. Starting from what emerges within the session, how trust is or is not built up, how the client reacts to certain questions or comments, can serve as a springboard to the particular way the client forms interpersonal relationships.

Working in this way puts a lot of pressure on the therapist to understand and be aware from moment to moment of how he or she is feeling and reacting to the client. The therapist cannot absent himself or herself from the process – he or she is part of the relationship and must therefore recognize what assumptions and blockages he or she might be bringing to the process. Bracketing is of paramount importance. It is all too easy to jump in and vocalize one's first thought, which might be seen as an interruption to the client's flow but may also serve to enhance the therapist's sense of self, rather than that of the client.

In essence we started from a theoretical, philosophical background and extrapolated and connected these ideas not only to an existential approach, but to that of working within a time-limited frame. The book then moved forward to explain how each of these concepts is applied, not only with client vignettes, but also with longer and more intricate case studies, which we hope give the reader a fuller understanding of the way time-limited existential therapy works in practice.

Existential concepts represented by the wheels were analysed segment by segment, connected and explored both in relation to theory and therapeutic methods. Case vignettes were brought in as further illustration. Following this, case studies were presented and world views were dissected and interconnected with behaviour patterns, value systems and all the rest of the segments of the existential wheels. Three of the case studies, Sue, James and Couples, added their own summaries and were able to connect their changes of perception, value system and behaviour patterns to all of their issues and all the other ontological 'givens'.

As must be evident by now, the learning process which we described in the book was not confined only to our clients, but was a reciprocal endeavour. We learned that our own structure of being in the world and our own issues and fallibility did not, as is sometimes believed, impede our therapeutic endeavour. On the contrary, they were a catalyst to connect with our clients.

We learned that this connectedness was an important element creating an inter-subjective relationship. Conversely, this relationship was conducive for clients to challenge their contradictions of their value system and become aware of their own world views. Through this method clients could establish their own structure, gain insight and thus challenge their behaviour patterns. During this continuing interaction between experiences, comprehension and grasping of AHA experiences, clients will undergo a learning process which they will continue to exercise, well after therapy.

BIBLIOGRAPHY

Adler, A. (1969). *The Science of Living*. New York: Doubleday, Anchor Books.

Beck, A.T. (1976). *Cognitive Therapy and the Emotional Disorders*. New York: International University Press.

Bohm, D. (1965). *Physics and Perception in the Special Theory of Relativity*. New York: Benjamin.

Bonaparte, M. (1938). *Time and Timelessness*. (P. Hartocliss, ed.). New York: International University Press.

Boscolo, L. & Bertrando, P. (1993). *The Times of Time*. New York: W.W. Norton.

Boss, M. (1979). *Existential Foundation of Medicine and Psychology*. Northvale NJ: Jason Aronson.

Budman, S.H., Hoyt, M. & Friedman, S. (1992). *The First Session in Brief Therapy*. New York: Guilford Press.

Bugental, J. (1987). *The Art of the Psychotherapist*. New York: W.W. Norton.

Camus, A. (1984). *The Myth of Sisyphus*. New York: Penguin Books.

Corsini, R.J. (Ed.) (1984). *Current Psychotherapies*. Itasca: F.E. Peacock.

Deurzen-Smith, E. van (1987). *Everyday Mysteries*. London: Routledge.

Deurzen-Smith, E. van (1988). *Existential Counselling in Practice*. London: Sage.

Dryden, W. & Feltham, C. (1992). *Brief Counselling*. Buckingham: Open University Press.

Ellis, A. (1962). *Reason and Emotion in Psychotherapy*. New York: New American Library

Ellis, A. (1992). 'Time-limited therapy: the rational emotive method.' In S. H. Budman, M. Hoyt & S. Friedman. *The First Session in Brief Therapy*. New York: Guilford Press.

Foulkes, S.H. (1975). *Group Analytic Psychotherapy Methods and Principles*. London: Karnak.

Frankl, V. (1963). *Man's Search for Meaning*. New York: Pocket Books.

Freud, S. (1900). *The Interpretation of Dreams*. In standard edition of the *Collected Works of Sigmund Freud 4, 5*. London: Hogarth Press.

Friedman, M. (1964). *The Worlds of Existentialism: A Critical Reader*. London/New Jersey: Humanities Press.

Greenson, R. (1967). *The Technique and Practice of Psychoanalysis*. London: Hogarth Press.

Gustafson, J.M. (1986). *The Complex Secret of Brief Psychotherapy*. New York: W.W. Norton.

Haley, J. (1990). *Strategies of Psychotherapy*. 2nd edn, Rockville MD: Triangle Press.

Hegel, G.W.F. (1952). *The Philosophy of Right*. Chicago/London: Encyclopaedia Britannica.

Heidegger, M. (1962). *Being and Time*. Trans. J. Macquarrie and E. Robinson. Oxford: Basil Blackwell.

Herink, R. (1980). *The Psychotherapy Handbook*. New York: New American Library.

Horney, K. (1951). *Neurosis and Human Growth*. London: Routledge & Kegan Paul.

Husserl, E. (1977). *Phenomenological Psychology*. The Hague: Nijhoff.

Ihde, D. (1986). *Experimental Phenomenology*. New York: State University of New York Press.

Jourard, S.M. (1971). *The Transparent Self*. New York/London: Van Nostrand Reinhold.

Kierkegaard, S. (1941). *Concluding Unscientific Postscript*. Trans. D.F. Swenson and W. Lowrie. Princeton NJ: Princeton University Press.

Kolb, D.A. (1984). *Experiential Learning*. London: Prentice Hall.

Laing, R.D. (1985). *Wisdom, Madness and Folly. The Making of a Psychiatrist*. London: Macmillan.

Locke, J. (1952). 'An essay concerning human understanding'. In R.M. Hutchins (Ed.), *The Empiricists*. Chicago/London: Encyclopaedia Britannica.

McCall, R. (1983). *Phenomenological Psychology: An Introduction*. Wisconsin: University of Wisconsin.

Macnab, F. (1991). *Brief Psychotherapy*. New York: John Wiley.

Malan, D.H. (1963). *The Study of Brief Psychotherapy*. New York: Plenum.

Mann, J. (1973). *Time-limited Therapy*. New York: Plenum.

Maslow, A. (1968). *Towards a Psychology of Being*. New York: Van Nostrand Reinhold.

May, R. (1961). *Existential Psychology*. New York: McGraw-Hill.

May, R. (1977). *The Meaning of Anxiety*. New York: Roland Press.

May, R. (1981). *Freedom and Destiny*. New York: Delta.

May, R. (1983). *The Discovery of Being: Writings in Existential Psychology*. New York: W.W. Norton.

Merleau-Ponty, M. (1962). *Phenomenology of Perception*. London: Routledge.

Michenbaum, D. (1977). *Cognitive Behavioural Modification: An Integrated Approach*. New York: Plenum.

Moustakas, C. (1994). *Existential Psychology and the Interpretation of Dreams*. Northvale NJ: Jason Aronson.

Perls, F. (1947). *Ego, Hunger, and Aggression*. New York: Vintage Books.

Perls, F. (1959). *Gestalt Therapy Verbatim*. New York: Bantam Books.

Rogers, C. (1961). *On Becoming a Person*. London: Constable.

Rogers, C. (1980). *A Way of Being*. Boston: Houghton Mifflin.

Sartre, J.P. (1958). *Being and Nothingness: An Essay in Phenomenological Ontology*. Trans. Hazel Barnes. London: Routledge.

Shazer, S. de (1985). *Keys to Solution in Time-limited Therapy*. New York: W.W. Norton.

Salvin, M. & Kriegman, D. (1992). *The Adaptive Design of the Human Psyche* . New York: Guilford.

Smith, D.L. (1991). *Hidden Conversations: An Introduction to Communicative Psychoanalysis*. London: Routledge.

Solomon, R.C. (1950). *A History of Western Philosophy: Continental Philosophy since 1750*. Oxford: Oxford University Press.

Spinelli, E. (1989). *The Interpreted World*. London: Sage.

Spinelli, E. (1994). *Demystifying Therapy*. London: Constable.

Strupp, H. (1992). 'Time-limited dynamic psychotherapy'. In H. Strupp *Psychotherapy in a New Key*. New York: Basic Books.

Sullivan, H. Stack (1953). *The Interpersonal Theory of Psychiatry*. New York: W.W. Norton.

Tillich, P. (1980). *The Courage To Be*. New Haven: Yale University Press.

Valle, R. S. & Hallings, S. (Eds) (1989). *Existential-Phenomenological Perspectives in Psychology*. New York/London: Plenum Press.

Yalom, I. (1980). *Existential Psychotherapy*. New York: Basic Books.

Yalom, I. & May, R. (1984). 'Existential psychotherapy'. In J. Corsini (Ed.) *Current Psychotherapies*. Itasca: F. E. Peacock.

Warnock, M. (1970). *Existentialism*. Oxford: Oxford University Press.

Watzlawick, P., Weakland, J.H. & Fisch, R. (1974). *Change: Principles of Problem Formation and Problem Resolution*. New York: W.W. Norton.

Weakland, J.H., Fish, R., Watzlawick, P. & Bodin, A. (1974). 'Brief therapy: focused problem resolution', *Family Process*, **12**: 141–168.

INDEX

Related titles of interest...

Paradox and Passion in Psychotherapy

An Existential Approach to Therapy and Counselling

Emmy van Deurzen

Challenging the dominant philosophy of psychotherapy and counselling as it has evolved over the past decades, the underlying assumptions of therapeutic culture are critically assessed and questioned, whilst an alternative perspective on the human predicament will be proposed, developed and illustrated throughout the book.

0-471-96191-4 170pp 1998 Hardback
0-471-97390-4 170pp 1998 Paperback

Case Studies in Existential Psychotherapy and Counselling

Edited by Simon du Plock

Looks at mental health care as we approach the millennium and explores how a philosophical approach can address the problems of living experienced by many people, even in the midst of relative wealth and material security, which medical approaches can only pathologize.

0-471-96192-2 170pp 1997 Hardback
0-471-97079-4 170pp 1997 Paperback

Brief Rational Emotive Behaviour Therapy

Windy Dryden

Practitioners will find useful insights and guidance on applying these methods throughout the process of therapy, including building the working alliance, assessment, formulation, and work in sessions and outside the sessions. Illustrated by a case study which reflects the problems of real life work with a client.

0-471-95786-0 244pp 1995 Paperback

Brief Therapy with Couples

An Integrative Approach

Maria Gilbert and Diana Shmukler

A concise, practical guide for couples with relationship problems, that relates therapy to the cultural, racial and religious context of relationships, as well as key issues like parenting and same-sex relationships.

0-471-96206-6 200pp 1996 Paperback

Visit the Wiley Home Page at http://www.wiley.co.uk